A BUSY DAY

1st

Act. I

Scene. I.

An apartment in an Hotel.

1st. Waiter, within. There! there! open that door! To the right, I say!

2d. Waiter. It's bespoke.

1st. Waiter. Open it, I say! the lady's fainting— Open it, when I bid you.

(A side door opens, & Eliza enters, with Deborah, who endeavours to support her.)

Deborah. Take care, take care, my dear young lady! O that Mr. Cleveland was but with us!

Eliza. (disengaging herself from Deborah) Hush, hush, good Deborah! why are you so alarmed! I am not hurt, I assure you.

A Busy Day

BY FANNY BURNEY

EDITED BY

TARA GHOSHAL WALLACE

Rutgers University Press
New Brunswick, New Jersey

The original manuscript, "A Busy Day,"
by Fanny Burney resides in the Berg Collection
of The New York Public Library, Astor, Lenox
and Tilden Foundations, and is printed
with the permission of the Library.

The frontispiece, manuscript page one
in the hand of General D'Arblay,
is used courtesy of the Berg Collection
of the New York Public Library, Astor, Lenox
and Tilden Foundations.

Library of Congress Cataloging in Publication Data

Burney, Fanny, 1752–1840.
Fanny Burney's A busy day.

Bibliography, p.
I. Wallace, Tara Ghoshal, 1952– II. Title.
III. Title: Busy day.
PR3316.A4B87 1984 822'.6 83-27023
ISBN 0-8135-1047-3

Manufactured in the United States of America

To my parents

CONTENTS

ACKNOWLEDGMENTS

I want to thank Dr. Lola Szladits and the New York Public Library for permission to reproduce the manuscript and for granting access to the wealth of materials in the Berg Collection. Like all Fanny Burney scholars, I owe the greatest debt to Joyce Hemlow, whose published work has inspired and illuminated my own, and who has always been generous and helpful. To the professors at the University of Toronto, who saw this in the early stages and who were unstinting in their encouragement, I owe a special debt; without the help of J. R. de J. Jackson, G. G. Falle, Jane Millgate and Michael Millgate, this work would never have been completed. I am particularly grateful to G. E. Bentley, Jr., who supervised my dissertation with care and acuity, and whose every suggestion was both practical and sensitive. Rea Wilmshurst was much more than a typist; I cannot sufficiently acknowledge her help in making editorial decisions. Finally I want to thank my husband, H. Scott Wallace, for his affectionate support and for his growing interest in Fanny Burney.

CHRONOLOGY

	Life	Novels and Prose	Plays
1752	13 June. Born in King's Lynn, Norfolk.		
1760	Burneys move to London.		
1762	Mrs. Burney dies.		
1767	Dr. Burney marries Mrs. Allen.	Burns first novel *Carolyn Evelyn.*	
1768		27 March. Begins writing diary "To Nobody."	
1778	27 July. Dr. Burney introduces FB to the Thrales.	*Evelina; or, The History of a Young Lady's Entrance into the World* published in January by Thomas Lowndes.	
1779			*The Witlings*
1778–1791			*Edwy and Elgiva*; *Hubert de Vere*; *The Siege of Pevensey*; *Elberta*
1782		*Cecilia; or, Memoirs of an Heiress* published in June by Payne and Cadell.	
1786	Becomes the queen's Second Keeper of the Robes.		
1787		Begins Windsor Journal for Susan Burney Phillips and Mrs. Locke.	

	Life	Novels and Prose	Plays
1788	Attends trial of Warren Hastings.		
1791	Resigns from royal service.		
1793	28 July. Marries General Alexandre d'Arblay.	*Brief Reflections Relative to the Emigrant French Clergy: Earnestly Submitted to the Humane Consideration of the Ladies of Great Britain*	
1794	18 December. Birth of son Alexander.		
1795			21 March. *Edwy and Elgiva* performed at Drury Lane.
1796		*Camilla; or, A Picture of Youth* published by subscription in July.	
1797	d'Arblays build and occupy Camilla Cottage.		
1798–1799			*Love and Fashion.* Accepted for production by Thomas Harris of Covent Garden.
1801–1802			*A Busy Day*; *The Woman-Hater*
1802	Moves to Paris.		
1812	Returns to England.		
1814	12 April. Dr. Burney dies. FB returns to France.	*The Wanderer; or, Female Difficulties* published in March by Longman and Rees.	
1815	d'Arblays return to England.		
1818	3 May. General d'Arblay dies.		

	Life	Novels and Prose	Plays
1823		*Narrative of the Illness and Death of General d'Arblay.*	
1832		*Memoirs of Doctor Burney.*	
1837	19 January. Alexander d'Arblay dies.		
1840	6 January. FB dies.		

INTRODUCTION

INTRODUCTION

An analysis of *A Busy Day* must address two general questions: what are Fanny Burney's main concerns in this play, and in what way does she accomplish her goals? The first question is not difficult to answer, for none of Fanny Burney's works is mysterious or inaccessible. *A Busy Day*, like her novels and other plays, aims to instruct as well as to amuse. Here, her subject has to do with manners and character; she wants to show that bad manners are a manifestation of a selfish heart and that they are not confined to any one social class. *A Busy Day* expounds on this theme in two ways: by bringing together the ill-bred of both upper and lower classes and allowing a natural interplay of vulgarity and prejudice; and by showing the effects of social and moral coarseness on the hero and heroine, who have both pride and delicacy of feeling. To accomplish the first object requires a situation that will naturally draw together members of both classes, and Fanny Burney creates this by having her lovers be from families which are socially diverse but equally boorish. The second object, which underlines the moral theme of the play, can only be achieved if the audience cares about the lovers, if the hero and heroine are credible, interesting, likeable.

A Busy Day is subtitled "An Arrival from India," and it is the arrival of the hero and heroine from Calcutta that begins the action of the play. There are references to India throughout the play, references which indicate that Fanny Burney's knowledge of British India was more than superficial. This knowledge came from various sources: her half brother Richard Thomas Burney had lived in Bengal;[1] her sister Charlotte married Ralph Broome, who had spent much of his life there;[2] and she took a great interest in the trial of Warren Has-

1. *The Journals and Letters of Fanny Burney (Madame d'Arblay)*, ed. Joyce Hemlow et al. (Oxford: Clarendon, 1972–82), 1: lxxiii; 3: 154.

2. *Journals and Letters*, 4: 174. Fanny Burney says of Ralph Broome: "To me, however, he was entertaining & informing, as we talked of India, & he permitted me to ask what questions I pleased upon points & things of which I was glad to gather accounts from so able a traveller." It is possible that she was already, in August 1798, accumulating materials for her projected play.

tings (for peculations as governor general of India), attending the proceedings as one of "the friends of the persecuted man."[3] These personal contacts with those who were familiar with India give the Indian references in *A Busy Day* a certain authenticity, but it would be a mistake to presume that Fanny Burney wanted only to display her familiarity with eighteenth-century India. The arrival from India or the Indies is a plot device familiar to audiences who had seen Richard Brinsley Sheridan's *School for Scandal*, George Colman the Elder's *Man of Business*, and Richard Cumberland's *The West Indian*, a device to bring together characters ignorant of each other's pasts and to introduce the uninitiated to the complexities of London social life. Just as the episodes in *Evelina* depend on having an inexperienced girl face "the great and busy stage of life,"[4] the incidents in *A Busy Day* are, to a great extent, dependent on Eliza's ignorance of her vulgar connections.

In drawing a parallel between Evelina's entrance into the world and Eliza's arrival from India, one must stress a crucial difference in their situations: Evelina is very young, very unsophisticated, and dependent on others for both financial security and social position. Eliza, on the other hand, is wealthy, fairly sophisticated, and confident of her social powers, and the first act is very largely devoted to exhibiting these qualities of the heroine. Almost the first thing we learn about her is her moral superiority to those around her, a superiority shown by her concern for her Indian servant Mungo. The English servants sneer unbelievingly at her request to look after him, and Deborah justifies her own indifference to his welfare—"for after all, a Black's but a Black; and let him hurt himself never so much, it won't shew, It in't like hurting us whites, with our fine skins, all over alabaster"[5]—but Eliza vows "my care of you shall be trebled for the little kindness you seem likely to meet with here" (I.39–40). And when Mrs. and Miss Watts show an ignorant horror of Indians, Eliza replies that "the native Gentoos are the mildest and gentlest of human beings" (I.493–94).

One of the qualities that clearly sets Eliza apart from Evelina or Camilla is her independence and self-confidence. Indeed, in the early expository scenes, Eliza is shown to be far more level-headed than

3. *Journals and Letters*, 1: 177.

4. Frances Burney, *Evelina; or, The History of a Young Lady's Entrance into the World*, ed. Edward A. Bloom (London: Oxford University Press, 1968), 7.

5. This edition, I.43–46. Subsequent references to this edition are given in parentheses in the text.

her lover, and she exhibits an almost distressing reluctance to act like a sentimental heroine. Rather than become distraught and helpless after the accident to her carriage, she quickly takes charge of the situation, being quite capable of giving orders for her own comfort and that of her servants. Eliza also shows her self-sufficiency when Cleveland joins her at the inn. She dismisses his eager admiration for her coolness—"My beloved Eliza! what a terrible accident! yet with what courage you seem to support it! what charming composure!" (I.50–52)—and gives a matter-of-fact explanation for having continued to travel without her companions (I.170–76). She shows no excessive distress when informed that she has wandered into a gaming house but takes practical steps to leave it quickly.

After the first act, Eliza's character conforms more to the pattern of the sentimental heroine, but one is constantly made aware of her good sense and forthright manner. As in many sentimental comedies, there is in *A Busy Day* an irritating tendency on the parts of the hero and heroine to misunderstand and misinterpret each other's actions, but Eliza takes longer than most heroines to succumb to suspicion and mistrust. Already confused by Frank Cleveland's solicitations, which are conveyed through Lord John, Eliza is further dismayed by witnessing the scene in which Miss Percival quite literally throws herself at Cleveland (III. stage direction preceding 428). But rather than give the scene the most negative interpretation, she simply expresses her sense of astonishment and doubt:

> How strange an adventure! They could not both be his sisters—yet how familiar a conduct to anyone but a Brother! I could hear nothing; but all I saw was most extraordinary. He is gone, too—and without speaking—Was it unavoidable? I must hope so; yet how dreadful the least doubt![6] (III.614–18)

Throughout the play, Eliza's good sense and her instinctive desire to trust Cleveland are systematically assailed in a series of distressing encounters. It seems to me that Fanny Burney has taken some trouble to show the progress of Eliza's feelings, so that her eventual rejection

6. See *Northanger Abbey*, in which Jane Austen mocks the impulsive conclusions drawn by romantic heroines. When Catherine Morland saw Henry Tilney at the Upper Rooms in Bath, he "was talking with interest to a fashionable and pleasing-looking young woman, who leant on his arm, and whom Catherine immediately guessed to be his sister; thus unthinkingly throwing away a fair opportunity of considering him lost to her for ever, by being married already": *The Novels of Jane Austen*, ed. R. W. Chapman, 3d ed. (London: Oxford University Press, 1933), 5: 53.

of Cleveland seems understandable rather than capricious. Summoned by Cleveland to the Tylney home, she is commendably tolerant of Lady Wilhelmina's ill-bred curiosity; but she is then forced to listen to the Tylneys' happy hopes concerning Cleveland's engagement to Miss Percival, as well as to their expressions of contempt for the merchant classes. Her suspicions are heightened by Frank, who not only confirms that Cleveland and Miss Percival are to be married but also asserts that Cleveland is aware of his own hopes of marrying Eliza. Cleveland proceeds to make matters worse by asking Miss Percival, in Eliza's presence, for a "two minute's hearing" (IV.520–21). Eliza leaves the Tylneys' home at the end of the fourth act feeling that she has been betrayed and deliberately insulted by her lover.

Having reached this not-unwarranted conclusion, Eliza tries to retain her self-possession and her control over her own life by avoiding any further contact with Cleveland and his family. But even here she is foiled and subjected to further pain before the resolution of the play. Summoned by an urgent note from Miss Percival, she arrives just in time to witness Cleveland kissing his hostess's hand and is then forced to discuss the oddness of her family with Lady Wilhelmina. Perhaps this relentless assault on her sensibilities is excuse enough for her refusal to give Cleveland a proper hearing when they do finally confront one another, but it must be admitted that this lapse into wounded coldness rather works against the rational and straightforward character that Fanny Burney has so carefully drawn. As if aware of the unpalatable effect of this change, Fanny Burney has kept the scene of mutual recrimination and misunderstanding quite short (much shorter than a similar scene between Beaufort and Cecilia in *The Witlings*) and has followed it by a clarification scene with Jemima. In this scene we have again the honest and sensible Eliza, who is eager to hear explanations and has no false delicacy about her desire for a reconciliation:

> [H]as any misapprehension involved my judgement in errour? Ah, Miss Cleveland! Dear and blessed, should I call the conviction of misapprehension which should clear your brother to my view noble, firm, and honourable as I thought him this morning! (V.698–702)

After this she quickly forgives and accepts Cleveland without any excessive coyness or resentment. Perhaps the strength of Eliza's character is most clearly shown by her last words in the play. She does not make a sentimental speech about true love overcoming barriers, nor even does she resolve to win the approval of Cleveland's family. On the contrary, her final words are censorious, an indictment of her new relations: "Ah! Cleveland! Were you less dear to me, how could I have courage to meet a prejudice so chillingly unkind, so indiscriminately unjust?" (V.990–92).

In her scenes with Cleveland, Eliza seems to be forced by circumstances to act a role that is neither congenial nor natural to her character: the conflict between her natural good sense and her rather melodramatic suspicions is created largely by external forces. It is in her dealings with her family that we see signs of the internal conflict between Eliza's sense of independence and her desire to be an unexceptionable sentimental heroine. Having been raised by an adoptive father, and having acquired both social position and wealth without the help of her natural family, Eliza quite understandably feels independent of them. On the other hand, both her natural feelings and her sense of duty compel her to give them not only her affection but also a measure of control over her actions. The conflict between Eliza's sense of independence and her sense of the proper way to behave towards newly rediscovered relations gives rise to what seems to me to be the emotional centre of the play. The fact that the reunion is complicated by the Watts family's vulgarity also contributes vastly to the comic tone of *A Busy Day*.

Eliza's problematic relationship with her family becomes clear from her first encounter with them. Even before she meets her relations, her speeches to Cleveland indicate her perception of the dual relationship. On the one hand, she claims, in rather fulsome language, to feel a natural and powerful sense of kinship: "A Father,—A Mother—my dear Cleveland! what sacred ties! Even though my memory scarcely retains their figures, my heart acknowledges their rights, and palpitates with impatience to shew its instinctive duty" (I.98–101). But in spite of her efforts to be properly dutiful, Eliza's language betrays her sense of distance from her family. She talks of their having "relinquished" their power over her, the implication being that she now voluntarily returns it to them; that is, she herself is now in control of her actions, but she chooses to defer to her family. She also concentrates on the way things look rather than on the way they really are: to acknowledge Cleveland openly as her lover will "*appear* like triumphing in my independence" (I.87–88); the power they once had had may *seem* to belong to her family once more; their claims on her "must to themselves *seem* so complete" (I.96–97, my italics). Clearly, Eliza does not feel that it would be proper to seem to be independent of her family, but she does in fact feel herself to be so.

Of course, much of Eliza's sense of distance from her family may be justified by their vulgarity, and, in spite of her determination to be a dutiful daughter, Eliza cannot help but recoil from their ill manners and even exhibit some snobbishness regarding their social position. Even before meeting them, she expresses her sense of their social inferiority when she is confident of her father's consent to the match with Cleveland: "His consent, his approbation cannot be doubted. Your high family, their rank in life, and your noble connexions, will make him proud of such an alliance, and of the honour which it will reflect upon his Daughter"[7] (I.210–14). After meeting her family and becoming aware of their ill-breeding, Eliza is doubtful of her acceptance by Cleveland's family, and indeed by Cleveland himself: "Alas! alas! Cleveland! How will his friends permit—how will he himself endure an intercourse so new to him!" (I.567–68).

That intercourse with her family is new and disagreeable to herself becomes clear as Eliza tries, rather unsuccessfully, to hide her dismay at being part of such a vulgar family. In Kensington Gardens, after a particularly harrowing display of the Watts's vulgarity, she seems involuntarily to cry out for rescue: "O Cleveland! that once I were but yours!" (III.229). This exclamation can be interpreted to mean that Eliza fears a rejection by Cleveland and wishes they were already married so that the eccentricities of her family might not dissuade him from the match. On the other hand, as seems more likely, Eliza may be wishing that the marriage with Cleveland were accomplished so that she herself need not be exposed to the vulgarity and meanness of the Watts circle. In case one is apt to condemn Eliza's desire to separate herself from her family, it is helpful to remember that one of our best-loved heroines of fiction shows just such a desire in similar circumstances. Elizabeth Bennet, wishing to shield Darcy from the unwelcome civilities of Mrs. Bennet and Mrs. Philips,

> was ever anxious to keep him to herself, and to those of her family with whom he might converse without mortification . . . and she looked forward with delight to the time when they should be

7. There are some interesting manuscript changes here. Originally, Eliza says her father "must be proud of such an alliance." By inserting details about that alliance—high family, rank, noble connections—Fanny Burney enumerates the qualities that would be appreciated by the Wattses, as if to emphasize that it is not merely Cleveland's own character or industry that would impress them.

> removed from society so little pleasing to either, to all the comfort and elegance of their family party at Pemberley.[8]

If Elizabeth, long inured to the comparatively mild crudeness of her relations, should feel such embarrassment, it is not astonishing that Eliza, gently reared by her adoptive father, should recoil from the sudden confrontation with her far less acceptable family.

It is this conviction of her family's inferiority that makes Eliza so willing to assume that Cleveland is about to rescind his vows to her; in fact, she is attributing to him her own feelings of revulsion and dismay, and her shame regarding her family makes her leap to the wrong conclusions. Her obsession with the inferiority of her own family renders her blind to Cleveland's real situation; she can only see his actions in the context of her own embarrassments.[9]

Eliza's family difficulties are indeed painful and do give rise to great uneasiness in her mind, but, fortunately for the audience, they also provide some of the most amusing moments in the play. One of the strengths of *A Busy Day* is that Fanny Burney, unlike many other comic dramatists of the time, is willing to give us laughter at the expense of her hero and heroine. Eliza's confrontations with her family provide comic scenes, not only because they expose the vulgarity and narrow-minded folly of the Wattses, but also because they deflate Eliza's rather melodramatic sense of duty and proper affectionate behaviour. Each time Eliza reacts with exaggerated emotion, the Wattses counter with placid, even callous equanimity. On first seeing her father, Eliza "runs to Mr. Watts, takes his hand, and drops upon one knee to him," to which exhibition Mr. Watts calmly replies, "How do do, my dear? You're welcome home again" (I.406). The first encounters with her sister and mother are even more anticlimactic. While Eliza rushes to embrace her sister, Miss Watts clearly has other things on her mind: "How do do, Sister? What a pretty hat you've got on! I'll have just the fellow to it. Pray who are those two smart beaus you've got with you?" (I.416–18). And Mrs. Watts, to whom Eliza runs "with open arms," manages to subdue her maternal feelings

8. *Novels of Jane Austen*, 2: 384.

9. In Richard Steele's *The Conscious Lovers* (1723), Bevil and Indiana find themselves in a situation which is similar in emotional content though not in plot. Though they are in love with each other, he cannot make any advances to a woman who is living, however chastely, under his protection, and she cannot bring herself to ask for romantic assurances from one who has already shown her such kindness. *The Plays of Richard Steele*, ed. Shirley Strum Kenny (Oxford: Clarendon, 1971), 323.

enough to reject physically Eliza's proffered embrace: "Take care, my dear, take a little care, or you'll squeeze my poor new Handkerchief till it won't be fit to be seen" (I.428–29). Later, when Eliza begins to weep over the memory of Mr. Alderson, Mrs. Watts interrupts her with "Pray, my dear, have you got over much Indy muslin? I ha'n't bought a morsel since I knew you was coming" (I.454–55). Even this gross materialism cannot wholly stem the tide of Eliza's overflowing emotions, and when she rather grandly replies, "You will permit me, I hope, to lay all my stores at your feet," her mother dampens her ardour with a prosaic "I'm sure that's a very pretty thought of you, my dear" (I.456–57). The truth is that Eliza *is* indulging in "pretty thoughts," and if these responses from the Watts family serve to show their insensitivity and superficiality, they also show that Eliza's effusive behaviour has its ridiculous side as well.

If Fanny Burney has taken care to present a heroine who is both sympathetic and credible, it seems at first that she has not taken the same pains with her hero Cleveland. Indeed, the character of Cleveland seems at times to be drawn so carelessly as to be at the same time conventional and inconsistent. If one were to attempt to assign a series of adjectives to him, one might say he is sensitive, gentlemanly, and liberal in social views; at the same time, he can be considered to be obtuse, inarticulate, and indecisive. These seemingly disparate qualities can be reconciled, not by seeing them as separate and conflicting tendencies (as in the case of Eliza's sense of independence and her sense of duty), but by regarding them as different manifestations of the same qualities. It is Cleveland's chivalry and good manners that often make him seem weak, and his sensitivity, to his own feelings and to those of others, that makes him so annoyingly, though comically, inarticulate. Like Eliza, Cleveland is greatly desirous of acting properly, a desire which hinders him from quickly putting an end to her doubts and his own perplexities.

Cleveland's scrupulousness regarding her feelings and wishes colours all his conduct towards Eliza, sometimes inhibiting their clearer understanding of each other's position. When he learns of Sir Marmaduke's plans for a match with Miss Percival and sees the family's reaction to Frank's plans to marry a "cit," Cleveland abandons his original intention of presenting himself to Eliza's family and concocts instead what appears to be an elaborate plan to have Jemima arrange a meeting:

> I must entreat you to wait upon the lady I have mentioned to you, and conjure her, in my name to grant me a five minutes audience immediately. The confusion this hair-brained coxcomb may create in the house by his unintelligible assertions can only be prevented, or cleared away, by an instantaneous meeting. Nor shall I think myself at liberty to declare our connexion, till I have revealed to her the disappointment of my expectations from Sir Marmaduke. (II.577–84)

Cleveland's seemingly excessive cautiousness is largely clarified by the last part of this speech. He will not presume to present himself as a suitor to the Wattses until Eliza expresses her indifference to his altered fortunes. Nor can he see her openly without raising questions which might prevent her complete freedom of choice. To guard both her reputation and her independence, he must arrange for his sister to be an intermediary between himself and Eliza. That this plan goes awry is not entirely Cleveland's fault; circumstances and Frank's machinations get in the way of the meeting he so carefully arranges. The abortive confrontation at the Tylney home, though marred by Frank's presence, owes its failure too to Cleveland's acute sensitivity to Eliza's emotions. When Jemima urges Cleveland to disabuse Miss Percival of her mistaken notions regarding himself, he can only reply, "Alas! Jemima, the averted eyes of Eliza unfit me for everything!" (IV.512–13).

Cleveland's determination to respect Eliza's feelings turns into a proud decision not to appeal to those feelings, a decision which is noble in itself but apt to be misconstrued. It is this sensitivity that makes Cleveland so quick to conclude that her coldness is a result of his sudden poverty, just as Eliza's consciousness of her family's vulgarity makes her misinterpret his actions. Each of them acts out of a proud and essentially generous impulse to release the other from a possible burden, with the result that there is acute misunderstanding and resentment on both sides.[10]

If Cleveland's inability to communicate clearly with Eliza stems from his sensitivity to her feelings, his general difficulty in verbalizing

10. This misplaced sensitivity on the part of lovers is the central concern in Hugh Kelly's *False Delicacy*, 4th ed. (London: Baldwin, Johnston, and Kearsly, 1768), in which two pairs of lovers (Winworth/Lady Betty and Sidney/Miss Marchmont) seem ready to give up their chance for happiness in marriage in order to avoid appearing selfish or indelicate.

his feelings seems to be the result of a gentlemanly politeness and reticence about private affairs. At times, Cleveland's politeness makes him appear to be a hypocrite, as when he assures Sir Marmaduke that he has no financial expectations from his uncle, though he has journeyed from India in expectation of being designated Sir Marmaduke's heir. I do not believe, however, that this sort of hypocrisy is meant to be condemned; Cleveland is following the dictates of social convention as well as his own sense of what is due to his benefactor. His is not the systematic and malevolent scheme of deception that Joseph Surface practises in *School for Scandal*; rather, it is the kind of socially acceptable compliance towards elders exhibited by Captain Absolute in *The Rivals* and by Marlow in *She Stoops to Conquer*. Such conduct is a result of respect for one's elders and for the customs of society, and Cleveland's thorough commitment to proper conduct, in conflict with his feelings, creates the confusion and inarticulateness that prevents him from coming to an early explanation with his family.[11]

Again, it is Cleveland's gentlemanly scruples which prevent him from openly rejecting Miss Percival. Having been told of her affection for him, and realizing that she assumes that the match is settled, Cleveland cannot, in public, reject her coy yet obvious advances. Therefore, he does not, in her presence, approach Eliza in Kensington Gardens, and he cannot abruptly disengage himself from her all-too-literal clutches (III.573ff). When, goaded by Frank and Miss Percival herself, he finally stammers out his love for Eliza, his outburst shocks him:

> I am in the deepest confusion—but I have been tortured out of all propriety. I dare not, madam, now address you; I am choaked by my own abruptness. But my feelings have been worked so cruelly, that every barrier of prudence and every consideration of delicacy, are irresistibly broken down by invincible, imperious Truth. Pardon—pardon me! (IV.643–48)

11. In *She Stoops to Conquer* (1773), Marlow finds himself in much the same quandary when he believes that his choice of a wife conflicts with his father's wishes: "Were I to live for myself alone, I could easily fix my choice. But I owe too much to the authority of a father, so that—I can scarcely speak it—it affects me": *The Collected Works of Oliver Goldsmith*, ed. Arthur Freedman (Oxford: Clarendon, 1966), 5: 186. The same perplexity is felt by Bevil, in *The Conscious Lovers*, who, because of his affection for his father, is torn between his own and his father's choice of a bride.

If it seems odd that Cleveland should be so thoroughly disconcerted by having avowed his attachment to Eliza and defended her character, Miss Percival's strong resentment shows the seriousness of his lapse from good manners. Clearly, Miss Percival's dignity, if not her affection, is seriously wounded, and Cleveland is at fault for having subjected her to a rejection in front of a witness, especially one so indiscreet as Frank. It is an action at odds with Cleveland's good breeding and concern for others' feelings, which shows how sorely his own feelings have been tried.

The rather incoherent conversations between Frank and Cleveland serve to show more than their lack of mutual understanding; they emphasize Cleveland's delicacy regarding personal relationships. We see that Frank has no scruples regarding his proposed bride's dignity or sensitivity and will talk at length and disrespectfully of her and her family, thus exposing them to the contempt and derision of his family and friends. Cleveland, on the other hand, scrupulously avoids naming Eliza, and it is his gentlemanly reticence that causes the confusion regarding Eliza's identity to continue up to the end of the fourth act.[12] Again and again, we see that the qualities that seem most irritating in Cleveland—his inability to communicate clearly and his postponement of explanations—not only serve to keep the plot going but also have an internal logic: they are directly related to his sense of delicacy and his commitment to social propriety.

Fanny Burney treats Cleveland with the same sort of comic sympathy that she does Eliza; she allows her audience to accept his foibles but to laugh at them too. The first scene in the play establishes Eliza as an independent and strong-minded character, in part at the expense of the hero. Here, Fanny Burney is working within a long-established and recognizable convention: from Rosalind to Célimène to Kate Hardcastle, heroines have exhibited their strength of character and their wit at the expense of their sometimes hapless lovers. In *A Busy Day*, Eliza does not exactly appear as a wit, but in the encounters with Cleveland, it is often she who seems to control the relationship. She rejects his role as protector (I.79–82), and even his covert surveillance of her is useless, since not only is he unable to prevent the accident to her carriage, but he is also unable to rescue her

12. See William O'Brien's *Cross Purposes* (1772), in which the three Bevil brothers are unaware that they are wooing the same woman: the socially inferior but wealthy Emily Grub.

from it: "the unlucky intervention of another carriage impeded my immediate view or knowledge of the accident which befel you; and when I got sight of it, you were already in the House" (I.183–86). Cleveland's inability to be of service to Eliza is also gently mocked by the fact that he cannot deal with servants. He certainly is unable to stem the tide of Deborah's constant chatter (although, to be fair, this might be beyond the abilities of even the imperious Tylneys), and the waiters at the hotel treat his commands with sneering indifference:

> 1ST WAITER. . . . What wine did you say, sir?
> CLEVELAND. Wine? I said pen and ink.
> 1ST WAITER. Pen and ink sir?
> CLEVELAND. Yes; make haste.
> 1ST WAITER. Certainly, sir. I wonder I don't. Pen and ink, indeed! (I.120–4)

Clearly, Cleveland's self-appointed task of protecting Eliza is neither necessary nor effective, and one can understand why she does not need his support at the moment of her reunion with her family.[13]

Of course, Cleveland's most obvious characteristic is his inarticulate embarrassment, and it is on this trait and on the confusion proceeding from it that Fanny Burney concentrates her comic treatment of him. The early encounters with Sir Marmaduke and Lady Wilhemina leave him tongue-tied, and his attempts to make sense out of Frank's tales leave him in pitiable but comic confusion. The stage directions implicit in Frank's speeches indicate how extreme are Cleveland's reactions to Frank's plans for marriage: "Nay, don't jump so!"; "Why you jump higher and higher!"; "You start like a Ghost in a Tragedy" (II.503, 517, 525). Part of the comedy in this play lies in the fact that Cleveland can only react, not being able to initiate any action himself. He is so easily confounded that, in every confrontation with a person of less sensitivity and politeness, he becomes the sufferer. Thus Miss Percival and Frank easily torment and tease him, and even the ill-bred Miss Watts throws him into confusion. Her forwardness interrupts his only chance to address Eliza in Kensington Gardens (III.465–66), and later, when Miss Percival mischievously sends Miss Watts rather than Eliza to a tête-à-tête with Cleveland, he falls easy prey to the hoax:

13. This watching over the heroine by the hero is treated with greater seriousness in *Camilla*, in which Edgar often secretly watches Camilla, not only to protect her, but also to assess her delicacy and propriety. Eliza, of course, has none of Camilla's flaws; she is neither impulsive nor easily duped into misbehaviour.

MISS WATTS. La, how droll! He's fell in love with me without knowing my name! (*aside*)

CLEVELAND. What execrable vengeance is this! (*aside*)

MISS WATTS. He looks quite the gentleman; but it's odd he don't begin. (*aside*)

CLEVELAND. What am I to do now? How cruel is an angry woman! (*aside*)

MISS WATTS. I dare say he'll say something pretty, when he's got it ready. (*aside*)

CLEVELAND. Madam, I—my confusion—

MISS WATTS. La! he's quite the lover. (*aside*) (V.639–49)

By the time Cleveland disentangles himself from this confusion, he has angered Miss Watts and thoroughly embarrassed himself. Miss Percival's intention to avenge herself has been entirely successful in this regard, and the audience has been given the opportunity to share in the joke.

The complexity of characterization in *A Busy Day* is not echoed in the simple construction of the plot, which depends almost entirely on the impediments which postpone the inevitable marriage of Eliza and Cleveland. These difficulties, which extend the action to five acts of comedy, are due to two kinds of misunderstandings: those which arise between the hero and heroine, and those which disturb each character's relationship to family. Eliza and Cleveland, who in the beginning of Act I seem ready for marriage, jeopardize their engagement by succumbing to mistaken suspicions of each other. As I have suggested in my discussion of the hero and heroine, these suspicions are due not to deliberate masquerading, as they are in *She Stoops to Conquer* or *The Rivals*, but rather to their inability to communicate openly with each other. Of course, none of these misunderstandings, whether due to misrepresentation from others or to accidental encounters, could cause any problems between Eliza and Cleveland if each were not so ready to misconstrue the actions of the other. Their willingness to believe the worst about each other creates a greater block than any external imposition could; and this mistrust comes, of course, from their sensitivity about their own perceived shortcomings: Cleveland's poverty and Eliza's vulgar connections. So in this case, plot devices are firmly tied to characterization. We can accept that Cleveland and Eliza are kept apart by these misunderstandings, not because the evidence is overwhelming, but because we can believe that Cleveland and Eliza are convinced by the flimsy evidence.

To the extent that there is any plotting by characters in the play, it comes from Frank Cleveland, whose intrusion into his brother's affairs contributes to the misunderstandings which keep the lovers apart.[14] Frank, whose profligacy and fertile imagination connect him with such eighteenth-century stage figures as Charles Surface (in *The School for Scandal*) and Aimless and Archer (in Sir George Farquhar's *The Beaux' Stratagem*), begins the blocking action by deciding to woo Eliza's eighty thousand pounds. This in turn causes Lady Wilhelmina to bring forth all her prejudices against the merchant class and prevents Cleveland from openly avowing his own attachment. Again, it is Frank who precipitates a break between the lovers when he convinces Eliza that Cleveland has turned her over to his brother, and of course, Frank's mysterious and impertinent references to Eliza and the Watts family render Cleveland more awkward and tongue-tied than even the Tylneys' open contempt for City connections can. Up until the last act, however, even Frank's interference is unwitting; he is no less confounded by Cleveland's impetuous anger than Cleveland is by Frank's seeming mockery. But in the fifth act, Frank, together with Miss Percival, becomes a true plotter, manipulating the other characters and setting the scene for their discomfiture. In this last act, Frank and Miss Percival become the managers of the action, directing the other players without their knowledge, making sure that the various characters are appropriately juxtaposed in order to give the desired comic effect. In doing this, they reflect, and to some extent take over, Fanny Burney's own concern to present comic confrontations.

The plot developments throughout *A Busy Day* seem to be unimportant except as they provide occasions for delineation of character or comic confrontations. The first act in the hotel serves two purposes. First, it economically establishes the background of the action by informing the audience about the engagement of Cleveland and Eliza and indicating the possible difficulties which may arise from the two families. It is a conventionally expository first act. But it also serves to demonstrate Fanny Burney's comic method: it begins the cycle of confrontations between members of different social classes, confrontations that provide both laughter and social commentary.

Before going on to examine the depiction of various social classes

14. An indication of Frank's importance in *A Busy Day* is the rather surprising fact that he has the greatest number of speeches.

in *A Busy Day*, it is important to establish two points: for Fanny Burney, bad manners and bad morals are inextricably intertwined, and she does not spare any class in her satiric indictment of bad manners. By bad morals I do not mean sexual or religious immorality; Fanny Burney is not concerned in *A Busy Day* with chastising the immorality of rakes or blasphemers. What she is concerned to show is that social insensitivity indicates a kind of moral obtuseness, a selfishness as ethically improper as it is socially unacceptable. Whenever she shows vulgarity and rudeness, she also implies moral coarseness, and in the depiction of this there are no class boundaries.

Joyce Hemlow calls *A Busy Day* "a devastating and comprehensive satire on bad manners of high and low alike."[15] Fanny Burney, in setting up the confrontation of classes, does not treat either side gently. The first act introduces the ill-bred arrogance of two representatives of the upper class, Frank Cleveland and Lord John Dervis; but it concentrates on the vulgar manners and lack of sensitivity of the Wattses, the newly rich merchant class.[16] I have already indicated that the Wattses' coarseness of manner when meeting Eliza reflects an indelicacy of feeling; their reception of her advances shows their indifference to her feelings. The Watts ladies are also guilty of the sin of snobbery when they refuse to acknowledge their cousin Joel Tibbs:

> MR WATTS. . . . Peggy, my dear, turn about and shew yourself. Here's your old Cousin Joel Tibbs.
> MISS WATTS. La, Pa', why can't you hold your tongue? What do you call me Peg for? How often have I told you I'm Margerella?
> MR TIBBS. What's that Cousin Peg! Good lauk! who'd have thought it! Dressed out like a fine lady in the front boxes! well, I'm glad the World goes so merrily with you all. But what, don't you know me, Cousin Aylce?
> MRS WATTS. Why indeed, as to that,—I can't pretend to say I remember everybody I see. (I.542–51)

15. Joyce Hemlow, "Fanny Burney: Playwright," *University of Toronto Quarterly* 19 (1949–50): 185.

16. The particular class to which the Wattses belong is more easily placed in a literary context than a historical one. Newly wealthy, uneducated, and aggressively vulgar, they are like the merchant classes depicted in John Burgoyne's *Heiress* (1786), George Colman the Elder's *Man of Business* (1774), George Colman the Younger's *Heir at Law* (1797), Hannah Cowley's *Who's the Dupe?* (1778), and Arthur Murphy's *Citizen* (1761). Fanny Burney herself, of course, had used characters like the Wattses before; they are clearly the legitimate heirs of the Branghtons in *Evelina*.

Here the Wattses engage in just the kind of cruel snobbishness they themselves suffer at the hands of the upper classes; any sympathy one might feel for their plight in subsequent confrontations with the upper class is thus reduced by this example of their own arrogance.

The two Watts ladies are also ridiculed because of their pretensions to gentility, and the laughter they elicit is not the laughter of affectionate sympathy but of contempt. Mrs. Watts uses her wealth to dress herself expensively and thereafter becomes concerned only with possible damage to her own finery and the possible cost of that of others. Miss Watts, who has been "finished at a boarding school" (III.293), exhibits the sort of grotesque gentility that Mr. Smith shows in *Evelina*. Cries of "pray" and "La, Pa'" punctuate all her conversations, and she changes her own name from Peggy to Margerella and insists on calling Eliza Eliziana.[17] Unlike Eliza, she is eager to dissociate herself from her socially unacceptable parents: "I intend, when you [Eliza] are married, you should *Shaproon* me everywhere, for I hate monstrously to go out with Ma'! Don't you think Ma's monstrous mean? And Pa's so vulgar, you can't think how I'm ashamed of him" (III.347–51). Her own vulgarity lies in her disrespect for her parents and in her eager pursuit of men. Mother and daughter share an enthusiasm for making genteel acquaintances, and both consider that social acceptance can be gained by a display of wealth. When faced with the evident contempt of the Tylneys, they try to impress them by speaking of their possessions:

> MISS WATTS. . . . They look as if they thought we were just a set of nobodys. Let's talk of our Coach. . . . I wonder if our Coach stops at the Door. . . . I dare say, (*aloud*) Robert's forgot to tell Thomas to order Richard to stop.
>
> MRS WATTS. Yes, I dares to say Robert's forgot to tell Thomas to order Richard to stop. (V.318–28)

Although their pathetic eagerness to be accepted by upper-class society is pitiable, our sympathy for them is effectively undermined by the coarseness of their methods.

17. Cf. Miss Alscrip's objections to being called Molly by her father: "Oh! hideous, Molly indeed! you ought to have forgot I had a christened name long ago; am not I going to be a countess?": *The Heiress*, in *The British Theatre; or, A Collection of Plays, Which Are Acted at the Theatres Royal, Drury-Lane, Covent Garden, and Haymarket. Printed under the Authority of the Managers from the Prompt Books*, ed. Mrs. Elizabeth Inchbald, 25 vols. (London: Longmans, Green, Hurst, Rees, and Orme, 1808), 22: 41.

Nor is Mr. Watts a more admirable figure. He seems at first to be more tolerable than his wife and daughter, since he does show some slight affection for Eliza, and since he does not repudiate the relationship with Joel Tibbs. He also gains our sympathy because he articulates the difficulties encountered by the newly rich and can therefore be seen as a victim. Mr. Watts's difficulties are twofold: his new wealth has created domestic strife, and the new social class he wishes to join openly despises him. The nature of his domestic difficulties suggests that the man who has no occupation loses both self-respect and the gratitude of his family. Speaking of the joylessness of his luxurious life, Mr. Watts describes himself as idle and lonely:

> I can't divert myself no way! Ever since I left off business, I've never known what to do. They've [his wife and daughter] made me give up all my old acquaintance, because of their being so mean; and as to our new ones, it's as plain as ever you see they only despise me: for they never take off their hats if I meet them in the streets; and they never get up off their chairs, if I ask them how they do in their own houses; and they never give me a word of answer I can make out, if I put a question to them. (III.297–305)

Clearly, as victim of his family's social ambitions, Mr. Watts is a figure to be pitied, but his passivity in the face of domestic tyranny must lessen our sympathy for his predicament. A more serious point against him is that his wealth has made him mercenary. One of his first concerns when meeting Eliza is to ascertain the amount of her inheritance—"Did he leave much over your fourscore?" (I.447–8)—and his immediate response to a letter of proposal for Eliza is: "But what has he got, my dear?" (III.179). Even this preoccupation with money would not necessarily cause withdrawal of sympathy from Mr. Watts if he were not also shown to be miserly; when a porter asks him for a tip, Mr. Watts refuses in no uncertain terms:

> PORTER. Why, your Honour! won't you give me something to drink, your Honour? (*following*)
> MR WATTS. To drink? Why, what, are you dry friend?
> PORTER. We always have something to drink, your Honour, from gentlefolks.
> MR WATTS. Have you? Well, then,—here! Waiter!—bring the lad a jug of water. (I.589–95)

Mr. Watts's new wealth has not increased his generosity to those less fortunate than himself, and Tibbs shows himself to be more truly "gentlefolk" when he himself fulfills the porter's expectations. Mr. Watts does not see, as the audience does, that his refusal to share his wealth is parallel to the refusal by the upper classes to share their social position with him and his family.[18]

Given the unattractive portrait of the social encroachers, one might perhaps expect the aristocrats who are trying to keep them out to be presented sympathetically. But here again Fanny Burney shows that vulgarity and moral insensitivity can be found in any class. With the exception of Cleveland and his sister Jemima, all the members of the upper classes are depicted as selfish, arrogant, and foolish.[19]

Sir Marmaduke, who is characterized by his nephew as "self-occupied" (I.199), is indifferent to anything that is not conducive to his personal enrichment and comfort. He blithely orders Cleveland to marry Miss Percival because she will pay off Sir Marmaduke's mortgage and orders him back to India when these plans fail: "Why what's half a dozen years, or so, in the life of a young man? . . . a voyage more or less to the East Indies—What is it, at your time of life?" (V.612–16). Sir Marmaduke's egoism is so unrelenting that even as a "humour" character he may seem overdone—there are very few variations on the theme of straightforward selfishness, and his harping on one string does become irksome. But Fanny Burney wants to make a moral point through this portrait of a comic eccentric. Thus his lack of interest in his nephews and his dependents is an abrogation of responsibility, for he does stand in the place of a parent to them. His indifference has a moral dimension because it harms those who depend on him for survival and comfort.

Lady Wilhelmina Tylney, the quintessential social snob, in no way ameliorates this picture of a selfish and morally faulty upper class. Her idiosyncrasy is that she worships the aristocracy and despises the lower classes. She reacts with horror to the accidental burning of a nobleman's wig, but the far more serious affliction of a poor old man leaves her unmoved: "persons of his class must naturally expect to be exposed, now and then, to some disagreeable events" (II.112–13).

18. Mr. Watts's mercenary outlook on life is like that of Mr. Sterling in George Colman the Elder's *The Clandestine Marriage*, of whom Lovewell says, "Money . . . is the spring of all his actions": *The Dramatic Works of George Colman* (London: Becket, 1777), 1: 5.

19. See Thomas Holcroft's *He's Much to Blame* (1798), in which Lady Jane is drawn sympathetically but her parents, Lord and Lady Vibrate, are foolish and arrogant.

Like Sir Marmaduke, she has no interest in the happiness of her nephews, caring only that they make alliances which are socially acceptable, and her views on friendship are summed up in her assertion that "Sympathy of character, Miss Cleveland, is mere romance" (II.138–39).

The other representatives of the upper classes—Frank Cleveland, Lord John Dervis, and Miss Percival—are presented with fewer details than the Tylneys, but here again Fanny Burney shows her contempt for the superficial and the insensitive. Frank is selfish and heartless, and though he is not a vicious manipulator like Joseph Surface, he is just as indifferent to others. Lord John, whose bored indifference to all around him reminds one of such characters as Mr. Lovemore in Arthur Murphy's *The Way to Keep Him* (1760) and Ennui in Frederic Reynolds's *The Dramatist* (1789), is idle and foolish, equally bored in company and alone. He and Frank Cleveland affect an idleness of manner like that of Mr. Meadows in *Cecilia*, and a fashionable slanginess of speech which Samuel Foote characterized as "a manner of speaking devised and practised by dulness, to conceal the lack of ideas, and the want of expressions."[20] Miss Percival is as voluble as Miss Larolles of *Cecilia*, and she adds to this a coyness of manner and a vindictiveness of temper which both amuse and alienate her audience. Like Miss Watts, Miss Percival is an inveterate man-chaser; but being better versed in the conventions of romance, she strives to hide her obsession by affecting a maidenly panic at the notion of being wooed:[21]

> That Wretch, my dear Jemima, desires a private audience. How abominable! As if I could ever bear to see him alone! . . . O no! no! no!—I can't think of it these six years, at least. Besides, what can he want to say? Can you form any guess, Jemima? (IV.210–23)

The reader's reaction to Miss Percival's antics is to agree with Cleveland, who says "she is vain and fantastic, and has won from me neither . . . esteem nor . . . confidence" (II.438–39).

20. Samuel Foote, *Devil upon Two Sticks: A Comedy in Three Acts. As It Is Performed at the Theatre-Royal in the Haymarket* (London: Cadell, 1778), preface.

21. The maiden with a consuming interest in men is a familiar figure in late eighteenth- and early nineteenth-century literature. The most thorough examination of such a character can be found in the novels of Jane Austen, which provide a gallery of coy and flirtatious women, from Isabel Thorpe (*Northanger Abbey*) and Miss Steele (*Sense and Sensibility*) to Lydia Bennett (*Pride and Prejudice*) and Mrs. Clay (*Persuasion*).

When the lower-class vulgarity of the Wattses meets the upper-class coarseness of the Tylneys, it becomes difficult to judge which side is more ill-mannered. In these confrontations between the two social classes lies most of the comic force of *A Busy Day*; and the contrast of manners, which is in essence no contrast at all, provides the social commentary in the play. The comic confrontation of social classes is not an unusual occurrence in English drama; from Shakespeare to Tom Stoppard, English dramatists have exploited the comic possibilities in these encounters. The fact that there is so much of this kind of comedy in late eighteenth-century drama has perhaps social and cultural significance which it is not my intention to explore, but one can speculate that it was a way to cope, *after* the fact, with the assimilation of merchants into the upper financial and social structure. Whatever the reason, it is clear, at least, that playwrights from Goldsmith to Burgoyne deal particularly enthusiastically with this phenomenon of the meeting of two classes of society. Fanny Burney, therefore, does not take on a new subject for comedy, but there are two aspects of the social confrontations in *A Busy Day* that make the play more than a copy of others. First, as I have already noted, she spares neither class in her exposé of bad manners and bad feeling, and second, she stages these confrontations before a witness whose reactions and embarrassments are at least as interesting as the encounters themselves.

In the satire of both classes, Fanny Burney goes further than many of her contemporaries, who often emphasize the shortcomings of only one social group. John Burgoyne's *Heiress* shows the pretentious vacuity of the newly rich without making much fun of the class they aspire to join; Colman the Elder's *English Merchant* extols the virtues of the merchant Freeport at the expense of the aristocrats Lord Falbridge and Lady Alton; and Hannah Cowley's *Who's the Dupe?* shows the nimble-witted aristocrat Granger making a fool of the merchant Doiley. This is not to say that other dramatists of the period never include a foolish merchant and a corrupt nobleman in the same play, but it seems to me that *A Busy Day* does this more systematically than most. Each encounter between the Wattses and the representatives of the upper class shows how little there is to choose between the two. In the first act, when Frank Cleveland and Lord Dervis witness the reunion of Eliza and her family, they are appalled by the Wattses' vulgarity. In a series of asides to Lord John, Frank expresses his horror at their manners, but he has little awareness of the vulgarity of his own role as eavesdropper until the robust curiosity of the Wattses makes it painfully obvious:

MRS WATTS. Pray, my dear, who are these two young gentlemen with you?
FRANK (*advancing*). I—I—I—
MR WATTS. Did they travel over in the same ship with you, my dear?
MISS WATTS. La, Pa', I wish you wouldn't talk. The gentleman's going to speak himself.
ELIZA. They are entirely strangers to me, sir.
FRANK. I beg a million of pardons—but I have only waited for a moment's opportunity to express my concern and confusion, and—and—I beg an hundred thousand pardons—I am so utterly confounded—the accident—but the waiter—
(I.460–71)

Here the impertinent curiosity of Frank is countered by the more straightforward yet equally vulgar inquisitiveness of the Wattses. Eliza, the neutral party here, must watch her family expose themselves to two strangers who have already distressed her by their impertinent behavior.

The next time the two classes meet, both Eliza and Cleveland are suffering observers. This encounter takes place in Kensington Gardens, one of the few public places where the socially ambitious Wattses can be sure to find "genteel" company. They are not disappointed, for this is where the Wattses meet Cleveland, Jemima, and Miss Percival, and here again the vulgar manners of the lower classes are matched and even surpassed by the insensitive rudeness of the aristocratic Miss Percival. Miss Percival, impelled by natural cruelty as well as by a desire to attract Cleveland through her wit, openly mocks the appearance of the Watts ladies and affects a swoon of horror at Mr. Watts's "bob jerun" wig (III.541–48). The latter antic has unexpected consequences, for the Wattses, who are literal-minded, deduce that she is "subject to fits" (III.566), and Mrs. Watts kindly offers to cure her—"It's only just the littlest touch in the World of the top of the nose, with the tip of the finger" (III.568–70)—an offer which sends Miss Percival shrieking off the stage.

The presence of Cleveland and Eliza at this encounter is crucial, not only for the comic value of their embarrassment, but also for dramatizing for the reader the consequences of the clash of social backgrounds. Poor Cleveland's plight here is both comic and pathetic, as he gradually recognizes the lowness of Eliza's connections and is prevented, by the exigencies of his relationship with Miss Percival, from approaching Eliza. The combination of the Wattses' coarseness and the constant demands of Miss Percival makes Cleveland a comically pitiable figure, and of course his chagrin is increased by the knowledge that his own actions are under the sensitive scrutiny of that other witness, Eliza.

The final encounter between the two classes is both more pointed and more comic than the previous confrontations. It is a meeting deliberately staged by Miss Percival and Frank, who quickly foresee the comic value of such an encounter. In this encounter, though their modes of expression vary, each side is equally vulgar and insensitive. The languorous indifference of Frank and Lord John, who deliberately ignore the awkward social advances of the Wattses, is an illustration of the kind of rudeness which Mr. Watts has described (III.297–305, already quoted here);[22] and when Lady Wilhelmina meets the Watts ladies, it is difficult to decide who is the most ill-bred:

> MRS WATTS. Dears, my dear, I wish she'd receive us, like; for I'll be whipt if I can think of a word to say for a beginning.
> MISS WATTS. Why, ask her if she's going to Rinelur. That's the genteel thing to talk about in genteel Company.
> MRS WATTS. I will, my dear. Pray, good lady, may you be going to Rinelur tonight?
> LADY WILHELMINA. Sir Marmaduke!
> SIR MARMADUKE. Lady Wil?
> LADY WILHELMINA. Did anybody—speak to Me?
> MRS WATTS. Yes, it was me, my good lady, as spoke; it wasn't the gentleman.
> LADY WILHELMINA. How singular! (*turning away*) (V.294–305)

Perhaps the most effective comic confrontation in the play is one that matches Lady Wilhelmina against the irrepressible Mr. Tibbs, who, on a dare from Miss Watts, apes the manner of Lord John and Frank:

22. The indolent and affected aristocrat is a figure Fanny Burney mocked in both *Evelina* (Mr. Lovel) and *Cecilia* (Mr. Meadows). She would have been familiar with such characters on the eighteenth-century stage: the Fine Gentleman in David Garrick's *Lethe* (1749), Mr. Lovemore in Murphy's *The Way to Keep Him* (1760), Ennui in Reynolds's *Dramatist* (1789), and Sir Loftus and Opal in Joanna Baillie's *Tryal* (1798) are all variations of the languid and rude gentleman.

MR TIBBS. . . . (*struts round to face* LADY WILHELMINA) How do do?
LADY WILHELMINA (*staring*). What?
MR TIBBS. I hope you are confounded well?
LADY WILHELMINA. Heavens!
MR TIBBS. O the Doose, and the Devil, and the plague and consumed! (*ludicrously imitating* LORD JOHN)
LADY WILHELMINA. What inscrutable effrontery! I'll look him into a statue. (*fixes her eyes upon him and frowns*)
MR TIBBS. How do, I say? (*nodding familiarly*)
LADY WILHELMINA. Dignity is lost upon such ignorance. 'Twill be better to awe him by authority—draw me that sofa this way, sir! (*imperiously*)
MR TIBBS. Sofa? Tol de rol. (*singing*)
LADY WILHELMINA. Astonishing! Did you not hear me, sir!
MR TIBBS. O the Doose!
LADY WILHELMINA. This is a class of person beyond any I have met with yet!
MR TIBBS. O the Divil! (*throws himself full length upon the sofa*) (V.742–60)

The irony is, of course, that this is precisely the "class of person" that Lady Wilhelmina associates with, and in the face of Mr. Tibbs's determined impertinence, she is as helpless as the Wattses are when confronted with the insolence of Frank and Lord John. One of the points made in *A Busy Day* is that snobbishness can be to some extent in the eye of the beholder and that the Wattses' cringing attitude towards the upper classes is in some part responsible for their constant discomfiture.

For this final confrontation, the circle of witnesses is much enlarged. Cleveland and Eliza are, as usual, the suffering third parties—after all, the encounter has been engineered by Miss Percival in order to mortify them. Cleveland, on the one hand being introduced to the Wattses by Miss Percival with arch pleasantry, and on the other being assailed by Lady Wilhelmina's indignation at being in such low company, can only wail "O that I were again in Calcutta!" (V.503–4). And Eliza, being earnestly solicited by Lady Wilhelmina to "conjecture who these singular persons are" (V.541–42), finds herself too overcome to remain in the room. But the other witnesses relish the encounters. Frank's love of mischief finds ample satisfaction in the distress of his own relations and in that of the Wattses;

and Miss Percival, busily causing distress for all the parties, finds it is "balm to me" to see their chagrin (V.564–65). Even the scene between Mr. Tibbs and Lady Wilhelmina has an appreciative audience in Miss Watts, who, much as she wants to be included in the Tylney social world, cannot help but enjoy the routing of the imperious lady by the impertinent social inferior.

I hope it is clear from the preceding discussion that, for Fanny Burney, social behaviour is inextricably intertwined with morality. Her novels, from *Evelina* to *The Wanderer*, clearly demonstrate that, for her, good manners are tied to good principles, and the depiction of social classes in *A Busy Day* reiterates her moral positions: that class boundaries are not what separate the well-bred from the vulgar, and that essential delicacy springs from minds and hearts rather than from pedigrees. Thus the coarseness of the Wattses is matched by the self-centered insensitivity of the Tylneys, and the delicate sensibility of Cleveland finds its equal in the noble pride and delicacy of Eliza. Though Fanny Burney quite rightly and wisely shows these parallels largely through the dramatization of vulgar or noble behaviour, the point is so important to her that she also has Cleveland speak directly of it:

> Sweet lovely Eliza! from weeds so coarse can a flower so fragrant bloom? How beautiful, O Nature, are thy designs! how instructive is thy study! Avaunt all narrow prejudice. Elegance, as well as talents and virtue, may be grafted upon every stock, and can flourish from every soil! (III.649–53)

The scenes of confrontation in *A Busy Day* show the truth, not only of this statement, but also of its corollary: that vulgarity, as well as vapidity and viciousness, may arise quite naturally from the most purebred and carefully nurtured seeds.

A Note on the Names

There does not seem to be significance attached to many of the names in *A Busy Day*. Cleveland and Tylney are both names of ducal families. Watts seems to be a typical name for families of no distinction; in Samuel Foote's *The Commissary* (1765), Zac Fungus boasts about the lineage of his intended bride by saying, "Ay, such a name, Lord, we have nothing like it in London: none of your stunted little dwarfish words of one syllable: your Watts, and your Potts, and your Trotts."[23]

There is an exchange in Hugh Kelly's *False Delicacy* (1768) which may throw light on two of the other names:

> MRS HARLEY. Deborah! O I should hate such an old fashioned name abominably!
>
> CECIL. And I hate this new fashion of calling our children by pompous appellation . . . a fellow who keeps a little alehouse at the bottom of my avenue in the country, has no less than an Augustus Frederick, a Scipio Africanus, and a Matilda Wilhelmina Leonora, in his family.[24]

23. Richard W. Bevis, ed., *Eighteenth-century Drama: Afterpieces* (London: Oxford University Press, 1970), 265.
24. Kelly, *False Delicacy*, 13.

A BUSY DAY

PERSONS OF THE DRAMA

LORD JOHN DERVIS	Knight
SIR MARMADUKE TYLNEY	
CLEVELAND [Sir Marmaduke's nephew]	Pope
FRANK [Cleveland's brother]	Lewis
MR WATTS	Munden
MR TIBBS [cousin to Mr Watts]	Fawcett
AARON, servant to Sir Marmaduke	
VALET of Lord John	
1ST WAITER / 2ND WAITER at an Hotel	
A SERVANT of Miss Percival	
A PORTER	
[FOOTMAN TO THE TYLNEYS]	
LADY WILHELMINA TYLNEY	Mrs Mattocks
MISS PERCIVAL	
JEMIMA CLEVELAND [sister to Cleveland and Frank]	
MRS WATTS	Mrs Davenport
MISS WATTS	
ELIZA WATTS	Mrs Pope
DEBORAH [Eliza's servant]	

[Actors' names in FB's hand]

ACT I

An apartment in an Hotel.

1ST WAITER (*within*). There! there! open that door! To the right, I say!

2ND WAITER. It's bespoke.

1ST WAITER. Open it, I say! the lady's fainting—open it, when I bid you. 5

A side door opens, and ELIZA *enters, with* DEBORAH, *who endeavours to support her.*

DEBORAH. Take care, take care, my dear young lady! O that Mr Cleveland was but with us!

ELIZA (*disengaging herself from* DEBORAH). Hush, hush, good Deborah! why are you so alarmed! I am not hurt, I assure you.

DEBORAH. O, you don't know yet—nor I neither; but I dare say 10 I'm bruised all over, when I come to examine. Mercy on us what a thing to travel so many thousands and thousands and millions of miles only to be overturned at last! If Mr Cleveland had but been with us—

ELIZA. Be quiet, dear Deborah. Pray where are we now? (*to the* 15 WAITER) I am entirely a stranger to London.

1ST WAITER. In St James's Street, meme. I thought nobody so ignorant as that! (*aside*)

ELIZA. How far are we from Bond Street?

I.17 **St James's Street** Built in 1650, St. James's Street became the site of White's Club (1755) and Boodle's Club (1765). Hugh Phillips, in *Mid-Georgian London* (London: Collins, 1964), says that "despite its adjacency to the Palace, St. James's Street was never an outstandingly residential street for the wealthy and great" (p. 69).

I.19 **Bond Street** The Wattses probably lived not on the commercial New Bond Street but on "the aristocratic end" (Phillips, *Mid-Georgian London*, 252), which was old Bond Street. Bond Street is the address of the well-connected Willoughby

1ST WAITER. Just by, meme. 20
ELIZA. Can you procure me a carriage to convey one thither?
1ST WAITER. O dear, yes, meme.
ELIZA. See for one, then, I beg. And pray assist my servant in taking care of my trunks.
1ST WAITER. What, the Black? 25
ELIZA. Yes; be so good as to see if he wants any help.
1ST WAITER. What, the Black?
ELIZA. Yes. He is the best creature living. I shall be extremely concerned if he should meet with any accident.
1ST WAITER. What, the Black? 30
ELIZA. I shall be much obliged to you for any service you may do him. Pray make haste.
1ST WAITER. Certainly, meme. Good Lord!

Exit sneering.

ELIZA, DEBORAH, 2ND WAITER.

2ND WAITER. Any commands for me, meme?
ELIZA. Only that you will see also if you can be of any use to him. 35
2ND WAITER. What, this Black—gentleman?
ELIZA. Yes.
2ND WAITER. By all means, meme! To be sure I shall!

Apart and exit.

ELIZA, DEBORAH.

ELIZA. Poor Mongo! my care of you shall be trebled for the little kindness you seem likely to meet with here. 40
DEBORAH. Why, that's very good of you, my dear young lady, to be so kind to him, being my late master's wish: but, for all that, these gentlemen mean no harm, I dare say; for after all, a Black's but a Black; and let him hurt himself never so much, it

---

in *Sense and Sensibility* (*The Novels of Jane Austen*, ed. R. W. Chapman, 3d ed., London: Oxford University Press, 1933, 1: 183).

I.25 **the Black** A term used to refer to Asians from the Indian subcontinent as well as Negroes.

I.39 **Mongo** "Mungo" in lines I.60 and I.128. "A typical name for a black slave. Hence, a negro" (*OED*). Fanny Burney may have been thinking of Isaac Bickerstaffe's *The Padlock* (1768), in which there is a Negro servant called Mungo. The term is used in Burney's *Camilla*, when Sir Sedley calls Othello "honest Mungo."

won't shew. It in't like hurting us whites, with our fine skins, all over alabaster. I dare say if you was only to look at my arm up here— 45

Enter CLEVELAND.

Mercy on us! if here i'n't Mr Cleveland his own self!

ELIZA. Cleveland!

CLEVELAND. My beloved Eliza! what a terrible accident! yet with what courage you seem to support it! what charming composure! 50

ELIZA. It was but the panic of a moment. I escaped all injury. But how can you have heard—

DEBORAH. O Mr Cleveland! that ever my dear young lady sent you away from us. We've had nothing but the ill luck of being broke down and overturned ever since: and I don't know yet half how bad I am; but I dare say— 55

CLEVELAND. Dear Mrs Deborah, will you have the kindness to ask Mungo if the baggage is all right? 60

DEBORAH. Ay, ay, Mr Cleveland, I understand you well enough! you've only a mind to get rid of me, that you may say pretty things to my dear young lady here. As if you could not just as well say 'em before me. I warrant you suppose I have never had a sweetheart myself. Lord help your poor young heads both of you! 65

Exit.

CLEVELAND, ELIZA.

CLEVELAND. I must at least confess her penetration to be less deficient than her delicacy. My dearest Eliza! (*kissing her hand*) how anxiously—

ELIZA. Tell me, I beseech you, by what chance you were in this house? By what chance you discovered— 70

CLEVELAND. I was not in this house; nor must you, my Eliza, one unnecessary moment remain in it. Though nominally an Hotel, it is, in fact, a notorious Gaming House.

I.74 **Gaming House** Obviously, Eliza cannot have strayed into one of the noted men's clubs such as White's; Cleveland must be referring to one of the less respectable gambling houses that sprang up on St. James's Street. In any event, Cleveland's

ELIZA. Let me, then, hasten from it instantly. I have sent for some carriage— 75

CLEVELAND. Send rather for your Friends;—unless, indeed, you will accept me as a guard to convey you to them.

ELIZA. Not for the Universe! ignorant of our connexion, uninformed of its sanction from my generous adopted Father, what could they think of seeing me with a Guardian so little . . . venerable? 80

CLEVELAND. They would but think what, I flatter myself, they will almost immediately know, that I aspire at a claim for that honour which no age can dispute, no authority supersede. 85

ELIZA. But so abruptly, and after an absence of the greatest part of my life—will it not appear like triumphing in my independence? The power which they relinquished to my kind adopted Father may seem again, now I have lost him, to return to its first channel— 90

CLEVELAND. But did not He, did not Mr Alderson himself make over to me the tenderest as well as most solemn powers of protection? And has anything, but our sudden deprivation of him, prevented those powers from being rendered indissoluble?

ELIZA. 'Tis true; but they know not all this; and, till properly informed, their claims are so near, and must to themselves seem so complete that the communication cannot, I think, be made with too much circumspection. A Father,—A Mother—my dear Cleveland! what sacred ties! Even though my memory scarcely retains their figures, my heart acknowledges their rights, and palpitates with impatience to shew its instinctive duty. 95 100

CLEVELAND. I will not oppose an impulse which I revere. Send for them, however; it is improper, it is unsafe, stranger as you are to the Hydra-headed dangers of this vast metropolis, that you should trust yourself and your effects to a common hired carriage, with no other guards than this loquacious old soul, and an inexperienced black servant just imported from Calcutta. What can have induced you to part from Mr and Mrs 105

---

agitation is understandable, for in the eighteenth century, "no lady who valued her reputation was to be seen walking down Bond Street or St. James's Street": Stella Margetson, *Regency London* (New York: Praeger, 1971), 67–68.

I.107– **Calcutta** From 1757 to 1931, Calcutta was the capital of British India. It was also the most important commercial centre in India; "its trade exceeded a million pounds sterling a year, and upward of sixty vessels annually visited the port":

Brown who were to have delivered you into the hands of your Parents? 110

ELIZA. Let me write to my Father; I will then explain how it happened.

CLEVELAND. Is there no bell in this room? Here! Waiter!

Enter 1ST WAITER.

1ST WAITER. Your commands, sir?

CLEVELAND. A pen and ink for this lady. 115

ELIZA. And pray be so good as to contradict the orders I gave for a carriage.

1ST WAITER. A carriage, meme?

ELIZA. Yes; I begged you to let me have me one immediately.

1ST WAITER. Did you, meme? What wine did you say, sir? 120

CLEVELAND. Wine? I said pen and ink.

1ST WAITER. Pen and ink, sir?

CLEVELAND. Yes; make haste.

1ST WAITER. Certainly, sir. I wonder I don't. Pen and ink, indeed!
Aside, and exit loiteringly.

ELIZA, CLEVELAND.

CLEVELAND. Whoever comes hither but for wine, or for dice, is only in the way. 125

Enter DEBORAH.

DEBORAH. Well, I suppose I come too soon, according to the old story; but Mungo is safe, and the trunks are safe, and so—

CLEVELAND. Will you, then, have the goodness to get your lady a pen and ink? 130

DEBORAH. Now that's fudge again, just to get me off! Why I tell you, I should like to hear what you're to say as well as your-

---

J. H. Furneaux, ed., *India: A Grand Photographic History of the Land of Antiquity, the Vast Empire of the East. . .* (London: International Art, 1896), 166.

I.131 **fudge** "nonsense" (*The English Dialect Dictionary* [hereafter *EDD*], ed. Joseph Wright, London: Oxford, 1961).

selves. However, I'll call the waiter. Here, Waiter! (*opens the door and calls*)

CLEVELAND. How perverse! 135

Enter 2ND WAITER.

2ND WAITER. Commands?

CLEVELAND. A pen and ink, sir. This lady is waiting for a pen and ink.

2ND WAITER. This moment, sir. Is that all you called for, sir?

CLEVELAND. Yes, sir. I beg you to be expeditious. 140

2ND WAITER. This moment, sir. Curious people enough, these!

Aside, and exit yawning.

ELIZA, CLEVELAND, DEBORAH.

DEBORAH. Well, I must say I was better served by half in Calcutta, little as I like those Negro places. Though, to be sure,—

CLEVELAND. This is too fatiguing! I will be back instantly.

Exit.

ELIZA, DEBORAH.

DEBORAH. There, now! if he had not rather fetch the pen and ink himself, than talk to you before me! And here he is already! I believe he deals with a conjurer. 145

Re-enter CLEVELAND.

CLEVELAND. I have seized this from the adjoining room.

ELIZA. A thousand thanks.

She seats herself at a table and writes.

DEBORAH. If you'll believe me Mr Cleveland if it had not been for my old master's promising to be the making of me, if I'd take care of my dear young lady here across those seas, I'd no more have gone to the land's end, there, than I'd have flown in 150

I.153–54 **flown in the air** The allusion may be to "Balloon ascents from St George's Fields on the south side of the river [which] drew enormous crowds of spectators": Margetson, *Regency London*, 117. The first ascent was made by Vincenzio Lunardi on 15 September 1784. Dr. Johnson received three letters on 18 September about the new marvel (James Boswell, *Life of Johnson, Including Boswell's Journal* the air. But what my young lady sent you off for, as soon as we got on dry land, I don't know; for lord! as to being so afraid to let people see one's got a sweetheart. I never minded it, for my part, when it was my own case. And I don't know that I should now, if it was to happen to me over again. 155

ELIZA (*rising*). I have entreated their directions how to proceed. Deborah, pray find a messenger. 160

DEBORAH. Ay, ay; I'll go. If I can't make sport, at least I won't spoil it. I always suppose the case my own. So, if you won't talk before me, I'd as lieve go and look about me below. "To Thomas Watts, Esquire Bond Street." Well, I'll warrant you an answer in ten minutes. So talk fast; for I suppose they must not hear you no more than I. Lover's whims, lord help 'em! However, I've had my own. And nobody knows but what I may have 'em again. 165

Exit.

ELIZA, CLEVELAND.

CLEVELAND. Now, then, my Eliza, suffer me to learn why you have left your party?

ELIZA. Mr Brown was taken ill upon the road and obliged to stop last night at Guildford. His amiable wife, you will believe, could not quit him; but the distance from London was so short, that we travelled on separately this morning without scruple. We arrived in perfect safety; but as we passed through this street, and just opposite to this house, the chaise, which perhaps was overloaded, broke down. Tell me, now, by what means— 170 175

CLEVELAND. When I left you, as so rigidly you commanded, at Portsmouth, a thousand nameless fears prevented my proceeding, and I loitered, that, at least at every change of horses, I might gather news of your safety. But when I found, at Guild- 180

---

of a Tour to the Hebrides and Johnson's Diary of a Journey into North Wales, ed. George Birkbeck Hill, 6 vols., Oxford: Clarendon, 1887, 3:413).

I.171 **Guildford** Twenty-nine miles southwest of London in the county of Surrey, Guildford was an important staging post. A guidebook of 1800, *The History and Description of Guildford, the County-town of Surrey* (2d ed., Guildford: Russell [1800]), lists six coaches in addition to the mail coach which passed through Guildford every day between Portsmouth and London (p. 39).

I.178 **Portsmouth** Portsmouth in Hampshire was a major port for both the navy and trade vessels. See *Mansfield Park* for a description of Portsmouth's activity and noise (*Novels of Jane Austen*, 3:375–447).

ford, that you continued your journey without the Browns, my surprise and alarm made me order my driver to pursue your chaise closely till it stopt. Nevertheless the unlucky intervention of another carriage impeded my immediate view or knowledge of the accident which befel you; and when I got sight of it, you were already in the House. 185

ELIZA. You must not reproach my desire of a short separation. It is only that my Friends may hear the history of our engagement before you meet them; and that you may pay to your own the respect of soliciting their concurrence, ere you venture to present me to them. Ah! you know not how I tremble when I reflect upon what has dropt from you of the total apathy of your uncle Sir Marmaduke, towards everything and everybody where he has no personal interest; and of the exclusive partiality for rank and birth—so ill adapted to me and my connexions! of your Aunt, Lady Wilhelmina. 190 195

CLEVELAND. They will, they must adore you. Though Sir Marmaduke, I confess, were your virtues not seconded by your splendid independence, might at first, be too much self-occupied to perceive them; nor dare I feel any great security that my Aunt Wilhelmina would be conquered, even by the most endearing of your attractions, if your family still resided in the heart of the City: but since your last letters inform you that they are retired from business, and removed to this end of the Town, the same narrow pride may lead her now to respect, which, then, would have urged her, most illiberally, to scorn them. But when will you permit me to present myself? 200 205

ELIZA. When you have written to my Father. A line will suffice to make an opening. I will then completely develop the whole history: but I shall never have the courage to begin the subject. His consent, his approbation cannot be doubted. Your high family, their rank in life, and your noble connexions, will make him proud of such an alliance, and of the honour which it will reflect upon his Daughter. 210

CLEVELAND. Generous, noble Eliza! from you springs all of honour the connexion can boast; for what is honour if its source is not virtue? How do I now bless the parsimonious reserve of my 215

I.203 **the City** The mercantile centre of London, the heart of which is at the intersection of Poultry and Cornhill (Margetson, *Regency London*, 13).

Uncle, which compelled my Indian expedition! Without it, I had never known my Eliza! Yet how sick were my feelings when driven, by the fatigue of suspence, to seek a competence upon such distant shores, from the mental toil of dependence, upon one who perpetually warned me to expect nothing, though he brought me up to expect anything! 220

ELIZA. With what anxiety shall I long to hear the motive that has caused his so sudden, yet so imperious recall! 225

CLEVELAND. I cannot have any doubt but it is to announce me at length, openly for his heir. He would else certainly not have broken up, in so peremptory a manner, the rising promises of my own industry.

Enter DEBORAH.

DEBORAH. Well, I hope I've stayed away long enough now? Though I can't say you look very glad to see me. However, I forgive you; for a true lover's never very polite; except to his sweetheart. I know I'd never have spoken to mine again, if he had not been as rude as a bear to everybody else. But as the Porter said he'd be back in five minutes, I thought it best to give you a hint, for ten of them are over already. 230 235

ELIZA. O hasten away, then, I beseech you! you must not add the confusion of an explanation of this nature, to the perturbation of a meeting so affecting to my heart. I entreat you to begone!

CLEVELAND. Retain your firmness my Eliza! I obey. 240

Kisses her hand, and exit.

ELIZA, DEBORAH.

DEBORAH. He takes her hand with a very pretty air, that's the truth. If he were to do so my mine, I don't know for certain that I should send him away. I can't be sure.

ELIZA. Are you satisfied, Deborah, you found a safe messenger for my note? 245

DEBORAH. O, I made sure of that. Bring me an answer, says I, or bring the company along with you, and I'll give you half a crown; and the gentleman you go to will be sure to give you a handsome reward besides, for the good news you take him. That's the only way, my dear young lady; for as to trusting to 250 their promises—lord! what's a man's promise? I'll go and see if he's coming.

Exit.

ELIZA.

[ELIZA.] What an interview am I awaiting! what fears, what chilling doubts check my fondness and my hopes! Their approbation I think secure: but that of the friends of Cleveland— 255

1ST WAITER (*within*). Not there, sir, not there!—

ELIZA. Ah! they are come—Joy, now, takes place of all else! (*hastily opens the door*) Yes, here! here! here!

1ST WAITER (*as the door opens*). Very well, meme. O ho, is it so! (*Turns off singing while*

LORD JOHN DERVIS *and* FRANK *present themselves.*)

FRANK. Your servant, ma'am. 260

LORD JOHN. How dost do, Child?

ELIZA. Good Heaven!

FRANK. I am happy in the honour of your commands. What a pretty young thing, my Lord.

LORD JOHN. Consumed pretty. 265

ELIZA. What a cruel mistake!—I thought—I expected—

FRANK. No excuses, my dear. An adventure may save me from hanging or drowning. O Lord John! if you knew the diabolic run of ill luck I have had!— Not been in bed all night!

LORD JOHN. O the plague! 270

ELIZA. Gentlemen, I hope—I beg—this apartment—

FRANK. She is immensely handsome.

LORD JOHN. Devilish handsome!

ELIZA. If you will not relinquish my room, suffer me at least to pass to some other. (*advancing to the door*) 275

FRANK (*offering his hand*). Any other you please. Whither shall I conduct you?

ELIZA (*retreating*). Gentlemen I insist—I—Deborah!—Waiters! —Deborah!—

Enter DEBORAH.

DEBORAH. Hey day, what's this? What's your business here, Misters? 280

FRANK. What is yours for the enquiry Mrs Notable?
ELIZA. Do not answer Deborah; but desire somebody to shew me instantly to another apartment.
DEBORAH. That I will, I warrant. Here, Waiters! Waiters! (*calling aloud at the door*) 285
FRANK. Nay, fair lady, if we are seriously in your way— Mighty odd this Lord John. What did she call us in for?
LORD JOHN. Confounded odd.

Enter 1ST WAITER.

1ST WAITER. Commands? 290
ELIZA. Be so good, sir, as to let me have some room to myself till the arrival of my friends.
1ST WAITER. Here's one here, meme.

Opens a door on the other side.

ELIZA. Are you sure I shall be unmolested, there, sir, for the few minutes I have to remain? 295
1ST WAITER. O yes, meme.
ELIZA. Come then, Deborah.
DEBORAH. Yes my dear young lady.

ELIZA *goes into the next room; but as* DEBORAH *is following,* FRANK *twitches her back by the arm.*

DEBORAH. O lord! you fright me to death! save me, Mr Waiter, save me! 300
1ST WAITER. He! He! He!

Exit.

LORD JOHN, FRANK, DEBORAH
LORD JOHN *and* FRANK *draw* DEBORAH *from the door.*

LORD JOHN. Come, no airs, you old cat.
DEBORAH. Old cat? O! (*screaming*)
FRANK. Nay, nay, don't be affronted, my dear, 'tis only a phrase

I.282 **Mrs. Notable** Used to refer to women who are "capable, managing, bustling" (*OED*). In Arthur Murphy's *The Citizen* (1761) (London: Kearsly, 1763), Sir Jasper Wilding, perhaps ironically, calls Maria "Miss Notable" when she acts flighty, and she uses the term to describe herself when she has managed to break off her match with Philpot (pp. 5, 34).

of his Lordship's to his particular favourites. Pray who is that young thing? 305

DEBORAH. I won't tell you: so let me go.

FRANK. Why then I suppose you don't know, my Angel?

DEBORAH. Not know? Why who went with her to the East Indies then? And who came back with her? 310

FRANK. East Indies? Has she been to the East Indies?

LORD JOHN. What the plague did she do in the East Indies?

DEBORAH. That's more than the old cat will tell, I promise you.

FRANK. Nay, nay, don't bear malice. You look the very picture of sweetness and gentleness. 315

DEBORAH. Nay, as to that, I never was reckoned wanting in affability. Though I've met with but base returns, often enough!

FRANK. But perhaps you never heard any of her private history?

DEBORAH. Never heard? Why was not I Housekeeper to Mr Alderson from the time he adopted her? Did not I buy all the fine 320 things he ordered for her when he took the maggot to make her his heiress? And did not I carry back all her old cloaths for her sister, because the family then was as poor as Job? Never heard, indeed!

FRANK. Heiress? What, is she an Heiress? I hope we have not 325 been impertinent. That waiter deserves to have his bones broke for not telling us.

LORD JOHN. O the Deuce! toss him in a blanket.

FRANK. So she's to have a pretty considerable fortune, is she, Mrs Abigail? 330

DEBORAH. What do you call pretty considerable? She has eighty thousand pounds if she has a penny. However, Abigail's no name of mine.

FRANK. Eighty thousand pounds!

LORD JOHN. O the plague! I'll horse-pond that waiter in five 335 minutes!

I.321 **took the maggot** "A whimsical or perverse fancy; a crotchet" (*OED*).

I.328 **toss him in a blanket** Cf. *Camilla* (ed. Edward A. Bloom and Lillian D. Bloom, New York: Oxford, 1972), in which Lynmere recoils from Sir Hugh's plans to marry him to Eugenia and threatens: "Does he want me to toss him in a blanket?" (p. 568).

I.335 **horse-pond** "To duck in or drag through a horse-pond" (*OED*). In Hugh Kelly's *False Delicacy* (4th ed., London: Baldwin, Johnston, and Kearsly, 1768), when Rivers overhears the maid Sally counsel his daughter to elope, he threatens: "I may chance to cool your transport in a horse-pond" (p. 40).

FRANK. And when is this to come into possession, Mrs Rachel?

DEBORAH. I shan't tell you. But as to the when, why it's all in her own hands at this very minute. However Rachel's no name of mine. 340

FRANK. All her's now? But then, I conclude those poor relations, Mrs Bridget,—

DEBORAH. Nay Bridget's no name of mine neither; so there you're mistaken again. But as to her poor relations, I believe you'd be pretty glad to be half as rich. Why they are like so 345 many Crecusses now.

FRANK. Are they so, faith?— And their names—O, I recollect, their names—ay, their names are Stevens?

DEBORAH. Stevens? You know much of the matter to be sure. Why their names are Watts. He was nothing but an errand boy, 350 or such like, at his beginning. And as to she he married, she was no more than his master's housemaid: a poor mean thing—

ELIZA (*within*). Deborah! Deborah!

DEBORAH. My young lady calls! Now I wish you were both at old Nick for keeping me so! 355

Exit.

LORD JOHN, FRANK.

FRANK. Eighty thousand pounds, my dear Lord John!

LORD JOHN. That waiter deserves the bastinado.

FRANK. Eighty thousand pounds!

LORD JOHN. What the D--l can she do here?

FRANK. Eighty thousand pounds! 360

LORD JOHN. What? Hast a fancy to 'em?

FRANK. 'Twould be convenient.

LORD JOHN. What, marry? O the plague!

FRANK. The very D--l! And yet, eighty thousand pounds! 'twould be rather convenient. 365

LORD JOHN. Deuced convenient.

FRANK. And one might have her without much trouble. She can

I.346 **Crecusses** Deborah's mispronunciation of Croesus, the king of Lydia known for his great wealth.

I.355 **old Nick** The devil (*EDD*).

I.357 **bastinado** "caning or cudgelling, to beat or cane" (*OED*). In Burney's *Evelina* (ed. Edward A. Bloom, London: Oxford, 1968), Willoughby threatens to bastinado Evelina's dancing partner (p. 42).

have seen nobody yet. She can know nothing. And I hate trouble.

LORD JOHN. So do I, confoundedly.

FRANK. It's worth a thought. What can I do to scrape acquaintance with her? 370

LORD JOHN. Horse-whip the waiter.

FRANK. What will that do?

LORD JOHN. Make him call to her to beg him off.

FRANK. Admirable! Here, Waiter! Waiter! 375

LORD JOHN. Waiter Waiter!

Enter 2ND WAITER.

2ND WAITER. Coming, sir. Where's the young lady?

FRANK. Frightened away by your impertinence, sir. How came you—

LORD JOHN. Yes, how came you— 380

2ND WAITER. Here's a coachfull of company enquiring for her.

FRANK. Ha? Let's find out what they are.

LORD JOHN. Yes; but bastinado the waiter: Don't forget that.

FRANK. I will. How came you, I say,—

Enter MR WATTS.

MR WATTS. Where's my Darter? 385

FRANK. Umph!

2ND WAITER. I'm positive, sir, I left the young lady here.

FRANK. Young lady, sir? Pray may I presume, sir,—Are you a relation of the young lady?

MR WATTS. Yes, sir. She's one of my Darters. I've two. T'other's coming upstairs. 390

FRANK. I believe then, sir, the excessive insolence of one of these waiters has obliged the young lady to take refuge in another room.

2ND WAITER. Pretty well for assurance that! That's just such a gentleman as I should like to be myself. 395

Apart, and exit.

LORD JOHN, FRANK, MR WATTS.

FRANK. Will you give me leave, sir, to make use of your name in acquainting the young lady she may return in safety?

MR WATTS. Sir, I shall take it kind. I don't know what she should go pottering a'ter, just as we're all come. 400

FRANK (*tapping at the door by which* ELIZA *has entered*). Madam! Miss Watts! permit me, I entreat, the honour of offering some apology, and of informing you that Mr Watts is now here.

ELIZA (*rushing out*). O where? Where? My Father! my dear Father! 405

She runs to MR WATTS, *takes his hand, and drops upon one knee to him.*

MR WATTS. How do do, my dear? You're welcome home again. Well! I should never have known you! But what have you been a'ter? I hope the waiter ha'n't been sarcy?

Enter MISS WATTS.

MISS WATTS. La, Pa', what did you leave us for so? We've been up the wrong stairs; and I dare say Ma'll be blundering on this 410 half hour.

MR WATTS. Why, my dear, I wanted to see your sister of the soonest, so I e'en put my best foot foremost.

ELIZA (*running to embrace* MISS WATTS). My Sister!

MISS WATTS. O dear, is it you, Sister Eliziana? How you're grown! 415 How do do, Sister? What a pretty hat you've got on! I'll have just the fellow to it. Pray who are those two smart beaus you've got with you?

FRANK (*apart to* LORD JOHN). What a vulgar tribe!

LORD JOHN. Consumed vulgar! 420

Enter MRS WATTS.

MRS WATTS. Well. I've found my way at last. But I can't think, Tommy, how you could be so rude as to go on at sich a rate, leaving one all alone so. And the stairs are all dirty! Here's all my nice petticoats—

MR WATTS. Why, my dear, I thought your Darter would think it 425 long till she saw us, so I thought—

ELIZA. Is that my Mother?—my dear Mother!—

Runs to MRS WATTS *with open arms.*

MRS WATTS. Take care, my dear, take a little care, or you'll squeeze my poor new Handkerchief till it won't be fit to be seen. And it cost me sich a sight of money— 430

MISS WATTS. La, Ma', what signifies? I hope you can buy another. (*whispers her*) What do you talk so mean for before those two smart gentlemen?

MRS WATTS. Nay, my dear, I don't do it to find fault, for I think it very pretty of your sister to be in sich a hurry; only there's no need to spoil one's things. Come, my dear Betsey— 435

MISS WATTS (*whispering*). La, Ma', what do you call her Betsey for? you're as bad as Pa'! You know I told you she's to be called Eliziana now.

MRS WATTS. Yes, Elizinneny I mean. I'm sure, my dear, I'm very glad to see you again. You've been a long ways. (*kisses her*) Why you're grown quite a woman my dear! 440

FRANK (*apart to* LORD JOHN). This won't do Lord John!

LORD JOHN. O confound it, no!

MR WATTS. I wonder why those two fine chaps can't as well go and find out another room! (*aside*) Pray, my dear Darter, what was it took old Alderson off? Did he leave much over your fourscore? What do you cry for, my dear? 445

FRANK (*apart to* LORD JOHN). Fourscore? Poor Girl! 'tis pity—

LORD JOHN. O, it's the Deuce! 450

MRS WATTS. I hope you a'n't sorry to see us, my dear?

ELIZA. O no!—but the remembrance of Mr Alderson—his virtues—his benevolence, his unceasing kindness— (*weeps*)

MRS WATTS. Pray, my dear, have you got over much Indy muslin? I ha'n't bought a morsel since I knew you was coming. 455

ELIZA. You will permit me, I hope, to lay all my stores at your feet.

MRS WATTS. I'm sure that's a very pretty thought of you, my dear.

FRANK (*apart to* LORD JOHN). If she i'n't seized quickly, she won't be worth capture.

MRS WATTS. Pray, my dear, who are these two young gentlemen with you? 460

FRANK (*advancing*). I—I—I—

MR WATTS. Did they travel over in the same ship with you, my dear?

MISS WATTS. La, Pa', I wish you wouldn't talk. The gentleman's going to speak himself. 465

ELIZA. They are entirely strangers to me, sir.

FRANK. I beg a million of pardons—but I have only waited for a moment's opportunity to express my concern and confusion, and—and—I beg an hundred thousand pardons—I am so utterly confounded—the accident—but the waiter— 470

LORD JOHN. O the rascal! come and let's murder him.
MISS WATTS. O la!
MRS WATTS. O dear!
FRANK. Don't be alarmed, ladies. We'll step into the next room before we proceed to action. It won't do, Lord John! it won't do! 475
Apart to LORD JOHN, *and exeunt together into the inner room.*

ELIZA, MR, MRS *and* MISS WATTS.

MISS WATTS. La, Pa', why didn't you ask 'em to stay? You're always so monstrous stupid!
MRS WATTS. Yes, indeed, Tommy, you're always very stupid: I must say that for you. 480
MISS WATTS. Pray, Sister Eliziana, where did you get that pretty travelling dress?
ELIZA. It was made in Calcutta.
MISS WATTS. La! can they make things there? I thought they'd been all savages. 485
MR WATTS. Yes, yes, they can make pretty good things there, I promise you! I suppose there's more hundred thousands made in Calcutta than in all the known world besides.
MISS WATTS. Pray, Sister, do the Indins do much mischief?
ELIZA. Mischief? 490
MISS WATTS. What kind of look have they? Do they let 'em run about wild? Wa'n't you monstrous frightened at first?
ELIZA. Frightened? The native Gentoos are the mildest and gentlest of human beings.
MISS WATTS. La, nasty black things! I can't abide the Indins. I'm sure I should do nothing but squeal if I was among 'em. 495
MR WATTS. There's no need for you to go among 'em now, my dear, for I can give you as handsome I war'nt me, as the Nabob gave your Sister.

I.493 **Gentoos** "pagan inhabitant of Indostan, opposed to Mohammedan; a Hindoo" (*OED*). Cf. Hannah Cowley, *Who's the Dupe?* (1779), where Granger's brother wants him to go to the East Indies to "take a sweating with Gentoos": Elizabeth Inchbald, ed., *A Collection of Farces and Other Afterpieces*, 7 vols. (London: Longmans, Hurst, Rees, Orme, and Brown, 1815), 1:266.
I.498 **Nabob** James M. Holzman describes a nabob as "a civil or military servant of the [East India] Company, who enriched himself by exploiting the advantages which the establishment of British political dominion in India gave to the officials of the ruling power on the spot": *The Nabobs in England: A Study of the Returned Anglo-Indian, 1760–1785* (New York: N.p., 1926), 8. The term came to mean

MRS WATTS. It's surprising, my dear Darter Elizeneny, that you didn't get a rich husband yourself there: for I'm told the men in Indy all want wives. 500

MR WATTS. I'm sure I wish we could send 'em some. I'd spare 'em mine! (*half aside*)

MRS WATTS. What's that you say Tommy? 505

Enter MR TIBBS.

MR TIBBS. I beg pardon, ladies and gentlemen—I was told there was one Mr Watts here. I'm sure I don't know how the waiter could make such a mistake. I beg pardon— (*bowing frequently and retreating*)

MR WATTS. Mr Watts? Why pray what do you want with— Oddso! if it i'n't Cousin Joel Tibbs! 510

MR TIBBS. Why what's it you my dear Tom! Good lauk! I can't believe my eyes!

MR WATTS. My dear Joel Tibbs! (*they embrace*)

MISS WATTS. La, how provoking Pa' is as if he couldn't have walked off, and made believe he did not know him! 515

MRS WATTS. Dear if itn't Joel Tibbs. Come, my dears, let's get away. Only just— (*pinning up her apron*)

MR TIBBS. Why how you be decked out! Why I shouldn't have known you if I'd met you anywhere upon the face of Earth. 520

MR WATTS. My dear Joel, why I ha'n't seen you these eighteen years!

MR TIBBS. Silk stockings, as I live!— And a ruffled shirt! well, if anybody'd have said to me That's Tom Watts, I'd have contradicted 'em as flat as a pancake! And how does Cousin Aylce do? 525

MRS WATTS. Come, my dears,—I've pinned up my apron. Now let's go.

MISS WATTS. Yes, and shew Sister Eliziana about a little, poor thing.

MR WATTS. Why there she is! why, my dear! why don't you see Cousin Tibbs? 530

MRS WATTS. Come, Girls; la, my dear, you tread o' my gown.

MR TIBBS. What that? Is that Cousin Aylce? Lauk a Day! why

---

anyone who "returned from India with a large fortune acquired there" (*OED*). Uncle Oliver in Richard Brinsley Sheridan's *School for Scandal* is referred to as a nabob.

the World's turned topsy turvy! Cousin Aylce in a silk gown! And pray what's become of the children? How does Peg do? And the little one, that was just beginning to prittle-prattle? 535

MISS WATTS. I declare Ma', you're enough to provoke a saint! why can't you come along?

MRS WATTS. Why you wouldn't have me go without wiping my gown? Why there's all the marks of your feet upon it! 540

MR WATTS. Why that's she! that's Peg! Only think of your not knowing her! Peggy, my dear, turn about and shew yourself. Here's your old Cousin Joel Tibbs.

MISS WATTS. La, Pa', why can't you hold your tongue? What do you call me Peg for? How often have I told you I'm Margerella? 545

MR TIBBS. What's that Cousin Peg! Good lauk! who'd have thought it! Dressed out like a fine lady in the front boxes! well, I'm glad the World goes so merrily with you all. But what, don't you know me, Cousin Aylce?

MRS WATTS. Why indeed, as to that,—I can't pretend to say I remember everybody I see. 550

MR TIBBS. Why then we're even: for I should no more have known you than the Pope. You're prodigious altered. Your nose is grown as big again as it was when Cousin Tom married you.

MRS WATTS. Pray, sir, be so good as to look at your own! It's none of the least, I can tell you, whatever you may think of it. 555

MR TIBBS. And your eyes—that used to be so sparkish,—why they're as dull! And there's ever such a heap of little wizen wrinkles round 'em.

MRS WATTS. Dear sir, I wish you'd please to look at home! You've not stood still, no more than your neighbours. Come let's go. Tommy! my dear, come, too. What do you stop for? 560

Exit.

MR WATTS. Well, Girls, do you at least—

MISS WATTS. La, Pa' what do you say Girls for? Can't you say young ladies? I really think Pa' grows worse and worse every day. He'll never be the gentleman. 565

Exit muttering.

ELIZA. Alas! alas! Cleveland! How will his friends permit—how will he himself endure an intercourse so new to him!

Apart and exit.

I.547 **a fine lady in the front boxes** Mr. Tibbs may be knowingly insulting the Watts ladies, since the *Theatrical Guardian*, no. 5 (2 April 1791), informs us that the front boxes of a theatre were usually used by prostitutes (pp. 27–28).

MR WATTS, MR TIBBS.

MR TIBBS. Well, I declare! who'd have thought of their flouncing off so! Do you think, Cousin, Aylce minded about her nose? I said it for no harm. 570

MR WATTS. Ah! my dear Joel Tibbs! I've a deal to tell you of our new ways! If you can but come to me tomorrow morning—before my wife gets up—

MR TIBBS. How lucky it was I should happen to go by just now! I was thinking of you no more than the post; but I saw a shay broke down, as I was walking along, so I stopt to ask who it belonged to; and they thought I asked whose the coach was— Good lauk, Tom, that ever I should live to see you keep your coach! Such a poor snivelling Boy as I remember you!— Well, they said 'twas 'squire Watts's. Watts?—says I; why sure— 575 580

Enter a PORTER.

PORTER. Sir, the gentlewoman that sent me to you with the note, says you'll give me a reward.

MR WATTS. Me? Why did not she pay you herself?

PORTER. Yes, sir; only she says I took you such good news, she's sure you'll give me something over. 585

MR WATTS. No, my lad, no; I never did that in my life. Goodbye, Cousin Joel.

PORTER. Why, your Honour! won't you give me something to drink, your Honour? (*following*) 590

MR WATTS. To drink? Why, what, are you dry friend?

PORTER. We always have something to drink, your Honour, from gentlefolks.

MR WATTS. Have you? Well, then,—here! Waiter!—bring the lad a jug of water. 595

Exit.

MR TIBBS, PORTER.

PORTER. Water? A jug of water!— There's a fellow! There's a Rogue!— If I don't go and give him his dues—

I.576 **shay** Chaise, a "regular family carriage . . . which could hold three persons": *Novels of Jane Austen*, 3:561.

MR TIBBS. Ha! Ha! Ha! Hark ye my lad! I ha'n't got so high up in the World as Tom Watts, and I never was so low down; but if you carried him good news, you shan't be disappointed of your Pot, my boy. There! (*giving him money*) And take this with it; never yearn after over-riches; if they come when a man's young, they only make him a spendthrift; and if they come when he's old, they make him a miser or a fool. It's better be content with a little,—and ready to share it with them that have less. 600 605

Exit.

PORTER. Thank your Honour! Water, and be hanged to un! A jug of water! I wish he had it in his face!

Exit.

Re-enter LORD JOHN, *and* FRANK.

FRANK. What's to be done, my dear Lord John? What's to be done in this desperate moment?

LORD JOHN. O the very D--l of a moment! 610

FRANK. These people are so extravagantly vulgar—

LORD JOHN. O, confound it! don't think of them.

FRANK. Though it would not much signify, I should never see them, after the horrid bore of the ceremony. But then,—my aunt—Lady Wilhelmina—she'd never forgive it. Such a set of new Nephews and Neices and Cousins—I don't know if it would not cost her an apoplectic fit. 615

LORD JOHN. O the plague! Give it up.

FRANK. And yet my dear lord—'tis a barbarous temptation—she seems thrown into my very hands—and . . . I have not at this moment a guinea left in the World! 620

LORD JOHN. Not a guinea?

FRANK. Not a crown, by Jupiter!

LORD JOHN. Not a crown?

FRANK. Not a sixpence; by Mars, Jupiter, and Apollo! 625

LORD JOHN. O take her, then, take her! 'Tis better than the King's Bench.

FRANK. And she is really young and pretty.— 'Twould but a

I.601 **Pot** "small still" (*EDD*), probably used here to mean ale or beer.

I.627 **King's Bench** "A jail formerly appropriated to debtors and criminals confined by authority of the supreme courts at Westminster" (*OED*).

charity. I must positively think of it. A little rhodomontade is all she can require. Come, my Lord John, you can help me. You shall go and tell Sir Marmaduke and my Aunt Wilhelmina that 'tis my fixt resolve to take this measure: and then, either they will draw their purse strings and pay my debts, or I'll fairly put the eighty thousand pounds into my pocket. 630

End of Act I

ACT II

A drawing room at SIR MARMADUKE TYLNEY'S. SIR MARMADUKE *is discovered seated at a table reading a newspaper, and* MISS CLEVELAND *at work.*

SIR MARMADUKE. Now what an unfortunate thing is this! Stocks risen one per cent!

MISS CLEVELAND. How glad I am for poor Mrs Summers! She is obliged to sell out all she is worth this very day, to settle with her husband's creditors. Why should you be sorry, Uncle? 5

SIR MARMADUKE. Pish! What is Mrs Summers to me? 'Tis the very D--l. I had an odd fifty pounds lying by me, that I told Jacobs to buy in this very morning.

MISS CLEVELAND. But what, my dear Uncle, is fifty pounds to you, compared with a stake so important to Mrs Summers and her children? 10

SIR MARMADUKE. Pho, pho, don't make such an ado about her. What are her children to me? I may lose between thirteen and fourteen shillings by this unlucky rise.

MISS CLEVELAND. Forget it, at least, for the present, to think of the near approach of my Brother. We may now reasonably hope to see him in a day or two. The wind is so delightfully fair— 15

I.629 **rhodomontade** "a blustering and bragging speech; from Rodomont, the brave but braggart leader of the Saracens in Boiardo's *Orlando Innamorato*": *Brewer's Dictionary of Phrase and Fable*, rev. ed. (London: Cassell, 1959). General Tylney, in *Northanger Abbey*, has been "misled by the rhodomontade" of John Thorpe regarding Catherine Morland's fortune (*Novels of Jane Austen*, 4:26).

SIR MARMADUKE. Fair? And be hanged to it! It's so rough and harsh, it cuts me off from my ride.

MISS CLEVELAND. But if it facilitates his return, after a voyage so long, so dangerous, so painful— 20

SIR MARMADUKE. Pish! What's his voyage to my ride?

MISS CLEVELAND. I thought you were quite anxious to see him?

SIR MARMADUKE. Well, so I am: but there's no need I should lose my ride to hurry him home. 25

MISS CLEVELAND. O shocking! to have him tost to and fro' on that immense Ocean!—

SIR MARMADUKE. Pho, pho, don't make such a fuss about nothing. You know I can't bear to lose my ride. And what harm can it do a young man to be a week or two more or less in a warm comfortable Cabin? 30

MISS CLEVELAND. Pray, sir, has Aaron told you of poor Tomson's death?

SIR MARMADUKE. Death?

MISS CLEVELAND. Yes. He died last night. I was sure you would be much concerned. 35

SIR MARMADUKE. Concerned? Why, I hope it is not really true?

MISS CLEVELAND. Aaron saw his Mother this morning.

SIR MARMADUKE. The D--l! why, it is but two days ago that I lent him half a guinea! 40

MISS CLEVELAND. Poor worthy man!

SIR MARMADUKE. And I have no note for it!

MISS CLEVELAND. And his Mother, my dear Uncle—

SIR MARMADUKE. Pho, pho, what's his mother to me! I shall never recover that half guinea! 45

Enter AARON.

AARON. I am sorry, sir, to be the bearer of ill news, but Robert is just returned from Tylney Hall, and he says—

SIR MARMADUKE. Why what's the matter now? Are any of my tenants run away?

AARON. No, sir; but there broke out such a dreadful fire in the village yesterday morning— 50

SIR MARMADUKE. You don't say so? Has it done any mischief to Tylney Hall?

AARON. No, sir, not to Tylney Hall; but—

SIR MARMADUKE. You make me tremble! are any of the houses burnt belonging to my Estate? 55

AARON. No, sir, not one: but—

SIR MARMADUKE. Why then, what do you put on such a long face for? I hate a long face for nothing. Would you have just that single village in the whole World, exempt from mischief, lest that blockhead Robert should be frightened? 60

AARON. No, sir; but there are so many sufferers!—

SIR MARMADUKE. Well, don't make such a pother if there are. Everybody must submit to accident.

AARON. Poor old Mr Walters, sir, threw himself from his chamber window, and broke both his legs. 65

MISS CLEVELAND. O!

SIR MARMADUKE. Well, well, well, who can help it? What's the use of repining? I hate repining.

AARON. And that i'n't all, sir; Mrs Mark was overturned in her chaise by her horses taking fright in trying to pass the crowd. 70

MISS CLEVELAND. O poor Mrs Mark.

SIR MARMADUKE. Well, well, if people can't bear to risk an overturn, they have no business to keep carriages.

AARON. And Lord Garman has had the narrowest escape of all. A flake of fire fell upon his head just as he was getting into his carriage, and one whole side of his Hair has been singed off. 75

MISS CLEVELAND. How terrible!

SIR MARMADUKE. A mighty matter, truly! as if his barber could not furnish him with another. Learn to make light of little evils, Neice. If every trifling misfortune is to be aggravated in this manner— 80

AARON. And another flake, sir, light just upon our little Hay-rick near the Barn, and burnt it to the ground.

SIR MARMADUKE. What, what do you say? 85

AARON. A flake of fire, sir, light upon our little Hayrick, and consumed it in a minute.

SIR MARMADUKE. The D--l it did?

AARON. Yes, sir; but it's only the little one.

SIR MARMADUKE. Only? I wish it had been your own house, with all my heart! Only? There is not a thing I had a more particular value for. I had rather by half the whole village had been burnt! 90

AARON. Sir, the great stack is quite safe; and we have fared better than anybody else in all the neighbourhood, for Squire Pollard has lost three of his horses by the fall of a stack of chimneys; Squire Milton two of his cows, by— 95

SIR MARMADUKE. And pray what do I care for that? What are their horses and cows to me? My little Hay-rick!—There was never so unfortunate a thing since the World was formed! This year, too, of all others—My little Hay-rick!— 100

Exit, followed by AARON.

Enter LADY WILHELMINA TYLNEY.

MISS CLEVELAND. O Lady Wilhelmina! have you heard of this terrible fire that Robert brings the account of from Tylney Hall?

LADY WILHELMINA. Yes. It has extremely affected me. I find Lord Garman has nearly lost all his Hair. 105

MISS CLEVELAND. O, that's nothing! but poor old Walters has broken both his legs!

LADY WILHELMINA. Nothing, Miss Cleveland? I am surprised to hear you speak so lightly of a misfortune of that nature to such a Nobleman as Lord Garman, whose Hair was so deservedly admired. As to old—what is it the man calls himself?—persons of his class must naturally expect to be exposed, now and then, to some disagreeable events. 110

MISS CLEVELAND. Dear madam, does not your La'ship think it a greater evil for a poor man to lose his legs, than for a man of rank to lose his Hair? 115

LADY WILHELMINA. Certainly not. A man of rank is peculiarly susceptible to evil, because not brought up to vulgar vicissitudes; but a low person has so little leisure to reflect or refine, that a few disagreeable accidents can make but little impression upon him. 120

MISS CLEVELAND. Ah Lady Wilhelmina!— Pardon me—but because you do not enquire into the poor man's feelings, is it therefore to be concluded he has none?

LADY WILHELMINA. That is a point I do not investigate. And, indeed, Miss Cleveland, if you discoursed rather more rarely of people of that description yourself, I should think it more becoming a young woman of fashion. As to me, I confess I always feel degraded for the rest of the day, when I have been induced to converse upon any low subjects. 125 130

MISS CLEVELAND. May I beg your La'ship's permission for the carriage to call upon Miss Percival?

LADY WILHELMINA. Willingly. That is an acquaintance you cannot too much cultivate. I always encouraged it, even before the death of her noble Brother, and our views of affinity. 135

MISS CLEVELAND. Yet not, I should think, from much sympathy of character.

LADY WILHELMINA. Sympathy of character, Miss Cleveland, is mere romance. Miss Percival's connexions are of the first class. When I know that, I am unmoved by little excentricities. 140

MISS CLEVELAND. I am sure I wish everybody else would give her the same law.

LADY WILHELMINA. Everybody else, Miss Cleveland? I hope you don't hold it requisite that a young lady allied like Miss Percival, should consult the opinions of such persons as everybody 145 else?

Enter AARON.

AARON. Lord John Dervis.

Exit.

Enter LORD JOHN DERVIS.

LORD JOHN. Servant, good folks. Hope you're all well. What a confounded hot morning.

LADY WILHELMINA. I am extremely glad you were announced 150 Lord John; I might else have feared the Porter had admitted someone not upon my list.

LORD JOHN. How so, Lady Wil?

LADY WILHELMINA. The mode of your entry is so entirely new to me, Lord John, that it might have led me to apprehend one 155 of your Lordship's grooms—you'll pardon me, my lord—had taken the liberty to present himself before me in person.

LORD JOHN. What kept you from the Coffee Room last night? (*to* MISS CLEVELAND)

II.158 **Coffee Room** See *Evelina*, 39: "When the opera was over, we went into a place called the coffee-room, where ladies as well as gentlemen assemble. There are all sorts of refreshments, and the company walk about, and *chat*, with the same ease and freedom as in a private room."

MISS CLEVELAND. I was not at the Opera.

LORD JOHN. No? What in the World did you do with yourself? 160

Enter SIR MARMADUKE.

SIR MARMADUKE. Can you tell me which way the wind is, Lord John?

LORD JOHN. There's none.

SIR MARMADUKE. No wind? Ring the bell, then, Jemima, and order the horses. Come, now I shall get my ride. 165

LORD JOHN. Your horses, Sir Marmaduke? Why there's a pelting shower of rain.

SIR MARMADUKE. Rain?

LORD JOHN. Yes. I met old Farmer Dubbins just as I came in, blessing himself aloud that it would be the saving of the corn. 170

SIR MARMADUKE. Hang the corn! now I shall lose my ride again!

LORD JOHN. Sir Marmaduke, may I speak to you upon a little business?

SIR MARMADUKE. I never meddle with other people's affairs. (*going*) 175

LORD JOHN. O but this is an affair of your own.

SIR MARMADUKE. An affair of my own? (*turning short back*)

LORD JOHN. Yes; that is of your Nephew, my friend Frank Cleveland.

SIR MARMADUKE. What, he wants money, again, I suppose? 180

LORD JOHN. Plaguely.

SIR MARMADUKE. I thought so. Your servant, my Lord.

Exit.

Manent LADY WILHELMINA, LORD JOHN, MISS CLEVELAND.

LORD JOHN. O the D--l! I'll open the case to you then, Lady Wil.

LADY WILHELMINA. I am always happy to converse with your Lordship; but as to Mr Francis Cleveland's affairs, I make it a point never to interfere in them. (*going*) 185

LORD JOHN (*yawning*). Poor Frank! then he must e'en marry the little Cockney!

LADY WILHELMINA (*returning*). My Lord?

MISS CLEVELAND. Lord John! 190

LORD JOHN. Why it's a horrid bore; but what's to be done? A man must eat and drink.

LADY WILHELMINA. I trust, Lord John, it is not from you we shall receive intelligence of any disgrace intended to our family, for I cannot doubt but you would be shocked equally with ourselves at any degenerate alliance. 195

LORD JOHN. The Deuce a whit! If a man must needs be forced into the noose, it comes to the same thing if it's tied East as West. All points are one that do but replenish the coffers. Poor Frank's are plaguy low. 200

MISS CLEVELAND. But what is it you mean, Lord John?

LORD JOHN. That he has just met with a nice little Cit, who dies to have a woman of quality for her aunt.

LADY WILHELMINA. Lord John, permit me to say, you allow yourself to associate with persons beneath your dignity, till you acquire habits of familiarity that have rather an unpleasant effect. 205

MISS CLEVELAND. Do pray, Lord John, explain yourself. Has my brother Frank really had the good sense and the good fortune to form a connexion with any respectable family in the City? 210

LADY WILHELMINA. Miss Cleveland?

LORD JOHN. Respectable Family? Why they are as much below the City as us! They are as much outcasts with them as here. The vulgarest tribe!

MISS CLEVELAND. O fie, fie Frank! 215

LADY WILHELMINA. And is it possible, is it credible, Lord John, you can condescend to bear us such an embassy?

LORD JOHN. Why what the plague can a poor fellow do Lady Wil? He can't starve.

LADY WILHELMINA. And can you, my Lord, think mixing with persons of such a stamp— 220

LORD JOHN. Better than starving? Yes, I can faith.

LADY WILHELMINA. Intolerable! this must be put an end to. Lord John, assure him of our highest displeasure.

LORD JOHN. May I assure him you'll pay his debts? 225

LADY WILHELMINA. Impossible! we are just engaged in forming an establishment for his elder brother. But tell him we will make

II.202 Cit "short for citizen: usually applied, more or less contemptuously, to a townsman or 'cockney' as distinguished from a gentleman" (*OED*).

every exertion in his favour. Tell him I will myself intercede for sending him to the East Indies in his Brother's place.

LORD JOHN. What to fag? O the plague! no, no, Lady Wil! You won't catch Frank at fagging. 230

Enter AARON.

AARON. Mr Cleveland is arrived, my Lady.

Exit.

Enter CLEVELAND.

MISS CLEVELAND (*running to embrace him*). My dear Brother!

CLEVELAND. My dearest Sister!

LADY WILHELMINA. I am so much disconcerted, I can scarcely speak. Mr Cleveland, give me leave to congratulate you upon your safe return. 235

CLEVELAND. Your Ladyship is extremely good. I hope my Uncle—

Enter SIR MARMADUKE.

SIR MARMADUKE. My dear Nephew! 240

CLEVELAND. I have obeyed your summons, sir, with all the promptitude in my power.

SIR MARMADUKE. And you shall be well rewarded. I have not sent for you over upon a fool's errand. Give me credit for that. I think at last (*in a low voice*) I have got a handsome provision for you. 245

LADY WILHELMINA. If you wish to speak with Mr Cleveland alone, Sir Marmaduke, my Lord John will favour Miss Cleveland and me with his company in my dressing room. I can hardly breathe! To be connected with persons of such a class! 250

Exit.

MISS CLEVELAND. My dear Brother! (*shakes hands with* CLEVELAND *and follows*)

LORD JOHN. I've put her in the D--l of a worry.

Exit.

II.230 **fag** "To do something that wearies one; to work hard; to labour, strain, toil" (*OED*). At V.66, the word is used as a noun, meaning a junior schoolboy who must work for a senior one—"dare no more disobey her than a fag his monitor."

Manent SIR MARMADUKE *and* CLEVELAND.

SIR MARMADUKE. Well, my dear Nephew, and what now, do you think has made me send for you back? 255
CLEVELAND. I wait your own time for information, sir.
SIR MARMADUKE. What will you take for your voyage?
CLEVELAND. Your kindness, sir.
SIR MARMADUKE. Ay, ay; but how much will satisfy you?
CLEVELAND. Sir, I,—I— 260
SIR MARMADUKE. Come, what will do? Be honest.
CLEVELAND. Sir, I have not formed the smallest—
SIR MARMADUKE. Nay, speak out.
CLEVELAND. Whatever your goodness—
SIR MARMADUKE. Well, what say you to five thousand pounds? 265
CLEVELAND. My dear Uncle!
SIR MARMADUKE. Well, but what say you to ten thousand?
CLEVELAND. Sir!
SIR MARMADUKE. Come, speak; what say you to it?
CLEVELAND. You confound me, Sir Marmaduke! Munificence such as this— 270
SIR MARMADUKE. Well, if that flutters you, skip over to another five.
CLEVELAND. Sir?
SIR MARMADUKE. Skip over to another five I say, and tell me what you have to object to fifteen thousand? 275
CLEVELAND. My dearest Uncle, what can you possibly mean?
SIR MARMADUKE. Just what I say; fifteen thousand pounds.
CLEVELAND. O Sir Marmaduke! you distress, you overpower me!
SIR MARMADUKE. Well then, will you come to yourself if I say twenty thousand? 280
CLEVELAND. Sir!
SIR MARMADUKE. Will that bring you to yourself, I say?
CLEVELAND. Are you laughing at me?
SIR MARMADUKE. No. 285
CLEVELAND. You mean then,—you allude—I fancy, I now comprehend your generous though melancholy purpose.
SIR MARMADUKE. Melancholy? No. What is there melancholy in twenty thousand pounds? However if you think it so shocking, will it relieve you to double it? 290
CLEVELAND. Double it?
SIR MARMADUKE. Nay, then, treble it at once. And there ends

my lesson of Arithmetic for this morning. Sixty thousand pounds.

CLEVELAND. O my Uncle, you penetrate me to the quick! I see your full intention—but long may it be ere— 295

SIR MARMADUKE. Long? And what's your objection to its being short?

CLEVELAND. My dear Uncle, I am totally at a loss to comprehend you. My perplexity encreases every moment. 300

SIR MARMADUKE. There is only one condition annexed to it. You are to marry for it.

CLEVELAND. Marry?

SIR MARMADUKE. Yes, to take to you a wife. How you stare! Why, I am not going to propose to you an old Hag, like—(*in a* 305 *low voice*) your poor Aunt, God help me! Are you sure that door i'n't ajar?

CLEVELAND. Relieve me from this suspense, I conjure you, sir!

SIR MARMADUKE. Why it's to Miss— O you young rascal! What a happy thing it is to be a young rascal!— It's to Miss Percival. 310

CLEVELAND. Miss Percival?

SIR MARMADUKE. Yes. That pretty little frisky thing, Miss Percival. She has been violently in love with you these two years. We all saw that she had a hankering after you; but as she had next to nothing, we never noticed it. However you were hardly 315 sailed, when her rich brother, Lord Percival, departed, and left her all he had at his own disposal. Well! Why don't you jump?

CLEVELAND. I am in such amazement—

SIR MARMADUKE. As soon as she came into possession, she whispered her secret to your sister; and your sister whispered it 320 to your Aunt; and your Aunt whispered it to me; and I suppose, by this time, it is whispered into half a dozen news-papers. Jemima asked her leave to write for you over. She was too skittish to consent; but she did not say nay; only she insisted I should take the recalling you upon myself. Why don't you jump, 325 I say?

CLEVELAND. I am so astonished, so confounded, so disturbed—

SIR MARMADUKE. Yes, yes, you are badly off! well, not to be wanting on our side, upon so splendid an occasion, I agreed to make over to you my Lincolnshire Estate immediately.— 330

CLEVELAND. O Uncle! and upon these terms only must I hope—

SIR MARMADUKE. No, no; I made my own terms. I demanded ready money, in return, to buy off my mortgage. To this she consented; and therefore you have now only to take her fair hand. So off with your boots, and your travelling dress, and throw yourself at her feet. 335

CLEVELAND. Hear me first, my dear Uncle, and suffer my little narrative to meet with your indulgence. On my arrival at Calcutta—

Enter MISS CLEVELAND.

MISS CLEVELAND. Lady Wilhelmina begs to know, Uncle, if you will see Lord John before he goes, and hear from himself his very alarming account of Frank? 340

SIR MARMADUKE. What's his alarm to me? Don't interrupt us.

MISS CLEVELAND. She bids me say it has made her so ill—

SIR MARMADUKE. Pish! that's no business of mine. Pray leave us alone. 345

Enter LADY WILHELMINA.

LADY WILHELMINA. There was no detaining Lord John, Sir Marmaduke, while you hesitated whether to admit him. My good Cleveland, how opportune is your return at this distressing juncture! you know nothing, I imagine of this dishonouring plan of your graceless Brother? 350

CLEVELAND. Of Frank?

LADY WILHELMINA. O the most preposterous conduct! He is determined upon disgracing us all, by an ignominious alliance with a young woman out of the City! 355

CLEVELAND. The City? Confusion! (*walking away*)

LADY WILHELMINA. Your start satisfies me; you feel the indignity like myself.

CLEVELAND. Who I?— Indeed, madam, I—I—

LADY WILHELMINA. Your blushes revive me, my good Cleveland. I had feared you would have partaken of the romantic weakness of your sister, who, if the young woman were herself pleasing, would receive her at Temple Bar with arms as ex- 360

II.363 **Temple Bar** Archway for the state entrance of the king or queen into the City. It was located between Fleet Street and the Strand, and it marked the western limits of the City. Colloquially, it is used to distinguish the situation of gentlemen from that of a merchant. In Murphy's *Citizen*, Philpot rejects "this side of Temple Bar" (p. 38), and in George Colman the Elder's *The Clandestine Marriage*, Fanny tended, as if she were born a Peeress in her own right: but you, I see,— 365

CLEVELAND. Indeed, madam,—on the contrary—

LADY WILHELMINA. Spare yourself the violence of attempting to excuse him. The disorder into which you are thrown explains to me your real sentiments.

CLEVELAND. I protest, Lady Wilhelmina,— 370

SIR MARMADUKE. Is the girl rich?

LADY WILHELMINA. People of that sort commonly are; but I did not judge it necessary to enquire. I believe Miss Cleveland might hear what was said upon that subject.

MISS CLEVELAND. Yes, Uncle, she has a very large fortune. 375

SIR MARMADUKE. Why then where's the harm of Frank's entering it at his Banker's?

LADY WILHELMINA. The harm, Sir Marmaduke? The harm of mingling with people of that description? The very lowest, Lord John says,— 380

SIR MARMADUKE. Well, what's that to us? Who cares about the genealogy of a younger brother's wife? If it were my Nephew Cleveland, indeed, who may become the head of his house—

CLEVELAND. Distraction! (*still walking apart*)

LADY WILHELMINA. Cleveland, I exult in your honourable agitation. Let me see you in my dressing room, that we may deliberate what steps to take to preserve our family pure from an alliance with a native of the City. 385

Exit.

SIR MARMADUKE. Pho, pho, Cleveland, don't look so confounded. Make yourself up for paying your devoirs to Miss Percival, and leave Frank to his devices. If he can once manage his affairs, and pay his debts by himself, I shall never ask if his Banker lives at Cornhill or St James's. What difference does it make to me? 390

Exit.

---

says to Miss Sterling that, once Miss Sterling is married to the aristocratic Sir John, she must "never venture on the inside of Temple Bar again": *The Dramatic Works of George Colman* (London: Becket, 1777), 2:12.

II.390 **paying your devoirs** From the French "faire les devoirs," to pay one's duties or respects; see also IV.88.

II.393 **Cornhill** One of the major highways of the City, and the site of the Royal Exchange.

Manent CLEVELAND, *and* MISS CLEVELAND.

MISS CLEVELAND. I confess myself utterly astonished my dear Brother, at your altered sentiments, and to see you concur with such alacrity in prejudices you were accustomed to hold in contempt. How often have I heard you declare, that you knew many characters as well informed, as well educated, and as amiable, in the City as at our end of the Town? 395 400

CLEVELAND. Let me take you to my heart, my dear Sister, for the pleasure which the justness of your memory at this moment bestows upon me.

MISS CLEVELAND. Why, then, all this disturbance? And why so readily have you joined with Lady Wilhelmina in contemning poor Frank? As to Lord John's assertions of the peculiar vulgarity of the intended connexion, they may but spring from the idle love of ridicule in which almost all young men of fashion indulge themselves. 405

CLEVELAND. My dearest Jemima, what you mean as a reproof comes home to me as the most soothing flattery. I have been wholly misconceived by Lady Wilhelmina, and the surprise and confusion into which two incidents equally unexpected and embarrassing had thrown me, robbed me of presence of mind to rectify her mistake. 410 415

MISS CLEVELAND. And what are these two incidents? May I ask?

CLEVELAND. One is the discovery of the motive of my summons home; the other is the view of the displeasure excited by the project of Frank. 420

MISS CLEVELAND. The discovery relative to Miss Percival can give you, I think, nothing but delight?

CLEVELAND. Delight? O no, no! no!

MISS CLEVELAND. You are then fastidious indeed. And to what must I impute the extreme consternation so palpable in your countenance, upon hearing that Frank had elected a Partner from within the precincts of the City? 425

CLEVELAND. Not to disapprobation, on my part, but to alarm at that which was so haughtily proclaimed by Lady Wilhelmina, for O Jemima! within those precincts—within that City—was born the beloved object of every hope of my heart! 430

MISS CLEVELAND. Is it possible? Frank, then, is more than justified—but alas for poor Miss Percival!—your affections are engaged?

CLEVELAND. Why Miss Percival has honoured me with her choice I cannot tell: certainly not from any interchange of partiality; for though she is gay and agreeable, and I have taken pleasure in rallying and chatting with her, she is vain and fantastic, and has won from me neither the esteem nor the confidence I wish to repose in my wife. 435 440

MISS CLEVELAND. Ah, Brother, you men, at best, are but sad animals! How often do you make us think ourselves admired, nay adored, when we are only played with,—and despised?

CLEVELAND. My dear Sister, when women wish for lasting esteem, instead of fleeting admiration, let them but be pleased without flattery, gay without coquetry, and gentle without affectation, and then, take my word for it, the men will even gratefully rejoice to respect them as they deserve. 445

FRANK (*within*). Where is he?

MISS CLEVELAND. I hear the voice of Frank. 450

CLEVELAND. Leave us together a few minutes, my dear Jemima. He will, then, probably, be explicit as to his situation, and we may concur in forming some mutual plan to subdue the prejudices of Lady Wilhelmina.

MISS CLEVELAND. That will be a conquest indeed, for they are as wide from reason as from feeling. 455

Exit.

CLEVELAND.

[CLEVELAND.] O my lovely Eliza! how shall I claim you of your Friends, without the inheritance of which I thought myself so secure!

Enter FRANK.

FRANK. Brother, your hand! most heartily welcome back to England. 460

CLEVELAND. I rejoice to see you again, my dear Frank.

FRANK. Fair wind, fair fortune, and a fair lady have wafted you home most prosperously. I congratulate you upon them with all my heart, and that without spite or envy; though a more pitia- 465 ble contrast to such enjoyments never yet was offered by living wight than by your most obsequious servant.

CLEVELAND. Inform me how you are circumstanced, dear Frank, and accept my best services.

FRANK. You will feel, I know, for my distress; but have a care you do not draw back when you hear of my resource! 470

CLEVELAND. Fear me not. I am under much present embarrassment myself, and reciprocal confidence may lead to reciprocal relief. Speak without reserve.

FRANK. I have been so inhumanly hard run, that I am compelled, at length, to consent to the most horrid of sacrifices. 475

CLEVELAND. How so?

FRANK. Faith, I am ashamed to say.

CLEVELAND. No; no; trust me.

FRANK. 'Tis a violent measure; you'll never believe it. 480

CLEVELAND. Why not?

FRANK. I must marry.

CLEVELAND. Marry?

FRANK. Nothing less.

CLEVELAND. And is that the horrid sacrifice? 485

FRANK. Nay, what can be worse?

CLEVELAND. And who is the honoured object at whose shrine you are to be thus offered?

FRANK. Why that, Brother, is the D--l of the business. I must take up with—look another way, I beg! I never felt so bashfull before. I must take up with—now don't despise me,—a Cit! 490

CLEVELAND. Despise you, my dear Frank? What is there to despise? On the contrary, I honour you.

FRANK. Come, come, no derision. Consider, a little, what I have to go through to persuade myself to so barbarous a downfall: but I have no other way left to retrieve— 495

CLEVELAND. Frank, this is talking too idly. You know that I—that the City—that is that I—but what is the lady's name?

FRANK. Why there again, I suppose you will all fly out. However, that, you know, she will change. Meanwhile, 'tis short at least. What do you think of Watts? 500

CLEVELAND. Watts?

FRANK. Nay, don't jump so! 'Tis not in Lady Wilhelmina's Herald's office, I grant; but still—

II.503–4 **Herald's office** Office of the College of Heralds, "a royal corporation . . .

CLEVELAND. Hold, hold!— Has this lady a Sister? 505

FRANK. O yes; and a Father and a Mother,—and half a hundred Cousins and Uncles, and Aunts and Grandmothers.

CLEVELAND. Where does she live?

FRANK. In Bond Street.

CLEVELAND. In Bond Street? Nay then, my dear Frank she is probably— 510

FRANK. I must not deceive you, though; my little elect has no chance of being the more polished from her present vicinity to St James's; for, to own the truth, she is but just disembarked from the East Indies. 515

CLEVELAND. The East Indies?

FRANK. Why you jump higher and higher! Perhaps you knew her there?

CLEVELAND. From what part of the East Indies does she come?

FRANK. From the land of the Hottentots for aught I can tell. I never enquired. But hold! Perhaps you may have heard of her; for I now recollect gathering that her residence had been at Calcutta. 520

CLEVELAND. Calcutta!

FRANK. You start like a Ghost in a Tragedy! I hope you know no harm of her? 525

CLEVELAND. If you mean this for raillery, sir, give me leave to tell you 'tis the worst-timed, and most unfeeling—

FRANK. Raillery? I have not such a thought. But if I had,—must I turn a Methodist Preacher, because, while you pay your addresses to a fair honourable, I am reduced to taking up with a little City Gentoo? 530

CLEVELAND. A City Gentoo? Frank, this is an excess of levity that I find wholly beyond endurance. You will please to have done with it. And never let me hear that lady's name from you again. (*walking up and down*) 535

FRANK. And why not? What are you so fierce? 'Tis a pretty little name enough, I think, and too glib to the tongue to be very fatiguing to the ear. However, if it enrages you so, I must be the quicker in making her change it. 540

CLEVELAND. Frank—

FRANK. Really, Brother, though I expected to put Lady Wilhel-

---

exercising jurisdiction in matters armorial, and now recording proved pedigrees, and granting armorial bearings" (*OED*).

mina in flames, I was by no means prepared to see you thus irritated at my taking a rib out of the City.

CLEVELAND. I irritated at a connexion with the City?— Tell me, however, did you ever even see this young lady you speak of thus securely and presumptuously? Never; I am certain. 545

FRANK. Ha! Ha! why it is not an hour since I left her.

CLEVELAND. And where, pray, sir?

FRANK. At a rather ackward place; but 'twas where we chanced to meet. 'Twas at a house belonging to a friend of mine in St James's Street. 550

CLEVELAND. Impossible!

FRANK. 'Tis my last stake; so I beg you will not think me more a plebian than yourself. It has nothing to do with my taste, I assure you; for I hold a Citizen, and Temple Bar in as sovereign contempt as you can do for the life of you. 555

CLEVELAND. Insufferable! How dare you, sir—

FRANK. Hey day!

CLEVELAND. How dare you, I say, speak thus disrespectfully of the City? Of the first characters for worth and probity in the Kingdom? 560

FRANK. Hey day! Why then what are you in such a passion about?

CLEVELAND. Characters that are the nation's support by their affluence, and the nation's honour by their integrity? 565

FRANK. Why then what the Deuce do you object to?

Enter MISS CLEVELAND.

MISS CLEVELAND. What is the matter, my dear Brothers? Why do I hear you so loud?

FRANK (*walking apart*). He foams so with pride and fury, he knows not a word he says. 570

CLEVELAND. My dear Jemima where can I speak with you a few moments alone?

MISS CLEVELAND. I expect the carriage every instant to take me to Miss Percival. 575

CLEVELAND. You must not see her till I have conversed with you. I must entreat you to wait upon the lady I have mentioned to you, and conjure her, in my name to grant me a five minutes audience immediately. The confusion this hair-brained coxcomb may create in the house by his unintelligible assertions 580 can only be prevented, or cleared away, by an instantaneous meeting. Nor shall I think myself at liberty to declare our connexion, till I have revealed to her the disappointment of my expectations from Sir Marmaduke.

MISS CLEVELAND. But what is her name? And where does she live? And how shall I introduce myself? And whom am I to enquire for? 585

CLEVELAND. Drive slowly to Kensington Gardens. I will but stop to prepare you a note of introduction and join you at the Gate. In a quarter of an hour's walk we can arrange our proceeding. It will be taken for granted, here, you are gone to Miss Percival. 590

MISS CLEVELAND. It will make me happy to be of the smallest service to you.

Exit CLEVELAND.

Manent MISS CLEVELAND *and* FRANK.

FRANK. I'm heartily glad he's gone. This Indian expedition, Jemima, has actually turned his head with arrogance and vanity. He put himself into such desperate choler while I was talking to him of my little Cit, and took such an antipathy to her poor tiny name, that he ordered me never to pronounce it again; and I thought, once or twice, he would have knocked me down. 595

Enter LORD JOHN DERVIS.

LORD JOHN. What the plague did you give me the slip for, Frank? 600

MISS CLEVELAND. For the very reason, probably, I shall now do the same—to get rid of you!

Aside and exit.

Manent LORD JOHN *and* FRANK.

FRANK. I wanted to see my Brother. But we make no way here, my dear Lord John!

II.588 **Kensington Gardens** Bought by William III in 1689, the gardens to Kensington House were opened to the public in the 1790s, "but only on Sundays and then only to those formally dressed. Sailors, soldiers, and liveried servants were all denied entry": Christopher Hibbert, *London: The Biography of a City* (London: Longmans, Green, 1969), 153. Perhaps the restrictions explain why the Watts family mistakes Lord John Dervis's valet for a gentleman.

LORD JOHN. The D--l you don't. 605

FRANK. No; the house is as full of rage as a man need wish it; yet it has not slackened the purse strings!

LORD JOHN. The plague it hasn't? Why then, e'en take the girl.

FRANK. So I will, if the bait does not require much trouble. But how can I get at her? 610

LORD JOHN. Send her a ladder of ropes.

FRANK. No, not yet; that must be after the Papa has refused me. One must not break through old established customs. However, as I've all to ask and nothing to offer, the Papa won't fail to play his part in rejecting me. The only difficulty is how to get into the 615 house. It will demand but little skill how to get out of it.

LORD JOHN. Call and ask them how they do.

FRANK. They'll be all in bed—or out—or dressing—or at dinner. I may be a month without catching them.

LORD JOHN. Write to her, then, and come to the point at once. 620

FRANK. No. I'll write to her Father. One has no chance with a young Girl till her Family are all against one. Or suppose you should write for me, Lord John?

LORD JOHN. Deuce take me if I do!

FRANK. You can set me off much better than I can myself. Besides 625 a Lord is always identified; but who, on t'other side of Temple Bar, knows anything of Frank Cleveland?

LORD JOHN. O the plague! no, no, no, Frank. Anything but that. I hate writing.

FRANK. Come, my Lord, here's pen, and ink, and paper. 630

LORD JOHN. Faith, not I. I can't abide writing. I hate pedantry.

FRANK. Yes, yes, you must. 'Twill have a most pompous effect upon little Miss to be demanded through a Lord. Come, I'll take no denial—Here, sit down.

LORD JOHN. O the D--l. Write! 635

FRANK (*forcing him to sit, and putting a pen into his hand*). Yes; say my many amiable qualities have induced you to come forwards, upon this interesting occasion, as guarantee of my honour, and singularly estimable character. Come, say something handsome for me. 640

LORD JOHN. O confound it! I could not write all that in an hour.

FRANK. Well, then, only say, my very deserving and even meritorious young friend.

II.611 **ladder of ropes** i.e., elope with her.

LORD JOHN. Stop: stop! not so much at once. *my very deserving and even* (*writes*) What's the other word? 645

FRANK. Meritorious.

LORD JOHN. What should I write meritorious for?

FRANK. What for? Because it's a fine-sounding word!

LORD JOHN. How the D--l do you spell it? I always forget.

FRANK. I'll put it down for you. There. Now add young friend, Mr Francis Cleveland. 650

LORD JOHN. O the plague!—how I hate writing! I wish it had never been invented; young what, did you say?

FRANK. Friend; to be sure.

LORD JOHN. Do you spell it with an i, or an e? 655

FRANK. With both.

LORD JOHN. O the Deuce! I've only put an e; does it signify?

FRANK. Not much. Go on. Why now you've left out Francis.

LORD JOHN. I wish it was all at Jericho, with all my soul! Put it in yourself. I'm plaguy tired. 660

FRANK. Never mind. 'Twill sound more respectable without the christian name. Now say Nephew to Sir Marmaduke Tylney—

LORD JOHN. Stop stop! Is Nephew writ n.e.v. or n.e.f.? It's the oddest thing in the world, but I never can keep that stupid word in my head. 665

Enter MISS CLEVELAND.

MISS CLEVELAND. Miss Percival is just come, and as the carriage is waiting at the door for me, it is impossible I can refuse seeing her.

FRANK. Let's go to your house, then Lord John, and one of your servants can run with it as soon as it is done. Send a good smart fellow. 670

LORD JOHN. 'Tis a most deuced bore. I never was so consumed tired in my life.

Exeunt at one door, and enter MISS PERCIVAL *at another.*

MISS PERCIVAL. My dear Jemima, you must come and pass the day with me. I am dying of the vapours. These India ships are certainly all lost. 675

II.659 **I wish it was all at Jericho** "Anywhere out of my way" (*Brewer's*).

MISS CLEVELAND. I cannot possibly wait upon you this morning; but in the evening—

MISS PERCIVAL. O I shall be dead before the evening; if you don't come directly. I can only invite you by my executors. 680

MISS CLEVELAND. I have so particular an engagement—

MISS PERCIVAL. Break it, break it! How can you be so formal?

Enter AARON.

AARON. Miss Cleveland, my Lady desires to know if you will not unorder the carriage now Miss Percival is come?

MISS CLEVELAND. How excessively tormenting! Yes I suppose it 685 must be put up. (*exit* AARON) What in the world can I do!

MISS PERCIVAL. Why come home with me, to be sure. You don't want Lady Wil's carriage for that. I am in agonies to consult you about my first appearance before a certain horrid wretch of your acquaintance. I mean provided I ever happen to see him 690 again. But don't you think, Jemima, he is certainly drowned?

Re-enter AARON.

AARON. My Lady is waiting for Mr Cleveland and I can't find him.

MISS PERCIVAL. Cleveland? Heavens! Is he arrived?

MISS CLEVELAND. How unfortunate! Tell her Ladyship that I have no doubt but he will attend her presently. 695

Exit AARON.

MISS PERCIVAL. He is really, then, arrived? O the Wretch! Let me run away this instant. I would not see him for the Universe. Perfidious Jemima! was this a plot to take me by surprise?

MISS CLEVELAND. No, I assure you; it is only—

MISS PERCIVAL. I can't stay to hear you; I am fluttered to death. 700 I can't possibly see him these three months. (*going*) Pray what room does the Wretch inhabit? I am so terribly afraid of meeting him—

MISS CLEVELAND. He is gone out.

MISS PERCIVAL. Gone out? To Piccadilly I suppose? Well, then, 705 I'll stay here; for I can't possibly receive him. At least not this half year. How does the Monster look?

II.705 **Piccadilly** Margetson (*Regency London*) says that in the eighteenth century, "Pall Mall, St. James's Street, Piccadilly and Bond Street were the main arteries of [the] small, exclusive coterie of the beau monde" (p. 6).

MISS CLEVELAND. Extremely well.

MISS PERCIVAL. The Miscreant! I'm horribly mad you sent for him over. Ten to one if I like him now. How could I be such a fool? I have been upon the point of listening to twenty others since. He's like a husband already; in the way of everything. 710

MISS CLEVELAND. If you wish it, my dear Miss Percival, I can undertake to persuade him—

MISS PERCIVAL. O undertake nothing, I beseech you. You must not mind a word I say. Don't you know I doat upon him to distraction? But what do you think he'll do in Piccadilly when he misses me? 715

MISS CLEVELAND. I believe he is not gone to Piccadilly this morning. 720

MISS PERCIVAL. Not gone to Piccadilly?

MISS CLEVELAND. He had an appointment, I understood, in Kensington Gardens.

MISS PERCIVAL. An appointment in Kensington Gardens? Vastly well! vastly well! extremely well indeed! I am amazingly glad! 725

MISS CLEVELAND. Do not be offended, I beg. The appointment, to be sincere was but with me.

MISS PERCIVAL. O it's extremely well. Perhaps, when he has finished all his affairs, and his appointments, and strolled a few hours in Kensington Gardens, he may intend calling in Piccadilly? Do you think he will be so good? 730

MISS CLEVELAND. He is, besides, only in his travelling dress.

MISS PERCIVAL. Pretty matter! So he wants to bedizen himself! Is this his impatience? Thinking of his fine person? He ought to think only of mine. However, I hope he'll go back to India, for I am determined never to speak to him more. I wish he would come in this very minute, that I might tell him so. What a look I should give him! 735

MISS CLEVELAND. If you had not been so angry. I might have been tempted to beg the loan of your carriage for a quarter of an hour, after it had set you down in Piccadilly. 740

MISS PERCIVAL. What, to go to Kensington Gardens? Nay, if the appointment is really with you, and with you only, perhaps it is

II.733 **bedizen** "To dress out, especially in a vulgar or gaudy fashion" (*OED*). In Arthur Murphy's *Know Your Own Mind* (1777) (London: Roach, 1807), Mrs. Bromley says to Miss Neville: "you are dizened to go out, I think" (p. 22). Fanny Burney uses the word in *Camilla*, when Sir Hugh asks Eugenia: "an't you dizen'd yet?" (p. 563).

merely to make some enquiries concerning me? Now do tell me!

MISS CLEVELAND. It is certainly only to meet me. 745

MISS PERCIVAL. Why then, probably the creature wants to make you bring him to me at once! How could you tell it me in so lifeless a manner? My dear Jemima, you want a shaking prodigiously. Come, I'll carry you to the Garden Gate myself. But—does he know—has he any idea—I hope he does not dare 750 suppose— Come, speak! does he dare suppose anything?

MISS CLEVELAND. How shall I do to return?

MISS PERCIVAL. O you little Jesuit! You won't answer me. Well, however, I'll wait in the chariot till the conference is over, and then bring you home myself. Only take care he does not hand 755 you into the chariot! If he does, remember I shall die that very moment. You can jump out while I sit back, and jump in afterwards in the same manner. But come, we'll settle all that during the drive. I can peep at the Wretch through the back Glass, you know, without being seen. How delightful! Don't forget, though, 760 that I positively can't receive him these three weeks.

MISS CLEVELAND. If I had any other means to prevent my poor Brother from waiting in vain, I could not thus abuse your goodness.

MISS PERCIVAL. Come, then, run! fly! how slow you are! Heav- 765 ens, I wish you were in love, Child! I always think everybody looks fast asleep that isn't in love.

Exeunt.

End of Act II

ACT III

The Scene represents Kensington Gardens.
Enter MR WATTS, MRS WATTS, MISS WATTS, *and* ELIZA.

MR WATTS. Well, Bet, my dear, what say you to Kinsington Garden?

III.1 **Kinsington** The vocabulary and pronunciation used by the Watts family is not easily placed in a particular dialect. Words like "gownd" (III.16), meaning gown, and "sounded away" (V.216–17), meaning swooned or fainted away, can be

MISS WATTS. La, Pa', now you're calling her Bet again!

MR WATTS. Well, my dear, don't scold. I can't never remember that new name. 5

MRS WATTS. Why no more can I, my dear, as to that. Not that I mean to 'scuse your Pa' in the least. Why, my dear, why you look no how? What's the matter? (*to* ELIZA)

ELIZA. My long voyage has a little fatigued me. Nothing else.

MR WATTS. Why I told you so! bringing her out before a bit of 10 dinner, after crossing all them seas!

MISS WATTS. La, Pa', would you have her be as stupid as you? I'm sure I would not have lost such a morning for Kinsington Gardens for never so much.

MRS WATTS (*to* MISS WATTS). Dear, my dear, do but look at 15 your gownd! Only see how it trails!

MISS WATTS. La, Ma', I hope I need not be always taking care of my things now!

MR WATTS. Nay, my dear, nobody's by.

MISS WATTS. Yes, but somebody's coming; and a very fine gentle- 20 man, too. Only think, now, if he should have heard you! Making one look so mean!

Enter the VALET *of* LORD JOHN DERVIS.

VALET. Pray, sir, may I take the liberty to ask if you're the gentleman this letter's for?

MR WATTS (*reading the Direction*). —Watts Esquire—Bond 25 Street—Why it may be me and it may be not; for here's no Thomas. Pray, sir, can you tell me if Thomas was the other name that i'n't put down?

VALET. If you are Mr Watts, sir, most likely you are the gentleman; for I'm just come from Mr Watts in Bond Street, and the 30 Porter told me his master was in Kinsington Gardens.

---

ascribed to several regions, including Yorkshire, Somerset, and Devon (*EDD*). Others, such as "mad" (III.362), meaning angry, and "lolloping" (V.814), meaning lolling or lounging, are labelled as general colloquialisms. Still others, such as "Walley" (III.209), "kereless" (III.214) for careless, "notage" (V.212) for notice, and "cheze" (V.253) for chair, do not appear in the dictionaries I have consulted, and may be Fanny Burney's own interpretation of the verbal mannerisms of lower classes. Mr. Watts's "Muster" for Mister (III.211) is used by the lowly Daniel Dowlas in Colman the Younger's *The Heir at Law* (Elizabeth Inchbald, ed., *The British Theatre*, London: Longmans, Hurst, Rees, and Orme, 1808, 21:147).

MRS WATTS. Dear, Tommy, why are you so shilly-shally? Let me look at the letter myself.

MISS WATTS. La, Ma', you won't read it in half an hour. Give it to me, Pa'. 35

MR WATTS. No, my dear, I never shew my letters till I have read 'em, in case of private business. Why if it i'n't a whole half sheet of gilt paper wasted in a kiver! (*reads to himself*)

MRS WATTS. Come, let's sit down, young ladies, on this nice seat. Won't you sit down, too, sir? Peggy, my dear,—O Peggerelly I 40 mean—

MISS WATTS. Peggerelly? No, it's Margerella, I tell you!

MRS WATTS. Well, my dear, I mean Margarelly: make a little room for the gentleman.

MRS *and* MISS WATTS *seat themselves.*

MISS WATTS. It's a very pleasant day, sir. 45

VALET. Very much so, ma'am.

Sitting down by her.

MISS WATTS. Pray, sir, have you been long in the Gardens, sir?

VALET. Only a few seconds, ma'am. I was uneasy to put the letter into Mr Watts' own hand, and therefore, missing him at home—

MR WATTS. Well, here's a thing to make one stare if one will or 50 no! Why Bet—Elizenny, my dear, here's a gentleman wants to be coming a courting to you already.

ELIZA. To me, sir?

MISS WATTS. La, Pa', let's see. Are you sure it's to Eliziana?

MRS WATTS. More like it's to Margarelly, Tommy, for who should 55 know of Elizenenny's being here?

MISS WATTS. La, it means me I dare say!

ELIZA. Will you permit me, sir,—Will you—give me leave to see —to ask—by what—name the letter is signed? (*with confusion*)

MISS WATTS. It's Billy Bond, ten to one. But I'm sure, I won't 60 have him now.

MR WATTS. Why a name I never heard in my days, my dear, one John Dervis.

ELIZA. 'Tis certainly some mistake, then, sir. It cannot mean me. How prompt were my expectations to deceive me! (*aside*) 65

MISS WATTS. Why then it must be me! La, how droll! Why I never heard of John Dervis neither! I wonder where's he's seen me!

III.38 **kiver** "a cover; a frank for letters" (*EDD*).

MR WATTS. No, it can't mean you, my dear, for here's your Sister's name at full length.

ELIZA. It must be written, then, sir, for some foolish sport. Pray return it unanswered. 70

MR WATTS. So I will, my dear. Be so kind, sir, to take back this here letter to John Dervis, and tell him—

VALET. Who, sir?

MR WATTS. John Dervis, sir, as wrote me the letter. Tell him my darter says— 75

VALET. Do you mean my Lord, sir?

MR WATTS. Anan?

VALET. My Lord, I say, do you mean my Lord?

MR WATTS. My Lord? Not I! I never thought of a my lord. I mean nobody but this here John Dervis as has signed the letter. 80

VALET. The letter's signed by my Lord, sir.

MR WATTS. By my Lord? Why what do you mean? Here's nothing about a my lord here.

MISS WATTS. La, Pa', perhaps the letter's from a Lord? Pray let me look at it. 85

MRS WATTS. No, let me see it first Tommy. I never see a letter from a Lord in my life. (*takes the letter*)

MR WATTS. Why how can this here John Dervis be a Lord?

VALET. He's the second son of the Marquis of Wistborough. 90

MR WATTS. Son of a Marquis? What, John Dervis?

MISS WATTS. La, Pa', and how rude you've behaved!

ELIZA. Still I suspect some trick or some impertinence, for Lord John Dervis is utterly unknown to me. Will you permit me, madam, to look at the hand? 95

MRS WATTS. Dear, my dear, why I ha'n't made out hardly two words yet.

MR WATTS. Well, see but how people are upon the catch when one's got a little money! Please to tell his Lordship Lord John Dervis— 100

III.78 **Anan** "general mode of expressing that the auditor was at the speaker's service, or begged him to say on; and in later use, a mode of expressing that the auditor has failed to catch the speaker's words or meaning but is now alert and asks him to repeat" (*OED*). The expression seems to be used only by the lower classes or uneducated people: Dr. Last uses it in Samuel Foote's *Devil upon Two Sticks* (London: Cadell, 1778, 56); Moody the country clown in Sir John Vanbrugh and Colley Cibber's *The Provoked Husband* (ed. Peter Dixon, Lincoln: University of Nebraska Press, 1974, 34); and Lucy the maid in Thomas Holcroft's *He's Much to Blame* (3d ed., Dublin: N.p., 1798, 10).

MISS WATTS. La, Pa', don't give him the letter till I've looked at it. Why what signifies your holding it, Ma'? You know you can't read writing hand. (*takes the letter*)

MRS WATTS. Well, I might have made out some of it: snatching things away so! 105

MISS WATTS (*reads*).

"Sir,

"My very deserving and even meritorious young friend, Mr Cleveland"

ELIZA. Heavens!

MISS WATTS. "Nephew of Sir Marmaduke Tilney—" 110

ELIZA. Ah Sister, dear Sister, let me have the letter I conjure you!—

MISS WATTS. "has given me in charge to solicit the honour of your permission to declare the eternal devotion which he vows to your accomplished Daughter, Miss Elizabeth. His expectations from his Uncle, and other contingencies, he en- 115 treats an early enterview to set before you. I enter, therefore, into none of those particulars; but cannot conclude without begging to add my sincere testimony to the many virtues which modesty else might conceal in this truly exemplary young man. 120

"I have the honour to be, Sir.

"your most obedient Servent

"John Dervis."

MR WATTS. Why you see, now, he says nothing of his being a Lord. He only puts plain John. 125

ELIZA. How extraordinary! why has he not written himself? (*aside*)

MR WATTS. Are you sure, sir, as to that article of his being a Lord?

VALET. 'Pon my honour, sir. (*striking his breast*)

MRS WATTS. Well, I declare I wonder you can ask sich a question, 130 Tommy. Why one may see it's from a Lord as plain as can be.

MISS WATTS. Yes, it's exact the Lord. I should know it for a Lord's anywhere.

MR WATTS. Well, sir, you'll be kind enough to take it back to his Lordship Lord John Dervis and tell Lord John Dervis his Lord- 135 ship that my darter says—

ELIZA. No—Stop!—hold—my dear Father—

MR WATTS. Why, what now, Betsey?

ELIZA. Permit me to speak one word with you first.—

MR WATTS. Why what is all this, Betsey? Have you changed your mind? 140

ELIZA. I will explain myself fully, if you will only have the goodness to defer any answer till you have heard me—one moment—alone.

MR WATTS. Why then, my dear, let's ask the gentleman to take a turn or two the t'other way. 145

VALET. O Pray, sir,—ladies—no apology. (*walks to some distance*)

MISS WATTS. He's just as pelite as a Lord himself. I dare say he's the particular friend of Lord John Dervis.

MRS WATTS. Well, but, Elizennany, my dear, I suppose your Mamma may stay to hear you? 150

ELIZA. You are very right, my dear Mother—

MISS WATTS. And I'm sure I shan't go, for I want to know what it is myself.

ELIZA. You are all, my nearest Friends, and may command my confidence. This letter I now fancy—I now begin to believe—I now— 155

MISS WATTS. La, Sister Eliziana, what makes you stutter so?

ELIZA. This letter, I say, has been written . . . I rather imagine . . . at the request of—of—of a gentleman that— 160

MISS WATTS. Of a gentleman? La, who?

ELIZA. About a year ago, a Mr—Mr Cleveland came over to Calcutta . . . in a very advantageous post—and—and—and happened to form a particular intimacy with Mr Alderson—and—and in short my dear Father, the ship that brought me over myself, had been destined to bear to you letters meant to solicit your consent to—to . . . 165

MISS WATTS. La, if I don't believe you was going to be married to him?

ELIZA. But just before it set sail, a sudden cruel illness deprived me of that excellent adopted Parent. I then resolved upon returning myself—especially—to be wholly sincere—as Mr Cleveland had just received letters of recall from Sir Marmaduke Tylney his uncle. 170

MISS WATTS. So I suppose you both come over in the same same ship, then? 175

ELIZA. Yes, Sister.

MRS WATTS. Well, that was pretty enough.

MR WATTS. But what has he got, my dear?

ELIZA. Indulge him, sir, with an interview, and he will candidly acquaint you with the state of his affairs. He entertains the most reasonable expectations of inheritance from Sir Marmaduke. 180

MR WATTS. Expectations, my dear, did not make me one farthing of my fortune. However, if he had old Alderson of his side, most likely he has something of a substance, so I shan't object to the seeing him. 185

MISS WATTS. Ask him to dinner, then, Pa'; and ask the lord to come with him. And ask that smart gentleman.

MRS WATTS. No, no, tea will do very well, my dear. No need to be giving away one's dinners at sich a rate as that. 190

MISS WATTS. La, Ma', you're always so stingy!

MR WATTS. No, no, I shall ask him to call some morning. That's quite enough till I know what he's got. Sir! sir! I say—

VALET (*returning*). At your commands, sir.

MR WATTS. If you should happen to see Lord John Dervis his Lordship agen, sir— 195

VALET. O yes, sir! I always see my Lord when he dresses.

MR WATTS. Dresses?

VALET. He'd make but a poor hand without me, I believe!

MISS WATTS. La! 200

MRS WATTS. Dear!— Why sure, sir, you a'nt the footman?

VALET. Footman? O no ma'am! I am my Lord's valet.

MRS WATTS. Dear, Peggy, how could you be took in so?

MISS WATTS. La, Ma', it was all you! I thought he looked something quite mean at the first. And I was just going to say so, only something put it out of my head. I'll assure him! to sit himself down on the same bench with us! 205

MR WATTS. Well, well, my dear, time was I was not half as good. Mr Walley, you'll tell his Lordship Lord John Dervis I can't write, because of being in Kinsington Gardens; but my Darter does not deny to knowing of Muster Cleveland, and so, that being the case, he may call when it happens to suit. 210

VALET. Sir, your very obedient! Ladies,—yours.

Exit bowing.

III.206–7 **I'll assure him! to sit himself down on the same bench with us!** See John Burgoyne's *The Heiress* (Inchbald, *British Theatre*), in which Miss Alscrip mistakes Miss Alton for a fine lady and is then chagrined when she discovers that she is interviewing a lady's companion.

Manent MR, MRS, *and* MISS WATTS *and* ELIZA.

MR WATTS. He's a deal genteeler than I! I can't make that kereless bow for my life. I'm always afeard of a tumble, now I han't got my compter to lean upon while I do it. But Bet, my dear, pray tell me, now how old Alderson come to consent? 215

MISS WATTS. Pray, Sister Eliziana; do people ever see company in Indy, like in England?

MR WATTS. Why, if my eyes don't deceive me, if there i'nt Cousin Joel Tibbs! why Cousin Joel! Joel Tibbs! 220

MISS WATTS. La, Pa'! What do you call him for?

MRS WATTS. Indeed, Tommy, I do often wish your tongue was out! bringing about one sich a heap of people one's ashamed to be seen with! 225

MISS WATTS. I declare I'll walk on. Come, Sister Eliziana. And if he should speak to us before anybody, let's pretend not to know him.

Exit.

ELIZA. O Cleveland! that once I were but yours!

Aside and exit.

MRS WATTS. Stop, young ladies, stop! I can't go so fast, 'cause of my new shoes. But I'm sure I'll not stay behind, with that old Tibbs; ripping up every spiteful thing that can come into his head! I declare, Tommy, if it was anybody but me, they'd be in sich a passion!—however, I won't stay, I promise you. I'll go to t'other walk. 230 235

Exit.

MR WATTS *alone.*

[MR WATTS.] I'm sure, my dear Wife, you'd be welcome, for me, to go a pretty deal further!

Enter MR TIBBS.

MR TIBBS. Why I could have taken my oath I heard my own name!— What, Tom?— My dear Tom! why I went to your house just now—Good lauk, Tom, to think of that's being your house! when 'twas but t'other day, as one may say, you was 240

III.216 **compter** "Old spelling of Counter" (*OED*).

styed in such a little dirty hole! I wanted to tell you I could not come to you tomorrow morning, as you asked me, because of business. But they told me you was come here. So I e'en thought I'd come here too; for what's such a walk to me? 245

MR WATTS. Well, then, my dear Joel, as we're met so lucky, let's e'en sit down upon this here bench, and talk a little comfortable: for we may do it full as well here as at home; for, between friends, whenever anybody comes to me at home, my wife's rather apt to come a little nearish to the keyhole. 250

MR TIBBS. Does she? Why then why don't you tell her to go further off?

MR WATTS. O lauk, Joel, I can't do that! She's very pertickler as to what I say to her.

MR TIBBS. Why, what, has she forgot already how time was she 255 used to scrub the floor upon her knees, before you married her?

MR WATTS. Why if I was to say so much as a word about that, Cousin Joel, she'd go nigh to beat me.

MR TIBBS. Beat you? And would you let her?

MR WATTS. O no, I would not let her, to be sure. But if you'll take 260 my advice, Cousin Tibbs, you'll never be over persuaded by your wife and darters to leave off business.

MR TIBBS. Why, what a dickens, Tom, a'n't you happy, then, with your fine coach to rock you to sleep from one end of London to t'other? And your fine house that makes you look like a 265 lodger in it? And your fine servants standing by one by two, by three, to stare an old friend out of countenance? And your fine cloaths, that nobody can know you in?

MR WATTS. Ah, Joel, as long as business did but go on, all them things was a joy to me! For then I was somebody! And my wife 270 and darter did not dare give themselves such airs. I used to speak as sharp as they. Here's a nice dinner, says I; but who kivered the table? And what smart new gowns you've got on, says I; but who paid for 'em? And now let's all go, and take a ride in our own coach, says I; but which of us earned it? And 275 when first I got on in the world, I used to give 'em a crown at a time; and then, at last 'twas a guinea; and then, lauk! there was such kissing and joy! and there's a good Tommy! says one; and Thankee, dear Pa'! says the t'other: but now that once they've fooled me into giving 'em their pin moneys, as they call it, they 280 take it without never a word, just as if it was their own gaining!

MR TIBBS. Well, I never should have suspected such a thing of

Cousin Aylce. Why she used to be as meek, and as mealy-mouthed—

MR WATTS. Why lauk, Cousin Tibbs, so she is now, to everybody but me: but she uses me just like a cur dog! You'd know no difference!—And as to Peg, she's worse than her mother. She never thinks me genteel! 285

MR TIBBS. What, Cousin Peg?

MR WATTS. She takes me to task everything I say or do. It's nothing but La, Pa'! at every word. I can never talk two minutes together, but what I'm sure to say something wrong. Being finished at a boarding school herself makes her so mortal nice, there's no pleasing her. And Aylce always sides against me! 290

MR TIBBS. Why then, my dear Tom, if I was as you, I'd mind them no more than the cat, but divert myself my own way. 295

MR WATTS. Ah, Joel, that's the very thing! I can't divert myself no way! Ever since I left off business, I've never known what to do. They've made me give up all my old acquaintance, because of their being so mean; and as to our new ones, it's as plain as ever you see they only despise me: for they never take off their hats if I meet them in the streets; and they never get up off their chairs, if I ask them how they do in their own houses; and they never give me a word of answer I can make out, if I put a question to them. 300 305

MR TIBBS. Why then don't take off your hat to them; and don't get off your chair to them; and don't answer them when they speak to you. That's the way I should treat 'em, if any of 'em come across me. I should like nothing better.

MR WATTS. O, but you've no notion what it is, living in the great World! why I'm forced to leave off my things now as good, and better than I used to buy them at the first; or else they think me shabby. And I'm obliged to have my wig dressed every day! and to wear my best coat to dine in! And when all's done, nobody takes notice of it! It passes just for nothing. 310 315

MR TIBBS. Well, I would not lead such a life to be made the great Mogul!

MR WATTS. Nor I, neither, if I could chuse again; for these people in the great World don't know what they'd be at. There's nothing going on but spending. One can't wear a coat for a couple of 320

III.316–17 **the great Mogul** "the common designation among Europeans of the Emperor of Delhi. . . . A great personage; an autocratic ruler" (*OED*).

years, but what it's quite out of the mode! They'll turn you off a hat, before you can well know if it's been on your head! And if you talk to any of 'em of getting a shoe mended, or anything a little saving, they'll stare at you as if you was out of your mind.

MR TIBBS. They might stare like stuck pigs for aught I should care. Why, I declare— 325

MR WATTS. Hush! They're all coming back. Here's Betsey close by. Come along with me. I've a deal more to tell you. Only I'd as lieve my wife should not hear me.

Exeunt.

Enter ELIZA.

[ELIZA.] How heavily pass the minutes where anxiety takes possession of the mind! Why has he forborn all mention of our contract at Calcutta? Why omitted even to name Mr Alderson? Suspense, however, will soon be over; but what may be its result? Alas Cleveland, you little suspect the test by which your firmness will be tried! I never will forsake nor disavow my family; yet I feel for your surprise in an intercourse so new to you,—feel all your shame, your confusion, your blushes—tingling upon my own cheeks! 330 335

Enter MISS WATTS.

MISS WATTS. It's well they're gone! but pray, Sister Eliziana, what did you walk on for before I'd peeped? Come, let's sit down here. This is the best part of the Garden to wait in, for it's where all the best Company comes; only Pa' and Ma's always an hour too soon. Well, now let's talk. Pray how long may you have had this lover? 340

ELIZA. Pardon me, Sister; the narrative just now would extremely oppress me. 345

MISS WATTS. I want monstrously to see him. I intend, when you are married, you should *Shaproon* me everywhere, for I hate monstrously to go out with Ma'! Don't you think Ma's monstrous mean? And Pa's so vulgar, you can't think how I'm ashamed of him. Do you know I was one day walking in the Park, with some young ladies I'd just made acquaintance with, quite the pelite sort, when all of a sudden I felt somebody twitch me by the elbow: so I screatched, and called out La, how imper- 350 tinent! and when I turned round, saying Do pray, sir, be less free of your hands, who should I see but Pa'! 355

ELIZA. Was he there by accident?

MISS WATTS. No, he followed me o' purpose: and it made me so monstrous mad, if I had not bit my glove through, I should have fell a crying. Only think how provoking! for crying always makes my nose red; so I always resolve not to cry, if I am never so mad. And, but just before, I was in such prodigious spirits, I did not know what I said; for I was talking to a gentleman that I really believe, by his look, was a Baronet! 360

Enter MRS WATTS.

MRS WATTS. 'Pin my word, young ladies, I don't know what you walk on so fast for. There's no keeping up with you if 'twas never so. 365

MISS WATTS. La, Ma', I hope you're old enough to do without a Shaproon?

ELIZA. Will you take this seat, madam? 370

MRS WATTS. Thankee, my dear, I don't care if I do; for my new shoes are so strait over my toes—

MISS WATTS. Why now what do you offer it for? Now we can't talk without her hearing us!

ELIZA. I would rather not sit. My mind is too ill at ease for rest. (*walks about*) Heavens! Cleveland! With a lady! Arm in arm! It must be his Sister. O that he were alone! that I could learn his plans, and prepare him for the interview in Bond Street! They are advancing this way. I will keep in sight, yet leave it to his own discretion to address me or not. (*apart*) My dear Mother and Sister, I conjure you to let us all remove to that further seat. 375 380

MISS WATTS. La, why?

MRS WATTS. I'm very well here, my dear.

ELIZA. I have reasons of the highest importance,—I beg—I entreat— 385

MISS WATTS. Will you tell me what they are?

ELIZA. Yes, upon our return home; till then excuse me: but hasten, I beseech.

She goes to the further seat, MISS WATTS *eagerly following.*

MRS WATTS. Well, I never see the like! They can't let one sit still a minnet. And these new shoes do hurt my corns so! (*walks slowly to join them*) 390

Enter CLEVELAND *and* JEMIMA.

JEMIMA. I comprehend you perfectly, my dear Brother; but pray detain me no longer. I have told you Miss Percival is waiting for me. I give you my word, however, to be your messenger to Bond Street the first moment I can command the chariot. 395

CLEVELAND. Go in a chair, my dear Jemima. Do any thing rather than lose time thus critically circumstanced. Eliza expects me to address her through her Father immediately; but my apprehension lest Sir Marmaduke, when defeated in his own plan, should withdraw even all promise of favour, robs me of the courage to 400 proceed till I have conversed with her. If she cannot receive me alone in her own house, there can be no impropriety in her seeing me in your apartment, and your presence at Sir Marmaduke's. Send her in these lines: I wrote them before I left Albermarle Street. I am sure she will not refuse their request to 405 grant me a short audience without delay.

JEMIMA. But what will Lady Wilhelmina say to my bringing a total stranger to her house, without her leave or knowledge?

CLEVELAND. She will think it a little strange; but that is not material, as the cause must so soon be published. What do I see?— 410 Is it possible?— Jemima, yes! 'tis Eliza!—upon that seat—between those ladies—O look! Is she not most lovely?

JEMIMA. Her appearance is extremely interesting.

CLEVELAND. How fortunate an incident! I can now present you to each other, and tell her all my difficulties at once. 415

JEMIMA. I consent most willingly—But stop!— Who are those people with her?

CLEVELAND. I was just making that enquiry to myself.

JEMIMA. They look immensely odd. I don't much like to join them. 420

CLEVELAND. O Jemima, hold yourself superior at such a moment, to so little an objection!

III.404–5 **Albermarle Street** Named after the Duke of Albemarle, who originally owned the land (Blake Ehrlich, *London on the Thames*, Boston: Little, Brown, 1966, 279), by 1750 the street was "revered as an area of the rich and great. Behind the finely-carved doorways of Albemarle Street lived such eminent residents as the Earls of Pomfret and Grantham, the Marquis of Harrington and the Countess of Stafford": Phillips, *Mid-Georgian London*, 253.

JEMIMA. Indeed, Brother—I can't say I have much taste to making acquaintance with two such strange figures.

CLEVELAND. You distract me! It is impossible she should not have seen me; it is incumbent upon me therefore, to let her instantly know you are my sister. 425

He is drawing her towards the further seat; when MISS PERCIVAL *rushes in, and, catching the hand of* JEMIMA *throws herself against the shoulder of* CLEVELAND, *without looking at him.*

MISS PERCIVAL. O Jemima!— I am in a terror—an alarm—an agitation—I have been so dreadfully affrighted—

JEMIMA. But how, my dear Miss Percival? 430

CLEVELAND. Infortunate conjuncture. (*aside*)

MISS PERCIVAL. Twenty carriages, at least, have been just driving against the chariot; and alone as I was—without protector—without aid—the expectation of a sudden crush overpowered my spirits, and in the horrour of fainting without succour, I flew from the carriage to—your arms!— Bless me! (*starting*) Is it not you that are supporting me? Who have I been leaning against? (*drawing herself aloof but looking down*) I am all tremor and confusion. 435

JEMIMA. Let us go back together to the chariot. 440

MISS PERCIVAL (*looking up*). O all ye stars! What have I done? Traiterous Jemima! you have betrayed me into the arms of—your Brother!— Ah! never let me see him more!— I fly! I fly!

Exit running.

CLEVELAND. How perverse an encounter!

JEMIMA. Hasten after her, Brother!— Run! you will not, surely, suffer her to return to her carriage alone? 445

CLEVELAND. It is better she should surmize the mistake of her choice than foster it. I would not leave Eliza with an astonishment so great upon her mind as this scene must have produced for the Universe. 450

JEMIMA. And is this all your consideration for a young lady who has manifested towards you so noble, so disinterested an attachment?

CLEVELAND. I think of her with equal gratitude and concern; but my first consideration is due where my own love has been plighted by my honour. 455

JEMIMA. And must I, then, return to her alone?
CLEVELAND. Yes. Unless, first, you will permit me to introduce you to Eliza.
JEMIMA. Be quick, then, at least. 460

They move towards the further seat. ELIZA *looks down;* MISS WATTS *bends forward to stare; and* MRS WATTS *rises and courtsies low.*

MRS WATTS. Why don't you get up, my dears. Here's some company coming that looks us full in the face.
MISS WATTS. La, Ma', can't you sit still? They'll only get your place.
CLEVELAND. Miss Watts! (*looking at* ELIZA) 465

ELIZA *rises.*
MISS WATTS *starts up, and stands before her.*

MISS WATTS. La, does the gentleman know me?
JEMIMA (*drawing back*). Brother!
MISS WATTS. Pray, sir, did you want to say anything to me?
CLEVELAND. Ma'am?
MISS WATTS. Did not you speak to me, sir? 470
CLEVELAND. I? No, madam.
MISS WATTS. La, Ma'? Now did not you hear him as plain as could be?

Enter MISS PERCIVAL, *running.*

MISS PERCIVAL. O succour—succour me!
CLEVELAND. From what, madam? 475
MISS PERCIVAL. O I can't speak! I have seen such a frightful sight—Don't I look dying?— Protect me, I conjure you!
CLEVELAND. But from what? I see nothing. What has alarmed you?
MISS PERCIVAL. Support me to a seat. My feet totter. 480

CLEVELAND *and* JEMIMA *lead her to the nearest seat.* ELIZA *takes her place again.* MRS *and* MISS WATTS *stand still, occasionally whispering [to] each other.*

JEMIMA. Dear Miss Percival, what has thus again terrified you?
MISS PERCIVAL. O, two monsters! two shocking monsters, in something resembling human shape that, while I was slowly walking back to the Gate, looked at me with two such dreadful old wigs on, that, had I not fled hither for refuge, I really think must have demolished me with horrour. 485
JEMIMA. And was that all?
CLEVELAND. Amazing!
MISS PERCIVAL. I have the infirmity of a terrour about old men's wigs not to be expressed. Now do both of you sit down by me till I am a little recovered. 490

JEMIMA *sits;* CLEVELAND *only bows, looking uneasily towards* ELIZA, *whose head is turned another way.*

And now, do pray, Jemima, ask your Brother to tell me one thing sincerely. Does not he think me a terrible coward?
JEMIMA. What say you Brother?
CLEVELAND. Not absolutely an amazon, undoubtedly, madam. 495
MISS PERCIVAL. Pho!— Ask him, Jemima, if he does not think it very silly to be so fearful?
JEMIMA. Well, Brother?
CLEVELAND. I never judge a lady by any single trait.
MISS PERCIVAL. I protest if I hear one more such priggish answer, I shall yawn till tomorrow! Ask him—no, this one thing I must ask myself, for 'tis of the utmost moment. Pray, Mr Cleveland tell me, solemnly, have you, or have you not a serious aversion to wigs? 500
CLEVELAND. To wigs? 505
JEMIMA. To wigs?
MISS PERCIVAL. Yes, for old men, I mean—Young men have a pretty air enough in them, but an antique head with a bob jerun

III.508 **bob jerun** Bobs were "essentially short wigs without queues. They were first recorded in 1684, and became popular among those who could not afford long wigs. James Stewart, a hairdresser, wrote in the 1780s of the early eighteenth-century tradesman in his 'snug bob or natty scratch'": John Woodforde, *The Strange Story of False Hair* (London: Routledge and Kegan Paul, 1971), 33. Although they became acceptable for all classes by the 1760s (p. 37), they seem to be connected with the merchant classes. In Murphy's *Citizen* (p. 3), Wilding sneers at Young Philpot because he pretends to be a gentleman at night but wears a "frock

—if you would not rather encounter a brigand—a felon,—an assassin; I can never speak to you more. Why don't you answer? What in nature can you be contemplating? 510

Turning round she perceives MRS *and* MISS WATTS, *who intercept her view of* ELIZA.

Heavens, what two creatures! How can you bear to look at them?

CLEVELAND. Me?— I—I—I scarcely saw them. (*turning hastily away*)

MISS PERCIVAL. I believe they are two things just animated out of a Shew Box. Did you ever see such drolly horrid frights? 515

CLEVELAND. Confusion! Can they be Eliza's relations? (*aside*)

MISS PERCIVAL. This foremost, in particular, seems absolutely dressed out for a caricature shop. I dare say she's paid for shewing herself. Now don't you think so? 520

CLEVELAND. I really—have not taken—much notice of her.

MISS PERCIVAL. What can thus abash and confound him? (*apart*) O but do look. She seems so satisfied to be examined. She certainly fancies we are admiring her. Now don't be so cruel as to turn your eyes another way. 525

CLEVELAND (*apart to Jemima*). Dearest Jemima, persuade her to depart, I beseech you! Eliza will be so amazed at my distance—yet I dare not address her thus cruelly circumstanced.

JEMIMA. Is it not time, now, for us to return, Miss Percival?

MISS PERCIVAL. And pray look at the elder one! with what complacency she contemplates her own attire! how prim! how starched! how exactly like a painted old doll! 530

JEMIMA (*apart to* CLEVELAND). Propose handing her to the chariot.

CLEVELAND. How tormenting! (*apart*) May I not be allowed—Madam—to have the honour—to—to conduct you to your carriage? 535

MISS PERCIVAL. If he were not so embarrassed, I should think him an Iseecle. I must try to give him a little courage. (*aside*)

---

and bob-wig" during the day. See *Camilla*: "The effect of this full buckled bob-jerom which stuck hollow from the young face and powdered locks of the Ensign, was irresistibly ludicrous" (p. 264).

III.516 **Shew Box** "A box in which objects of curiosity are exhibited, especially a box containing a peep-show" (*OED*).

Well, I'll endeavour to rise. Your arm, Jemima. Heavens, how weak your arm is! Cleveland! will you not help to sustain me? 540

She rises between CLEVELAND *and* JEMIMA, *and is moving from the seat; but starts suddenly back.*

O heavens! O all ye stars! The monsters! The monsters!
JEMIMA. Where?—What?—Where?—
CLEVELAND. I see nothing.
MISS PERCIVAL. The Wigs! The very Wigs! 545

Enter MR WATTS *and* MR TIBBS.

MR WATTS. Well, if they an't all gone on!
MISS PERCIVAL. Do you not see them? Look! look there! they approach!—ah! Some hartshorn! some drops.

She throws herself again upon the seat, her head reclined against CLEVELAND.

CLEVELAND. I see nothing in the World—except two vulgar-looking men. 550
MR WATTS. Now which way can they be gadded to?
MR TIBBS. And somebody's took our places. But stop! Why, they're there!
MR WATTS. Why where?
MR TIBBS. Why, there! look yonder, man!— Why, what are you all here? (*going to the further seat*) How do do Cousin Aylce? What, Cousing Peg? And you, too my little Betsey? Why how you're grown since I used to have you o' my lap! 555

ELIZA *rises but keeps aloof.*

CLEVELAND. Heavens!—are those, also, her kindred?
MISS PERCIVAL. Are they gone? May I venture to raise my eyes? O, stand before me, Cleveland, stand before me! one of the monsters descends this way! 560

III.548 **Some hartshorn! some drops** Hartshorn is "the aqueous solution of ammonia . . . smelling salts," and drops refer to "volatile English drops, or Goddard's drops, a name of a medicinal liquor" (*OED*).

MR TIBBS. Dears, I'm afeard there's a lady taken bad. Pray, ma'am—

MISS PERCIVAL. O frightful! one of the Wigs is fixing me! 565

MR TIBBS. Belike the lady's subject to fits?

MRS WATTS. (*advancing*). Well, if she is, do you get to t'other side, for I know a way to cure her in a minnet. It's only just the littlest touch in the World of the top of the nose, with the tip of the finger; and if the young lady— 570

MISS WATTS. (*following*). La, Ma', can't you let me—

MISS PERCIVAL. (*starting up and screaming*). O the Savages are bearing down upon us!

Runs off, one hand covering her face, the other holding by CLEVELAND.

Exit.

CLEVELAND. How torturing an incident! (*aside as conducting her out*) 575

Exit.

JEMIMA. What an extraordinary set! Can Frank's new Relations be worse? (*aside*)

Exit.

MISS WATTS. La, Ma', what did you talk of touching her nose for? Now you've frightened her off. Do, Sister Eliziana, come along with me, and let's see which way she turns. 580

MRS WATTS. Why, now, I'm sure, my dear,—Why how you go on without hearing one! I'm sure I wish I had not bought these new shoes.

Exit, hobbling.

Manent MR WATTS, MR TIBBS, *and* ELIZA, *who keeps walking aloof.*

MR TIBBS. Why now I should be glad to know what that young lady gave that squall for, upon my coming up to her; just as if 585 I'd been something out of the way!

MR WATTS. My dear Cousin Tibbs, the great World is full of them things. You can't make 'em out no how. I could tell you such stories of how rude people's been to me, as would make you think nothing of anything. 590

MR TIBBS. Why then, why a'n't you as rude to them?
MR WATTS. They'll eat up all the best things, one after another, without caring for not leaving you a scrap: and they'll take all the best places, without minding if you have not a bit as big as my hand to sit upon: and they'll leave doors and windows open 595 upon one in the middle of a sneeze or a cough; and they'll let one speak half an hour, before they'll give one an answer; and they'll clean their teeth full in one's face, as if one was nothing but a looking glass; and they do such a heap of things—
MR TIBBS. Dickens, I'm glad you've told me; for if ever I come 600 across any of them, I'll take the best bit, and the best place myself, and pretend it's all only to be at the tip top of the mode.
MR WATTS. Why how do you think I was served one day by a gentleman of my Darter's acquaintance, that I met walking with her in the Park, and that hunched me plump out of my seat, 605 when I only got up out of peliteness to make him a bow?
MR TIBBS. Fegs, if he'd served me so, I'd have sat down jolt upon his lap, and Dickens! says I, what a nice cushion somebody's put me here!
MR WATTS. O, it's surprising what they'll do. They've no con- 610 science for that. But come a little this way, for fear of Betsey; for if she should tell Peg what I'm saying, she'll La, Pa', me for half an hour. It's a very troublesome thing the having darters.

Exeunt.

ELIZA *alone.*

[ELIZA.] How strange an adventure! They could not both be his sisters—yet how familiar a conduct to anyone but a Brother! I 615 could hear nothing; but all I saw was most extraordinary. He is gone, too—and without speaking—Was it unavoidable? I must hope so; yet how dreadful the least doubt! O Cleveland! with elegance like yours, founded on birth, education and intellectual endowments, can I wonder if your mind should involun- 620 tarily recoil from an alliance, in which shame must continually struggle against kindness, and Pride against Happiness?

III.605 **hunched** To hunch is to "push, shove, thrust" (*OED*).
III.607 **Fegs** "an (unmeaning) syllable in exclamatory phrases expressing asseveration or astonishment" (*OED*); a distortion of "faith" (*EDD*).

Enter MR WATTS *and* MR TIBBS.

MR WATTS. Betsey, my dear, our coach is up ready, and your sister says we must go, for there's no company, she says, this morning. So we're all going. Only do you walk on first, my dear. 625
There, that way,—don't you see 'em?

Exit ELIZA.

Manent MR WATTS *and* MR TIBBS.

MR WATTS. If you can come to me tonight, Cousin Joel, I'll be sure [to] be in my little parlour while my wife's upstairs, and then I'll finish you this story; and I'll tell you how I've been served twice besides, by two other gentlemen. As downright af- 630
fronted as ever you see. But I must not make my wife wait. Only remember this, Cousin Joel—Never leave off business!

Exit.

MR TIBBS *alone.*

[MR TIBBS.] Poor Tom! So he's only got all this money to be put out of his place, and held up as one ma[y] say, for a laughing stock to be made fun of! Why I, now, that am but a poor man 635
by his side, though time was I could have counted a guinea to his sixpence, I'd no more be trampled upon, at that rate, and elbowed, and flouted, and grinned at, as he says he catches 'em doing, than I'd be made the Pope of Rome. Why what's a Lord, and a Baronight, and Squire, and that to me? Not but what if 640
they'll be pelite, I'll be pelite too, but, fegs, if they ben't—we'll soon see which will be tired first of being t'other thing!

Exit.

Enter CLEVELAND.

[CLEVELAND.] Gone? How unfortunate! And the whole vulgar crew departed. Yet perhaps 'tis better so. Jemima will prevail with her to meet me at Sir Marmaduke's, and it might but have 645
embarrassed her to be addressed abruptly. Meanwhile, I will write to beg an audience with Miss Percival, and openly state to her my situation. These are certainly the relations of Eliza—I dare not doubt it.— Sweet lovely Eliza! from weeds so coarse

can a flower so fragrant bloom? How beautiful, O Nature, are thy designs! how instructive is thy study! Avaunt all narrow prejudice. Elegance, as well as talents and virtue, may be grafted upon every stock, and can flourish from every soil! (*going*) 650

Enter FRANK CLEVELAND, *singing*.

FRANK. O ho! you are here, are you? Why, master Cupidon has been mighty busy in these Gardens this morning. 655
CLEVELAND. Cupidon?
FRANK. Why, do you think I don't know whom you have been chasing? I met the beauteous fair one this moment driving off.
CLEVELAND. What fair one? Whom do you mean?
FRANK. You don't pretend to be smug I hope? Miss Percival, to be sure. 660
CLEVELAND. Pshaw.
FRANK. You are returned home in an immensely queer humour. Nothing pleases you. Is this the common effect of the Calcutta climate upon Europeans? If it is, I have dealt myself out a precious lot! 665
CLEVELAND. Calcutta? What, have you not done with that surfeiting absurdity yet?
FRANK. Nay, don't put me out of conceit with the business now it is irretrievable. I am but melancholy about it myself. 670
CLEVELAND. Irretrievable? What?
FRANK. Matrimony, man. Not but what the old codger may bluster a little, at first, about settlements, and pin money, and that; but I shall soon tell him—
CLEVELAND. What? 675
FRANK. That I'm not worth a penny.
CLEVELAND. That will be honest, at least.
FRANK. O, it i'n't worth a fib.
CLEVELAND. That's easy, however.
FRANK. Why what will he have to do with the business? Except just paying down the little yellow boys. 680
CLEVELAND. And do you conclude he will be so charmed with your fine person, that it will be all-sufficient to procure his favour?

III.672 **the old codger** Burney's *The Witlings* has a character called Codger, who is a choleric old man.

FRANK. O, the little girl will manage that. I shan't trouble myself about it in the least. The dear creatures take all those things upon themselves now. She'll pine, and sicken, and languish, and frighten the old codger; and then, you know, square-toes must call me into the consultation. That's the way now. 685

CLEVELAND. Frank, you are the most egregious coxcomb, without any exception, that ever I knew. 690

FRANK. 'Tis well to be perfect in anything. However, I must not stand trifling. Have you any commands in Bond Street?

CLEVELAND. In Bond Street?— Surely you have not the effrontery to really present yourself there? 695

FRANK. Effrontery? Why the affair is arranged I tell you. About an hour ago, I sent in my proposals; and the Papa himself answered he should be glad to see me, as soon as I pleased—in the name of his fair Daughter.

CLEVELAND. I certainly believe you are mad. However, ridiculous as all this is, I desire to have it cleared immediately and categorically. Who, once for all, is this Father? Who this Daughter? 700

FRANK. How can a man speak a name you have taken such a spite to? However, if you'll promise not to cut my throat, I'll tell you once more. The Father—but stand a little further off—the Father—is a certain—Mr—Watts of Bond Street. The daughter is just returned from the East and yclept Elizabeth. 705

CLEVELAND. Why then, Frank, if you are not mad yourself, you'll drive me so!

FRANK. If I had but arrived five minutes sooner, I might have introduced you to her, for she is but just gone hence. 710

CLEVELAND. Astonishing! How should you know of her being here?

FRANK. Why, having nothing better to do, and a tiresome fellow to get rid of, I scampered after my messenger, who I found pursued them hither. 715

CLEVELAND. This is all together the most unfathomable stuff—

FRANK. She has a barbarous set of relations. I must prepare you for that. You'll be devilishly ashamed of them.

CLEVELAND. Shall I? You know them, then? 720

FRANK. Quite as much as ever I intend to do. Lady Wilhelmina will faint away twice a day for a fortnight upon the first interview.

CLEVELAND. Are they so—so—so very bad then? Confusion! (*aside*)

II.688 **square-toes** "A precise, formal, old-fashioned person" (*OED*).

FRANK. O, past all description! I must not keep her waiting, though, pretty dear, that would be cruel. Don't you think so? 725

CLEVELAND. Frank—but no!— (*walking away*)

FRANK. Well, good morrow, and better humour to you my dear Brother. I am afraid Miss Percival is not quite so kind as my little Lizzy.

CLEVELAND. As who sir? (*turning back*) 730

FRANK. Why you are fiercer and fiercer! Can't you endure that name neither?

CLEVELAND. It is in vain I strive to be calm against so endless a rhapsody of folly and impertinence. Hear me, Frank! If you have ferreted into my affairs only to shew your wit by turning 735 them into ridicule, it is well for one of us, at least, that I can never forget you are my Brother.

Exit.

FRANK CLEVELAND *alone.*

[FRANK.] Comical enough! So a man can't talk of marrying now, but what it's ferreting into his affairs, and turning them into ridicule! What it can be that sets him thus a vapouring at the 740 least mention of my poor little Gentoo, I am really curious to know. I must go to her however, pretty melting soul! and swear that all the Fates and Destinies, the Loves and Graces—the Gods and Goddesses—brought her expressly from Calcutta to make her my Bride. 745

End of Act III

ACT IV

A dressing room at SIR MARMADUKE TYLNEY'S.
Enter JEMIMA, *leading in* ELIZA.

JEMIMA. I can never, dear madam, enough acknowledge this goodness; but, believe me, it is not my brother alone it will bind to you.

ELIZA. It was not possible for me to refuse a request to one who, but for my loss of my adopted Parent, would have had the power at this moment to have sent me a command. 5

JEMIMA. I left him seeking you, with the utmost anxiety, in Kensington Gardens. But if something important and unforeseen does not prevent him, he will be here, I am certain, almost immediately. I will not, therefore, anticipate his communications; he wishes, I know, to relate his difficulties to you himself. 10

ELIZA. Alas, I can too easily imagine what they may be! and should he think them insuperable—he shall not find me irrational to his representations, though I will not—to his Sister—pretend that they will leave me very happy! (*sighing*) 15

JEMIMA. Be assured—

LADY WILHEMINA (*within*). A young lady, do you say?

JEMIMA. 'Tis Lady Wilhelmina!

ELIZA. Lady Wilhelmina?

JEMIMA. Before my Brother arrives! How unfortunate! Before I know what he would have me say or do! 20

Enter LADY WILHELMINA.

LADY WILHELMINA. Allow me, Miss Cleveland, to enquire—but I beg pardon—I interrupt you—I intrude? (*looking at* ELIZA)

ELIZA (*courtsying respectfully*). It is I, rather, who intrude madam, and—and—How keenly she examines me! (*aside*) 25

LADY WILHELMINA. Pray don't let me discompose you. Don't mind me, I beg. Miss Cleveland, you will give me leave to speak with you. Don't mind me, I say, I beg. (*to* ELIZA, *still stiffly looking at her*)

ELIZA (*again courtsying low*). Ma'am I—I—what haughty affability! (*aside*) 30

LADY WILHELMINA. Who have you got here Miss Cleveland? What is this young woman? (*apart to* JEMIMA, *but always erectly staring at* ELIZA)

ELIZA. I cannot bear this unqualified scrutiny! (*aside*) Perhaps (*to* JEMIMA), I had better have the honour of waiting upon you some other time? 35

LADY WILHELMINA. By no means. I beg I may not be in your way. Don't let me give you any uneasiness. Who is it, I say? (*to* JEMIMA *in a half whisper*) 40

JEMIMA. Ma'am, it's a lady that—that—a young lady that I saw—that I met just now—in Kensington Gardens,—and—

LADY WILHELMINA. In Kensington Gardens?

JEMIMA. Yes, ma'am; Miss Percival took me to Kensington Gardens, and—and— 45

LADY WILHELMINA. If this young lady is an acquaintance of Miss Percival, how astonishingly ackward, Miss Cleveland, not to introduce me to her!

JEMIMA. Ma'am, I—

ELIZA. I beg— 50

LADY WILHELMINA. Can anybody under my roof be so uninformed how to conduct themselves? You really make me blush for you, Miss Cleveland. I hope, however, madam (*advancing smilingly and bowing her head to* ELIZA), you will have the goodness to forgive her. She means perfectly well; nobody means 55 better; but she is not yet entirely all I could wish. Give me leave, madam, to have the honour of hoping Miss Percival is well?

ELIZA. Miss Percival, madam?

JEMIMA. 'Tis a mistake that will delay all enquiry; let it pass a few minutes, I conjure you! (*apart to* ELIZA) 60

LADY WILHELMINA. Whispering too? You really make me nervous, Miss Cleveland! But you will allow, I hope, madam (*to* ELIZA), for early disadvantages. It is only within these very few years that I have been favoured with the company of Miss Cleveland under my own roof; for, till my alliance with Sir 65 Marmaduke, we were nearly strangers to each other. This you might, indeed, have conjectured.

JEMIMA. I hope so! (*aside*)

LADY WILHELMINA. You, madam, whose elegant deportment immediately announces your own connexions to be in the very 70 first style—

ELIZA. Mine, ma'am?—

LADY WILHELMINA. I never mistake in that particular. There is a certain air of reserve, a certain modesty of respect, in young people who are born and bred to know what is due to certain 75 distinctions in life, that immediately point them out to those who are conversant in discriminating the various classes of society.

ELIZA. Indeed, madam, I pretend not—I am far—

LADY WILHELMINA. Pardon me, madam; I needed not hearing 80 you were the friend of Miss Percival to understand your line: your manners, your look, convinced me at once you were accustomed to move in the first circle.

ELIZA. Alas, madam—

LADY WILHELMINA. But is it not extraordinary, Miss Cleveland, that your Brother has not yet been in my dressing room? I have waited there for him two hours and three quarters. But perhaps he is gone to pay his devoirs to Miss Percival? You say nothing? Perhaps as this young lady is Miss Percival's friend, she may know? 85 90

ELIZA. I, madam?

LADY WILHELMINA. Was Mr Cleveland, permit me to ask—of Miss Percival's party in Kensington Gardens?

ELIZA. Indeed I—I—

JEMIMA. My Brother, ma'am,—my brother was in Kensington Gardens—but it was— 95

LADY WILHELMINA. O, if he had the honour of attending Miss Percival, I must forgive him.

ELIZA. Attending Miss Percival! (*aside*)

LADY WILHELMINA. But else, to keep me waiting two hours and three quarters in my dressing room, is rather what I might have expected from his brother, Mr Francis. You have not, I presume, heard anything more of that disorderly young man. 100

JEMIMA. No, ma'am.

LADY WILHELMINA. Do you know if his degrading design has yet reached Miss Percival? 105

JEMIMA. I—I—fancy not ma'am.

LADY WILHELMINA. Can this young lady tell?

ELIZA. Ma'am?

LADY WILHELMINA. Did you happen, ma'am, to hear whether Miss Percival had received any tydings of a disgraceful nature relative to Mr Cleveland junior this morning? 110

JEMIMA. Ma'am, permit me to—to say—that Miss Percival has not—that this young lady has not heard anything—not the smallest—not anything ma'am. 115

LADY WILHELMINA. You relieve me. Yet, unhappily, what is known to that voluble Lord John Dervis can have no chance of secresy. Poor Cleveland! how virtuous a horrour did he manifest at the thoughts of a connexion so unfitting for our family. And how cruel must be his fear lest it should disgust Miss Percival with his house and himself! 120

ELIZA. What can this mean? (*aside*)

Enter SIR MARMADUKE.

SIR MARMADUKE. Hang his young family! what's his young family to me?

LADY WILHELMINA. Does anything disturb you, Sir Marmaduke? 125

SIR MARMADUKE. Disturb me? Why look at my greatcoat! See how the cape's sprinkled with rain! I dare say you may count nine or ten large drops upon it, and yet that booby, John Midge, stood in the hall, staring me full in the face as I got off my horse, 130 and rubbing his hands with joy, because, forsooth, he says this cursed shower will bring up peas and beans for his young family.

LADY WILHELMINA. Permit me, Sir Marmaduke, to present to you a friend of Miss Percival's.

ELIZA. Indeed, ma'am, your La'ship—(JEMIMA *stops her*) 135

SIR MARMADUKE. Miss Percival and her friends have us wholly at their command. Where's my Nephew?

LADY WILHELMINA. I imagine with Miss Percival. At least he has kept me waiting two hours and three quarters in my dressing room; and I can devise no other excuse for such inattention. 140

SIR MARMADUKE. Happy young rascal! Ah, I told him what it was to be a happy young rascal!

ELIZA. How strange! (*aside*)

LADY WILHELMINA. Unless, indeed, he is yet more nobly employed for us all, in trying to invalidate his brother's disgraceful 145 purpose of bringing that City-born girl into our family.

ELIZA. What do I hear! (*aside*)

SIR MARMADUKE. If she pays his debts, what's where she's born to us?

JEMIMA. Unfortunate subject. (*aside*) 150

LADY WILHELMINA. How any young person of that class can even think of coming among Us, often amazes me. What is it possible persons of that description, when once their fortunes are paid down, can expect from Us?

ELIZA. Miss Cleveland—suffer me, I beg, to retire. 155

JEMIMA. No, no! (*holding her*)

SIR MARMADUKE. I don't mean to praise the wisdom of such girls, Lady Wil, for I think them to the full as silly as you can do: but if they take our younger branches off our hands, and provide for our spendthrifts, what signifies their folly to us? 160

ELIZA. Indeed, Miss Cleveland—

JEMIMA. A moment! (*struggling to detain her*)

SIR MARMADUKE. Everybody knows those kind of matches are mere things of convenience: and as to Frank—who ever expected to hear anything better from such a prodigal? If Cleveland indeed had taken up with a girl of low extraction 'twould have nettled me; but Cleveland, ah! happy young rascal!— Give me leave, ma'am (*to* ELIZA), to commend myself to Miss Percival through your favour; and to assure her I have not forgotten her kind appointment for Piccadilly this—evening. 165 170

ELIZA. Sir—I— (JEMIMA *stops her*)

JEMIMA. Hush!

SIR MARMADUKE. And now I must get ready for this bore of a dinner. See here!—look—the marks of two drops of rain upon my sleeve! I wish the Devil had had that shower! Peas and beans for his young family, and be hanged to him! As if I cared for his young family. 175

Exit.

LADY WILHELMINA. It is impossible we should any of us forget what it is so much our happiness to remember as an appointment with Miss Percival. And permit me, madam, to hope I may there have the honour of confirming an acquaintance which I saw, in its very opening, would prove of the first class. I never mistake in that point. 180

Exit.

ELIZA, JEMIMA.

ELIZA. Indeed, madam, your La'ship is—is greatly—I am too much agitated—I cannot make myself heard!— 185

JEMIMA. I am extremely shocked, dear madam, that such perverse and provoking circumstances should damp the pleasure of our opening intercourse, and so ill repay the candid goodness with which you consented to its acceleration. How great will be my Brother's concern when— 190

ELIZA. Ah, madam! I see plainly that his situation, with respect to me, is unacknowledged to any part of his family but yourself! O Cleveland! so soon have you learnt to blush for her who so lately you delighted to exalt and to honour? Pardon me, madam—my heart is full. 195

JEMIMA. Let me, then, instantly explain—

ELIZA. I would fain begone; but my Father, who, indulging my request, was so good as to set me down, promised to call for me in half an hour, and—

MISS PERCIVAL (*within*). No, no; I'll go up to her room myself. 200

JEMIMA. Miss Percival! How tormenting!

Enter MISS PERCIVAL.

ELIZA. Ah! Heaven! Miss Percival, then, is the lady who was so familiar with him this morning! (*aside*)

MISS PERCIVAL. O Jemima, I die! do you know that Wretch —O you are not alone?— Pardon me. 205

ELIZA. Is there any other room where—

JEMIMA. By no means. This is a young lady, Miss Percival— that—that—

MISS PERCIVAL. O, I beg her pardon a thousand times. I hope she'll excuse my wild manner. That Wretch, my dear Jemima, 210 desires a private audience. How abominable! As if I could ever bear to see him alone!

ELIZA. I am sure I must incommode you. Pray, Miss Cleveland—

MISS PERCIVAL. O no, not in the least, I assure you. Nobody minds what I say. I rattle in all sort of ways. But Jemima, is it not 215 very presuming? What shall I do to punish him? See! he has had the impertinence to write to me. Tell me if ever you saw so priggish a little note in your life.

ELIZA. Heavens! It seems to me Cleveland's hand. (*aside*)

MISS PERCIVAL. See me alone? What can he mean? Surely, 220 Jemima, he can't flatter himself that—O no! no! no!— I can't think of it these six years, at least. Besides, what can he want to say? Can you form any guess, Jemima?

JEMIMA. I think—I can!

MISS PERCIVAL. O tell me, then!—no don't—I won't know. 225 Only don't fail to inform him I shan't write an answer. And as to seeing him and alone—I feel fainting at the very idea! Give me back the Wretch's note.

ELIZA. 'Tis Cleveland's hand indeed! I am sick at heart with strange surmizes. (*aside*) 230

MISS PERCIVAL. Well, what makes you so insipid, Jemima? Why don't you tell me what to do? Are you in the Creature's confidence?

JEMIMA. Sometimes—But I knew not this part of his plan.

MISS PERCIVAL. What part do you know, then? Pray tell me quick. I can't live a moment in any suspense. What part of his plan do you know? Do you think he dares ever imagine anything about me? O frightful! If you say yes, I shall certainly shut myself up!— But where? There are no Convents, now. Where can one be shut up, Jemima? 235 240

ELIZA. I know not what to conjecture. (*aside*)

MISS PERCIVAL. What a barbarous thing it is Jemima, that one has no shelter from those odious monsters the Men! I wish one could find some uninhabited Island, to which one could retreat from them in a Mass. But perhaps they would only pursue one. Men are amazing plagues. Do you think, Jemima, your Brother would take that trouble? 245

ELIZA. Heavens! her brother! (*aside*)

MISS PERCIVAL. Do you know I begin to take a great aversion to men. I am really afraid I shall quite hate them soon. And that will be very inconvenient, for one can't avoid sometimes seeing them. Do you hate them Jemima? 250

JEMIMA. Not—All!

MISS PERCIVAL. Why I'm not sure if I hate them All myself. But what in the World do you think this horrid creature will say to me, if I should trust him with an interview? Can you fancy to yourself what would be his subject? I am afraid this young lady thinks me very odd. 255

Enter a FOOTMAN.

FOOTMAN (*to* ELIZA). A gentleman, ma'am, desires me to tell you—O, he has followed me up! 260

Exit.

Enter MR WATTS.

MISS PERCIVAL. Ah!—one of my Wigs! Hide me dear Jemima—and be sure let it be where your Brother cannot find me!

Exit running.

JEMIMA. Excuse me, a moment, dear madam. (*to* ELIZA) I am glad to get her away!

Aside and exit.

ELIZA, MR WATTS.

MR WATTS. Why Betsey, my dear! why I hope I don't make the young lady run away? I only come upstairs to tell you—the young gentleman as got the lord to write me the letter, is below. 265

ELIZA. The young gentleman, sir?

MR WATTS. Why, as soon as I got home from setting you down, who should I see in the Entry a waiting, but he? So when he told me he was the young Muster Cleveland as came to court you, I told him I had just set you down at his Sister's here; so nothing would content him, but our both coming after you together. 270

ELIZA. O Cleveland! how critical is this moment!—and how happy should it clear away the dreadful suspicions that nearly overpower me! (*aside*) 275

Enter FRANK CLEVELAND.

ELIZA. Good Heaven! who is this? (*aside*)

MR WATTS. Now, sir, here's my Darter; and now I'm ready to hear what you've got to offer.

FRANK. Enchanting Fair! what exquisite happiness is mine to pay you thus my homage under this next-to-paternal roof! 280

ELIZA. What can this mean?

FRANK. Surely all the Elements—O Elements kind and fair!—united to forward my hopes, when they wafted to our sea-girt coast the destined object of my wishes! And surely . . . surely . . . what the Devil shall I say next? (*aside*) 285

ELIZA. Sir!

FRANK. Surely, I say madam, surely—surely if Love be the divine gift of felicity, the fates ordained my bliss upon the very hour you first set sail from India's soil. 290

MR WATTS. I dare say he i'n't worth a groat, he's got such a fluent tongue. (*aside*)

FRANK. Indeed, if it be possible to imagine bliss more—more—more joyful than mine—it must be—it must be—it must certainly be, I say—very—very extraordinary, indeed.— Rather lame that! (*aside*) 295

MR WATTS. I've no opinion of him. (*aside*)

ELIZA. Pray, my dear Father!!

FRANK. But if the most fervent devotion—the most tender homage—the most timid adoration, can move a fair bosom to 300 gentle sympathy, then shall I not find my ardent hopes all blasted, and blighted, and nipt in the opening bud.— Very well that, indeed! (*aside*)

MR WATTS. I dare to say he's a Swindler. I'll take up this here news-paper till he comes more to the point. 305

Takes a news-paper and sits in a corner reading.

ELIZA. How incomprehensible is this! Allow me, sir, to enquire why you address me in so singular a style?

FRANK. Ma'am?

ELIZA. If it is merely for sport—

FRANK. Sport, madam?— Ye Gods!— I had flattered myself, by your obliging attention to my blushing overtures, that I had your own fair permission for paying you my obsequious devoirs. 310

ELIZA. Overtures, sir? Good Heaven!—was that note to my Father from you?

FRANK. From my friend, ma'am, my Lord John Dervis. 315

ELIZA. And meant for you?— Amazing!— I thought—I imagined—it had been written for—for—Mr Cleveland?

FRANK. It was so, my dear madam.

ELIZA. How strange! Is your name, then Cleveland, sir?

FRANK. Most humbly at your command, madam. 320

ELIZA. Probably then,—permit me, sir, to ask—if you have—a brother?

FRANK. I have, ma'am: just returned, like your fair self, from the East Indies.

ELIZA. The East Indies? 325

FRANK. Yes, ma'am; and who is now upon that very pinnacle to which my fairest ambition rises; the pinnacle, madam, of connubial happiness.— A good handsome lie, that! (*aside*)

ELIZA. How wonderful! Can he behave thus yet know his Brother's situation? (*aside*) 330

FRANK. You probably saw, an hour ago, though without noticing her, my intended sister-in-law; for she was in Kensington Gardens at the same moment your own fair presence adorned them.

ELIZA. Intended Sister-in-law!—in Kensington Gardens!—Heavens! what stroke is now preparing for me! (*aside*) Will you allow me, sir, to make one more enquiry? 335

FRANK. How she softens! She's a good pretty Girl, really. (*aside*) Allow, madam? Ordain, enjoin, command, insist.

ELIZA. Has your Brother the slightest idea of the sort of discourse you now hold to me? 340

FRANK. Idea? He was the first confidant of my budding wishes, and your full-blown victory. I don't know how I shall get on much longer! (*aside*)

ELIZA. O Cleveland! have you but urged me hither to make me over to your brother! and to let me discover the perfidy you have not the courage to own? (*aside*) 345

FRANK. I have it now. (*aside*) Well may the East be celebrated for its fragrance, if thence issue Flowers of such exquisite odour! well may it supply Incense to the World, if for Incense it offers such objects! well— 350

CLEVELAND (*within*). May I be admitted Sister?

ELIZA. 'Tis Cleveland! How shall I bear to look at him? (*aside*)

FRANK. What a plaguy interruption! I may never attain the same energy again! (*aside*)

Enter CLEVELAND.

CLEVELAND (*in entering*). I have been barbarously detained— 355 she's here! and no Jemima! (*aside*) May I venture—(*to* ELIZA *who walks away and seats herself in a recess at the end of the scene*)

FRANK (*following and stopping him*). Prithee, Brother, go downstairs again! 360

CLEVELAND. Frank! In the name of Heaven, what is it you do here?

FRANK. Hush! Hush! don't you see? (*pointing to* ELIZA) Now do go down quick, there's a good fellow.

CLEVELAND. And on what pretence, sir, are you in this room 365 with—with—with—without Jemima?

FRANK. I'll tell you some other opportunity; but just now, do pray make haste and leave us.

CLEVELAND. Us, sir? Whom do you presume to include by Us? What have you to do with—with—with such a word as Us? 370

FRANK. How troublesome you are! I'll explain it, all by and by, I tell you; mean time, do pray run downstairs. I want to be alone.

CLEVELAND. So do I, sir!

FRANK. That is, not actually alone—you—you understand me? (*pointing to* ELIZA)

CLEVELAND. If I do, may I die this instant! 375

FRANK. Why, then the climate of India has dullified all your senses! Can't you conceive, when you find a man engaged with a fair lady, that you may do twenty things more agreeable to either of them than to come and look on?

CLEVELAND. Engaged with a fair lady?— Do you pretend to be here, then, by any permission? Any authority but your own? 380

FRANK. To be sure I do! Did I not tell you how the affair stood? I come by mutual arrangement. You have no memory, man!

CLEVELAND. Arrangement?

FRANK. Yes, reciprocal appointment to accelerate the noose. I told you so you know: but, untold, you might have been equally sure such a modest young man as I am could do nothing without encouragement. 385

CLEVELAND. This absurdity nearly maddens me! Prithee call Jemima. 390

FRANK. Call Jemima? Ha! Ha! facetious enough! And what for? To make a quartetto when a trio is already so out of season? Come, come, Brother, none of your jokes.

CLEVELAND. I protest, Frank—tell me, however, seriously, what you do in this—this—room? 395

FRANK. I have been telling you all day long, if you would but listen like a man of reason.

CLEVELAND. There is no enduring this trifling. What I cannot learn from you, I must solicit from this lady. Will you permit me— (*advancing to* ELIZA) 400

FRANK (*stopping him*). Hold, hold man! what are you thinking of? You may do mischief irretrievable. Can't you guess who that is?

CLEVELAND. That?

FRANK. Why it's my little Cit. 405

CLEVELAND. What!

FRANK. My little Gentoo, that I told you of! Have you forgotten it all? My Betsey Watts.

CLEVELAND. Frank, you'll provoke me to—

FRANK. Nay, don't be in a passion before her face. The poor thing can't help being born a Cockney, or bred a Hottentot. And, really, if you could but look at her divested of your prejudice, you'd think her a good pretty girl yourself. 410

CLEVELAND. Frank, I swear— (*raising his voice*)

MR WATTS (*looking round*). Anan! 415

FRANK. Hush, hush! what the Deuce do you speak so loud for? Now you've disturbed my Papa!

CLEVELAND. Who? (*looking about*)

FRANK. Nay, don't start and jump so. I tell you that's my Papa. He sits in that corner not to interrupt my soft speeches. 420

CLEVELAND. How inexplicable! What could bring him here?

FRANK. My coach and horses, my dear Brother.

CLEVELAND. Your coach and horses?

FRANK. That is, not mine in actual possession, but I doubt not mine by legacy: for he has promised, if my Uncle will come 425 down handsomely, not to oppose his Daughter's wishes.

CLEVELAND. His daughter's wishes?

FRANK. Yes. She was smit with me at a glance. The girl's not amiss in her taste. The old codger confessed himself she had owned her passion for me at the receipt of my proposals. 430

CLEVELAND (*stamping*). 'Tis false!

MR WATTS. Anan, there? Hay? What? (*coming forward*)

FRANK. Now see what you've done!— Nothing, sir, but a little raillery of my Brother. He affects to doubt your kind concurrence in— 435

CLEVELAND. Doubt? No sir! pardon me, I cannot doubt, I feel certain of the impossibility of your listening, even for a minute, to proposals for your inestimable Daughter from an utter stranger.

MR WATTS. Stranger? Bless you, no! why this here young gentle- 440 man knew my darter in Indy.

CLEVELAND. In India?— What Frank?

FRANK. Well done, honest old codger! (*aside*)

MR WATTS. Yes; he was old Mr Alderson's intimatest friend.

CLEVELAND. Mr Alderson's friend?— What Frank? 445

FRANK. Brava, my little Cit! the Girl must have invented this to favour her sudden passion. (*aside*)

CLEVELAND. This surpasses all else! And do you assert Frank, you were acquainted with Mr Alderson?

FRANK. Hand and glove together!— Never saw him in my life! 450 (*aside*)

CLEVELAND. I am overpowered by this effrontery!— And in India, sir? Was it in India you formed this friendship?

FRANK. In every part of the Globe alike. Whenever we met, we were equally cordial—I must not disgrace the little romancer. (*aside*)

MR WATTS. Why I told you as much! 455

CLEVELAND. What gross imposition—

MR WATTS. Imposition? Why, Betsey, my dear, pray come this

way. Did not you say that this here young gentleman was your sweetheart in Indy?

ELIZA (*advancing*). No, sir, I know him not. I was under a very great mistake. I beseech that we may instantly go home where I will try to rectify it. 460

CLEVELAND. Poor Frank.

MR WATTS. Good lauk, not know him! Why, pray, sir, i'n't your name Cleveland? 465

FRANK. I have that small honour, sir.

MR WATTS. Why, my dear, didn't you say as Muster Cleveland—

ELIZA. I spoke in errour. I know him not, sir, believe me.

FRANK. Who, o—o—o—o!

CLEVELAND. Permit me, then, now to speak for myself; and suffer me, sir (*to* MR WATTS) to entreat your sanction that I may address a few words in your hearing, to Miss Elizabeth. 470

MR WATTS. Servant, sir, servant! may I make bold first to ask your name, if it is not anywise disagreeable?

CLEVELAND. Cleveland, sir. 475

MR WATTS. Why, my dear, why now here's another of these Muster Cleveland's wants to speak to you. Pray do you hap to know him any better?

ELIZA. Once I thought I did!—but I find I judged too hastily. Indeed I know him not! 480

FRANK. Poor Cleveland!

CLEVELAND. Astonishing!

MR WATTS. Why there, now! Why my darter says she don't know neither one of you nor t'other!

FRANK. I wonder what the little Devil means! (*aside*) 485

CLEVELAND. How can I thus deeply have offended her. (*aside*) Allow me, madam, at least—

Enter MISS PERCIVAL.

MISS PERCIVAL. Miss Cleveland!—bless me! I thought to have found Miss Cleveland—and I see nothing but men!

Enter JEMIMA.

Jemima, you wicked thing, into what an horrible scrape have you drawn me! 490

JEMIMA. On the contrary, my dear Miss Percival, you know I told you—

MISS PERCIVAL. Hush! Hush! you abominable little mischief-maker! Would you lead that wretch there to imagine I could know he was in the house, and yet—not run out of it? 495

ELIZA. Heavens! (*aside*) My dear Father, are you not ready?

MR WATTS. Yes, my dear, yes; I'll only just pop my eyes over this here one more advertisement. "*For sale by the candle*." (*reading*)

MISS PERCIVAL. You don't tell me who that young lady is, Jemima. (*apart to* JEMIMA) 500

JEMIMA. A—a new friend.

MISS PERCIVAL. Of your own?

JEMIMA. I—I hope she will become so.

MISS PERCIVAL. I rather suspect—pray, Mr Frank, come hither. Let me speak to you in private. Do you think that young lady remarkably ugly? 505

FRANK. She stands so near to you, that I cannot judge.

JEMIMA (*apart to* CLEVELAND). My dear Brother, do you not perceive the necessity of explaining with Miss Percival immediately! Do you not see the cruel mistake she is nourishing? 510

CLEVELAND. Alas! Jemima, the averted eyes of Eliza unfit me for everything! but I believe you are right, and if she will allow me an audience less public—

MISS PERCIVAL. Now what are you two plotting together? Something about me, I dare say. However tell him, Jemima, I can't write to him—it's impossible. What should I write to him for? And as to seeing him—I can't see him neither. What should I see him for? 515

CLEVELAND. If, madam, I might presume to solicit a two minute's hearing— 520

ELIZA. My heart sinks! (*aside*) Have you not finished sir? (*to* MR WATTS, *who shakes his elbow in a token of a negative*)

IV.499 **For sale by the candle** "Traders of all descriptions used the coffee houses as a business address and found them a convenient meeting place where they could discuss their affairs with other merchants sharing the same interest; and the coffee house proprietors rendered them all kinds of services, handling their correspondence, advertising thefts and rewards, arranging passages on ships bound for the West Indies, Turkey and the Far East and conducting auction sales 'by Inch of Candle', the last bid before the candle flame went out securing the lot for sale" (Margetson, *Regency London*, 16).

MISS PERCIVAL. Two minutes? Horrible! I expire at the very thought. Jemima, do tell the creature I can't possibly grant such a request. No! I cannot give him more than—one minute at the most! (*smiling at him*) 525

ELIZA. Pardon me, Miss Cleveland,—I am pressed for time. I will wait for you sir, in the carriage. (*to* MR WATTS) O fatal blow!

Aside and exit.

CLEVELAND. May I not conduct you to the coach? 530

FRANK. No, no; (*holding him*) Don't you see, she goes first, purposely to give me opportunity to speak to her without squaretoes? And to explain her caprice? Don't be in the way so, man! look to your own affairs!

Exit.

MISS PERCIVAL (*patting him on the sleeve as he is following*). I am sure Frank has some design that way. Don't be a Marplot, Cleveland! 535

CLEVELAND. I shall lose my senses! (*aside*)

MR WATTS (*looking around*). Why what's this, now? Is my Darter gone? Why then I've no business to stay behind, I'm sure. Ladies and gentlemen, your humble servant, your servant, sir. And yours, ma'am. And your's too, ma'am. 540

Exit, bowing awkwardly around.

CLEVELAND, MISS PERCIVAL, JEMIMA.

MISS PERCIVAL. Bless me, Jemima, what's that man? And what in the Universe could he do in your room? Did you ever in your life see such an animal? And who is the fair Nymph? Some curiosity found out by Frank, I make no doubt. 545

CLEVELAND. How shall I contain my rage? (*aside*)

MISS PERCIVAL. Your Brother's grown horribly stupid, Jemima.

Re-enter FRANK CLEVELAND.

JEMIMA (*apart to* CLEVELAND). Seize this moment for an explanation with Miss Percival, Brother.— Frank, step this way! (*in a whisper*) 550

Exit.

IV.536 **Marplot** "One who mars or defeats a plot or design by officious interference or hinders the success of any undertaking" (*OED*). Mrs. Centlivre's *The Busie Body* (1709) has a character called Marplot.

FRANK. They'll soon have enough of each other, my dear! don't fear.

CLEVELAND, FRANK, MISS PERCIVAL.

MISS PERCIVAL. I'm glad you're returned, Frank, to keep us awake. Do pray tell me who that Quiz is! 555

FRANK. Don't ask me, I beg.

MISS PERCIVAL. Not ask you?— Why?

FRANK. Because I'm confoundedly out of countenance about him.

MISS PERCIVAL. Out of countenance about him, are you? Ah, ha! then I have conjectured right. And where, in Fortune's 560 name, did you light upon these two Things?

FRANK. Why I'll tell you the story, for it's really a good one.

CLEVELAND. May I entreat—

MISS PERCIVAL. No, no; I must hear the story first. Well, Frank?

FRANK. You must know I happened—by very great chance—for 565 it's what I make a point to avoid in general; to go into a sort of a kind of an Hotel—and there I saw them.

MISS PERCIVAL. Admirable! I was sure the Father was some Tavern keeper! And the carissima sposina elect—was she educated at the Bar? 570

CLEVELAND. Is it utterly impossible, madam, to hope for the honour of a single moment's hearing?

MISS PERCIVAL. Heavens Cleveland, don't speak in that solemn tone! Do tell on, Frank.

FRANK. Why, really, the adventure's amusing enough. Only my 575 Brother has taken an unaccountable antipathy to it. This little Thing, you must know, is just returned from the East Indies—

IV.569 **carissima sposina** Italian for "dearest little wife." See Austen's *Emma*, in which one of the pretentious Mrs. Elton's affectations is to call her husband her *caro sposo* (*Novels of Jane Austen*, 4:279).

IV.569–70 **educated at the Bar?** Miss Percival is no doubt making a pun on the two meanings of "Bar." The joke survives in George Bernard Shaw's *You Never Can Tell*, ed. S. N. Behrman (Lincoln: University of Nebraska Press, 1961, 54).

> DOLLY. Is your son a Waiter, too, William?
> WAITER (*serving* Gloria *with fowl*). Oh, no, Miss, he's too impetuous. He's at the Bar.
> M'COMAS (*patronizingly*). A potman, eh?
> WAITER (*with a touch of melancholy, as if recalling a disappointment softened by time*). No, Sir: the other bar—your profession, sir. A Q.C., Sir.

MISS PERCIVAL. From the East Indies, and not married? That's a bad sign! There must be some terrible flaw. Have a care, Frank!

CLEVELAND. I shall run wild! (*aside*) 580

FRANK. The sign may be bad, I grant, but the effect is tolerable enough: she has brought over eighty thousand pounds at her sole disposal.

MISS PERCIVAL. And you, I presume, have the kindness to propose taking the trouble and management of this sum out of her 585 hands?

FRANK. Why a lady may employ herself so much better than as a Steward, that I have not been without a little thought that way. However, I am not fixed. My Brother is so inordinately offended by the vulgarity of the connexion— 590

CLEVELAND. I offended at the vulgarity—at the—I?—

FRANK. He is ready to annihilate me every time I name it.— Yet, I remember the time when he called me a coxcomb and a witling, if I mentioned a Citizen or a merchant without respect! Ha! Ha! Ha! 595

CLEVELAND. And the time, sir, exists still—and will exist for ever, till I know two characters who deserve respect more than a merchant and a Citizen!

FRANK. There, again! now you'd think him all that was liberal! yet I've only to hint at my little Lizzy Watts— 600

CLEVELAND. Desist, if you please, sir, once and for all from naming her anymore!

MISS PERCIVAL. Bless me, how passionate!

FRANK. O, he has set his heart so completely against the poor little Girl, that I foresee, if I persevere, an inevitable breach, un- 605 less your charitable influence—

MISS PERCIVAL. My influence! my Command. Fie upon it Cleveland! how can you be so squeamish? For my part, I doat upon a little excentricity. Why should we be All born alike? Besides, think how amusing to see her and the Tavern keeper contrasted 610 with Lady Wil! If you don't place me where I may witness the first interview, Frank, I'll never forgive you. Won't it be delicious, Cleveland? Why, bless me, you look quite disordered? Why should you let it affect you so?

FRANK. Now do laugh him out of it, dear Miss Percival; for he's 615 in such a contradictory humour I scarcely dare approach him.

MISS PERCIVAL. Come, prithee, Cleveland, clear up. What signifies Frank's wife? Not but what Frank is a very good Frank, but still, why may he not please himself? And if he has a taste for a Nymph who knows something of the humours of a Tavern—why may he not be indulged? 620

CLEVELAND. Intolerable!— My head turns round! madam—

MISS PERCIVAL. Nay, nay, what is it to you? If she is vulgar, Frank is good natured. He'll let you laugh, I'm sure—and let me laugh too; for I think nothing half so comical. If she is pettish, also, I shall never want Sel Volatile again; and if she is pert— 625

CLEVELAND. She—she is an Angel!

MISS PERCIVAL. What? Hay? Did your Brother speak, Frank?

FRANK. Upon my honour, my Brother has been so extraordinary, that I won't take upon me to say whether he spoke or not; for why, all of a sudden, he should dub her an angel,—after so haughtily despising her— 630

CLEVELAND. Despising her? I despise?—no I adore her.

MISS PERCIVAL. How?

FRANK. Give me leave, in my turn, sir, to ask, now, whom it is you speak of? 635

CLEVELAND. Of one whom I regard as my Wife!—one whom I love to distraction!—one—

MISS PERCIVAL. Oh! (*screams*)

CLEVELAND. Pardon! Pardon!— I know not what I say. 640

FRANK. No more you have, all this morning. I'll bear witness for you to that.

CLEVELAND. I am in the deepest confusion—but I have been tortured out of all propriety. I dare not, madam, now address you; I am choaked by my own abruptness. But my feelings have been worked so cruelly, that every barrier of prudence and every consideration of delicacy, are irresistibly broken down by invincible, imperious Truth. Pardon—pardon me! 645

Exit.

MISS PERCIVAL, FRANK.

MISS PERCIVAL. Frank!

FRANK. Miss Percival! 650

MISS PERCIVAL. What can he mean?

IV.626 **Sel Volatile** i.e., sal volatile, "an aromatic solution of [ammonium carbonate] used as a restorative in fainting spells" (*OED*). General d'Arblay may have Gallicized the spelling.

FRANK. Nay, I don't know; but I begin to have a plaguy suspicion I can guess.

MISS PERCIVAL. An Angel? Love her to distraction—If I could believe him in earnest— 655

FRANK. Twenty things now recur, to make me wonder at my own supineness in not conjecturing there was some connexion immediately.

MISS PERCIVAL. Connexion?

FRANK. They both arrive from the East Indies, and at the same time—but what a Devil of a thing to be thus choused out of eighty thousand pounds, at the very moment I thought the dear little rouleaus were folding up for me! 660

MISS PERCIVAL. You treat this affair with tolerable levity, Mr Frank; but, give me leave to tell you should an insult of this nature be really intended for me, you, in common with the rest of your family, may learn to consider it more seriously. (*going*) 665

FRANK. Don't be offended with us All, dear madam. Distinguish the innocent from the guilty. Who, in this discovery and disappointment is so great a sufferer as myself? 670

MISS PERCIVAL. A sufferer? Upon my word! Do you suppose me, then, a Sufferer? Give me leave to ask what it is you may imagine to be my loss?

FRANK. How charming a spirit! The very type and counterpart of my own! Our situations, and our humours— 675

MISS PERCIVAL. Sir!

FRANK. Nay there's no denying the agreeable sympathy of our positions.

MISS PERCIVAL. What impertinence!— But if you, sir—or any part of your family—imagine that the whole of your race is not detestable to me—you—they—and all of you will soon learn of your errour— For though I feel nothing in this business but insensibility—indifference—apathy—I yet know what is due to myself—and never will rest till I am vindicated. 680

FRANK. My own exact sensation upon the subject. 685

MISS PERCIVAL. This is no season, sir, for frivolous raillery. You will please to acquaint your Sister—no! tell her nothing—but inform your Brother—no I will not deign him any message. He shall feel, unanticipated, my resentment, and my hate! (*going*)

IV.663 **rouleaus** "A number of gold coins made up into a cylindrical packet" (*OED*).

FRANK. Stop, dear madam! You give the exact process of what passes in my own mind. I find an absolute necessity of revenge. Not, indeed, of blood and slaughter; I won't meddle with bowls and daggers,—but I can never cast this business into the dulcest shades of oblivion, till I make them both feel at least as foolish as myself. 690 695

MISS PERCIVAL. Do you think you can do that? (*eagerly*)

FRANK. I'll do my best, and certainly not sleep till I succeed. The drowsy poppy would serve but to make me dance a jig, till I have turned upon themselves the tables of mockery and mortification.

MISS PERCIVAL (*returning and clasping her hands*). O Frank! Dear, delightful Frank, if you will but do that, and make Me the instrument of their humiliation and confusion, I shall adore you! 700

FRANK. Shall you faith! Why then so shall I you! which I have often longed to do before, but never dared.— Ah, my fair Miss Percival! how much sweeter a retaliation might we find for these offenders, than merely giving them back our torment! 705

MISS PERCIVAL. Pho, pho! now don't begin to be odious, the very first moment I find you endurable.

FRANK. Nay, as to that, my dear madam, I assure you that I have so little natural propensity to connubial bliss—that I only dropt the hint to prove to you my personal respect. 710

MISS PERCIVAL. If you were less ridiculous, your insolence would be insupportable. But tell me this moment what we can do?

FRANK. I hesitate whether to sketch them for a Caricature, or to portray them in a Farce. 715

MISS PERCIVAL. You are the most divine creature under the Sun! Follow me instantly to Piccadilly. I shall be senseless before morning if I attempt to pass the night with such an indignity unrequited. 720

FRANK. I am proud to attend you; and pray don't forget that, should you, at last, prefer to confound the traitor by a supplanter—my scruples against the state shall not, in so particular a case, stand in the way.

IV.693 **dulcest** This may be a mistake for dulcet, or, more probably, a form of dulse, meaning "dull, heavy" (*EDD*). The connotation seems to be "deepest."
IV.698 **drowsy poppy** See *Othello*, III.iii.330–32: "Not poppy nor mandragora, / Nor all the drowsy syrups of the world, / Shall ever med'cine thee to that sweet sleep."

MISS PERCIVAL. I could kill you for your effrontery,—if you were not, just now, so useful to me. 725

FRANK. 'Tis my standing maxim to sacrifice myself to my friends. (*bowing*)

MISS PERCIVAL. No nonsense! no nonsense!

Running off.

FRANK. Does she fly, now, to escape—or to be pursued? Modesty! thou art but a maidenly virtue—don't stand in the way of a young man's preferment!— I'll e'en go ask her! 730

End of Act IV

ACT V

An elegantly fitted-up apartment at MISS PERCIVAL'S, *splendidly illuminated.*

LORD JOHN DERVIS (*within*). If Frank Cleveland's here, I want to speak with him.

SERVANT. Please to walk upstairs, my Lord, and I'll see.

Enter LORD JOHN *and* SERVANT.

LORD JOHN. O the plague! What do you bring me hither for? I only want to speak with Frank Cleveland. 5

SERVANT. He was in this room just now, my Lord.

LORD JOHN. Ask if he's gone. But harkee! Don't say anything to Miss Percival of my being here. I would not disturb her. (*Exit* SERVANT) The D--l a word could I find to say to her. I hate talking. (*whistles*) 10

Re-enter SERVANT.

SERVANT. Mr Cleveland has been gone some time, my Lord.

LORD JOHN. The Deuce he has? Well, if he should happen to call again before I catch him, tell him I want to speak to him consumedly. Something of moment. Where the D--l shall I go now?

Exit.

Enter MISS PERCIVAL.

MISS PERCIVAL. Who's that? 15
SERVANT. Lord John Dervis, ma'am.
MISS PERCIVAL. What did you let him in for?
SERVANT. Ma'am, he—
MISS PERCIVAL. Don't answer! I can't bear to be answered. Go!— Stop!— If Frank Cleveland calls again, I'll see him. Nobody else. Yes,—stay! I expect the Tylney tribe. You must let them in. Nobody else. Go!— No, stop! If any queer-looking bodies come, you must not send 'em away. I don't know their names. Nobody else. Go, now—. Stay a minute! I have something I want to say. No; I've forgotten it. Go, can't you? 25

Exit SERVANT.

MISS PERCIVAL *alone.*

[MISS PERCIVAL.] What unspeakable pleasure it would give me to see that Wretch torn by wild beasts! And yet, were it not for the disgrace, the horrible disgrace, I should rejoice to have got rid of him, for he is grown so insipid, he made my head ache by his stupidity. But then—not to wait to be rejected!— A male creature,—destined for nothing but to die at one's feet.— 30

Enter FRANK CLEVELAND.

MISS PERCIVAL. Well, Frank, what ages you have been gone! Where have you been slumbering all this time? What have you done? Will they come? Have you had any success? If not, run out of my house directly. 35
FRANK. Can you form a wish in vain? They will all wait upon you.
MISS PERCIVAL. You enchant me! Dear Frank, you are the very best Friend I have upon Earth. I hate everybody else breathing. How did you manage? Whom did you see? Whither did you go first? 40
FRANK. To Bond Street; where instead of asking for the master or his dame, whom I had observed in my rencounter in the morning to be utterly powerless, I enquired at once for the Miss.
MISS PERCIVAL. What, that thing I saw at your Sister's?
FRANK. No; she is as little mistress as Papa or Mama. 'Tis the eldest hopes that takes the rule. 45

MISS PERCIVAL. But how in the world could you give the message?

FRANK. Nothing so easy. I told her, with a bow and a smile that went straight to her heart— 50

MISS PERCIVAL. Now don't be so conceited.

FRANK. That you begged the honour of her company to a small party in Piccadilly this evening.

MISS PERCIVAL. Does she not think me mad?

FRANK. She would come if she did, from excess of curiosity, but 55 she knows so little of the ways of this part of the Town, that, giving implicit credit to my report of your anxiety to make acquaintance with so agreeable a family, from the specimen you had just met with at Sir Marmaduke Tylney's, she accepted the invitation with the most vulgar joy: and I doubt not would have 60 been here ere now, had she not deemed it an happy opportunity to load her poor head with yet another tier of ornament: as if external weight were to make ballast for internal emptiness!

MISS PERCIVAL. But will the other come?

FRANK. They are all at her control, and dare no more disobey her 65 than a fag his monitor.

MISS PERCIVAL. And the Clevelands? And the Tylneys?

FRANK. I then returned to Albermarle Street, where I found my poor Sister in a terrible dilemma whether to wait upon you tonight or not. 70

MISS PERCIVAL. Bless me! could she suppose so unimportant an incident would influence my manner of passing the evening?

FRANK. I said so to her; I assured her you regarded it as an affair of no sort of consequence.

MISS PERCIVAL. You were perfectly right. (*fanning herself* 75 *violently*)

FRANK. I knew, I told her, your feelings by my own—and the little Gentoo was already out of my recollection.

MISS PERCIVAL. You are the very essence of impertinence! Go on however. 80

FRANK. She was in tribulation, also, about Sir Marmaduke and Lady Wil, who had gone out to dine a few miles from Town, just before this discovery was made; and in their utter ignorance of the state of things, had appointed to meet her and my Brother here this evening. Poor Jemima was distracting her brain for 85 some device to prevent their coming.

MISS PERCIVAL. But I hope she has taken no measure to that effect?

FRANK. No; I charged her to keep her own engagement, and to let them keep theirs; telling her, at the same time, that though the affair had been a little ackward at the moment, neither you nor I thought now anymore of our disappointment. 90

MISS PERCIVAL. Frank, I could kill you with pleasure! You are sure however, Lady Wil, and Sir Marmaduke will come uninformed of what has passed? 95

FRANK. Completely so.

MISS PERCIVAL. And—who else?

FRANK. My brother, from the moment he was awed out of your presence, has been employed in composing explanatory epistles to all the party. I found him in the act, and assured him he gave himself vastly too much consequence in addressing one of them to you, for that you had quite forgotten the morning's transaction, and expected, as a thing of course, the pleasure of his company, with the rest of his family, here this evening. 100

MISS PERCIVAL. Admirable! I forgive you everything now. Let me but be the first to name and present his new bridal relations, such as you describe them, to Lady Wilhelmina, and I acquit Fortune of spite! O, if I can but see him and them as mortified as myself—I shall become quite easy. 105

FRANK. Well, now let us talk of another scheme, and arrange how to surprise them in a new manner. 110

MISS PERCIVAL. With all my heart.

FRANK. To astonish, to strike them dumb.

MISS PERCIVAL. Tell me how.

FRANK. To make all their hairs 115

Like Quills upon the fretful Porcupine—

MISS PERCIVAL. No, how, I say?

FRANK. Let us pretend, nay, insist, that you never thought of my Brother at all.

MISS PERCIVAL. Pho! 120

FRANK. That the whole was a blunder of Sir Marmaduke's.

MISS PERCIVAL. O, if you can throw anything upon Sir Marmaduke—

V.115–16 **To make . . . Porcupine** *Hamlet*, I.v.20.

FRANK. Seconded by my dear Brother's own vanity and presumption. 125

MISS PERCIVAL. Ah, Frank! You are bent upon enchanting me! But how am I to do this?

FRANK. By publicly, and before them all,—giving your hand to his brother.

MISS PERCIVAL. You abominable wretch! how you disappoint and torment me! 130

FRANK. She calls me wretch!— I advance! (*aside*)

Enter a SERVANT.

SERVANT. Lord John Dervis desires to speak a word in great haste to Mr Cleveland.

MISS PERCIVAL. Send him away! Did I not charge you not to let any of those idle fools in? 135

SERVANT. He said it was about something of so much consequence—

FRANK. I'll run down, and dispatch him myself. Say I am coming.

Exit SERVANT.

MISS PERCIVAL. How can you suffer that Ideot to follow you? 140

FRANK. He's a good-natured fellow, I assure you. Empty and dull, to be sure, but a special good-natured fellow.

MISS PERCIVAL. Well, run and get rid of him.

FRANK. I go.— And yet,—might not his presence heighten the effect of the introductions? 145

MISS PERCIVAL. O, ay, true; bring him up. I shall have them all shewn into this room.

Exit FRANK CLEVELAND.

I won't receive the fool myself, however.

Exit.

Re-enter FRANK CLEVELAND, *with* LORD JOHN DERVIS.

LORD JOHN. O the D--l, don't bring me here. I hate company.

FRANK. We shall be quite alone. But what's the matter? Has anything happened? 150

LORD JOHN. I want to speak to you deucedly. What a plague I've had to trace you! Why did not you dine at Club?

FRANK. Particular business. But what's the distress, Lord John?

LORD JOHN. Why I'll tell you. I can't think where the D--l to go tonight. 155

FRANK. Why what's the matter with the Opera?

LORD JOHN. Sick as a dog of it.

FRANK. I'll cut you out some work to do for me, then. You may serve me essentially. 160

LORD JOHN. What, write another letter, I suppose? I'll be hanged if I do, though!

FRANK. No; that affair's at an end. It did not take.

LORD JOHN. I'm glad of it for giving me that bore of a letter to write. I have been yawning ever since. And what hast got into thy head now, Franciscus? 165

FRANK. A prize, my dear Lord John, of the first magnitude. The dantiest monied Girl of the Day.

LORD JOHN. What! Matrimony again? O the D--l! nothing better than that? 170

FRANK. Peculiar circumstances give me the temerity to attempt what, but an hour ago, I should have thought as much above my reach as the Sun. But hush!— Wait a moment.

Enter MISS PERCIVAL.

MISS PERCIVAL. They are come. What shall I do with them till the Tylneys arrive? 175

FRANK. Let them amuse themselves with gaping about the rooms.

MISS PERCIVAL. You don't suppose I shall undertake to entertain them?

FRANK. By no means. Let us all be at our ease. Whatever we do they will conclude to be the high ton, and consider as a favour. 180

MISS PERCIVAL. I shall not take the smallest notice of them till I can make them of some use. I hate trouble.

FRANK. My own motto! It is amazing what a congeniality of sentiment is perpetually breaking forth between us.

MISS PERCIVAL. No nonsense, I beg. I am in a dreadful ill humour. 185

FRANK. So am I. Our sympathy encreases every moment.

MISS PERCIVAL. I shall begin to detest you, Frank, if you go on so. (*throwing herself into a great chair*)

V.166 **Franciscus** The use of the Latin form suggests that perhaps Frank and Lord John's friendship began when they were schoolboys.

FRANK. There, then, our congeniality will end, for I feel myself beginning to adore you. (*throws himself into another, which he draws next to hers*) 190

LORD JOHN. I don't know what the D--l to do with myself. (*throwing himself full length upon a sofa*)

Enter MRS WATTS *and* MISS WATTS, *richly dressed.*

MRS WATTS. Dears, what a pretty house! Dears, if ever I see the like! Only look at them Pillows! But I wonder where's the lady that the gentleman said invited us, that she don't come to welcome us. 195

MISS WATTS. La, Ma', don't talk so loud. Don't you see there's Company? You always behave so vulgar!

MRS WATTS. Dears, so there is! And all sot down! I'm sure I never see 'em, or I should not have come in so rude. (*she makes three low courtsies*) 200

MISS WATTS. La, Ma', that stiff courtsie's quite old-fashioned now. Look at mine. I could make ten before you've done one.

MRS WATTS. Why, my dear, I must make 'em one a piece, you know. 205

MISS PERCIVAL (*to* FRANK). What curiosities! But I don't see the Dulcinea?

FRANK. Nor I. I begin to fear she is shaking off her leading strings, and won't come. 210

MRS WATTS. Well, my dear, I've done no harm, you find, for they take no notage of us.

MISS WATTS. There's the two gentlemen we see at the Hotel this morning; and this one is the one as come to invite us. I'm sure if he was to see me— 215

MRS WATTS. Dear, my dear, and that's the same lady as sounded away in Kinsington Gardens. I suppose she's come a visiting here.

MISS WATTS. La, so it is! La, how nice her hair's done! Mine's all of a clump to it. Stop! come this way, for here's Pa' with old Tibbs. 220

They retire to some distance.

V.208 **Dulcinea** See *Camilla*, p. 479, where Mrs. Arlbery admonishes Macdersey about his flirtations: "But is that perfectly delicate my dearest sir, to the several Dulcineas?"

Enter MR WATTS *and* MR TIBBS.
They both stand bowing low at the door.

MISS PERCIVAL. Heavens! here are my eternal Wigs.

FRANK. I forgot to tell you, that hearing Mr Watts was engaged with a friend, I left him, also, a message of invitation. But I see nothing of the little Gentoo. She has certainly refused to come.

MISS PERCIVAL. Undone, undone!— If I do not make her partake of my spleen, I shall never know peace again. Dear Frank, contrive but to bring her, and command me evermore. (*they whisper*) 225

MR WATTS. Now you'll believe another time, Cousin Tibbs! For all we've been making all them bows, they all sit as kimposed upon their cheres, as if we was no better than a mere dumb cretur come in. 230

MR TIBBS. Fegs, they shall bestir themselves a little, though, before I'll bob so for 'em agen. My neck's no looser than theirs, I can tell 'em. 235

MISS PERCIVAL (*to* FRANK). Do you think that will do?

FRANK. Perfectly. So mysterious an entreaty cannot fail to bring her.

MISS PERCIVAL. Why then write it for me. She don't know my hand. 240

FRANK. If you want a secretary, Lord John's your man. Lord John, Miss Percival begs you'll write a note for her.

LORD JOHN. O the D--l!

Gets up, and stalks out of the room.

MISS PERCIVAL. I'll do it myself. (*rises and passes by* MR WATTS, *while he is bowing to her*) 245

Exit.

MR WATTS. There agen, now, Cousin! The civiler one is, the ruder they be! You'd never believe what a push she gave me in going by.

MR TIBBS. Yes, but I can, though, for she's the same lady as squealed so at me in Kinsington Gardens. And the whole is all no how as one may say; inviting a body when there's never a mistress of the house, nor nobody to go to, nor to bring one a cheze, nor to make one a dish of tea.— 250

LORD JOHN *re-enters and retakes his seat on the sofa.*

LORD JOHN. I wish, Frank, you'd tell me what to do.

FRANK. I will. (*they whisper*) 255

MR TIBBS. Why now it's surprising how such a low person as that could get into company! whispering so that one can't hear him! I wonder if that's his manners!

MR WATTS. Why, lauk, Cousin, that's all the tip of the mode, I tell you. Nobody lets nobody hear what they say now; but just 260 their own peticklers. You may sit in a great room full of fine Gentry by the hour together, and think you're at a Quaker meeting.

MRS WATTS (*to* MISS WATTS, *apart*). Dears, my dear, only look down that t'other room! there's coming a purdigus fine lady, as 265 I dares to say is the mistress of the house.

MISS WATTS. La, so there is! And a gentleman just before her. Let's talk a little free and pelite with 'em.

Enter SIR MARMADUKE TYLNEY.

SIR MARMADUKE. She's as full of vagaries as a kitten! The house lighted up in this form, and no company! except these poor few 270 stragglers, who keep aloof from one another, as if fearful of some infection. She has a fine fortune, and she's a fine girl; but for all that—I'd rather my nephew had her than I.

Enter LADY WILHELMINA TYLNEY.

LADY WILHELMINA. Is it not somewhat strange, Sir Marmaduke, that a young person of the rank of Miss Percival should 275 not reflect, when she invites People of a certain class; that it would rather be civil if she were ready to receive them? Yet I have come through all the rooms, and—Bless me! what people are these?

SIR MARMADUKE. I can't imagine: unless those—(*pointing to* 280 MR WATTS *and* MR TIBBS) are two new men out of livery.

LADY WILHELMINA. Impossible she can have chosen two such grotesque figures. Besides, what do they stand there for? And look at those strange Women! how extraordinary! I can't turn my head round, but that odd body make me a courtsie! And 285 pray is not that Lord John Dervis, talking with Mr Francis Cleveland? And both sitting while we stand!

SIR MARMADUKE. Ay, ay; take no notice of them; they'll only come teizing again for money.

LORD JOHN (*to* FRANK). Who the plague are those old folks just come in? 290

FRANK. Only my Uncle and Lady Wil. Don't mind 'em. (*they continue whispering*)

MRS WATTS. Dears, my dear, I wish she'd receive us, like; for I'll be whipt if I can think of a word to say for a beginning. 295

MISS WATTS. Why, ask her if she's going to Rinelur. That's the genteel thing to talk about in genteel Company.

MRS WATTS. I will, my dear. Pray, good lady, may you be going to Rinelur tonight?

LADY WILHELMINA. Sir Marmaduke! 300

SIR MARMADUKE. Lady Wil?

LADY WILHELMINA. Did anybody—speak to Me?

MRS WATTS. Yes, it was me, my good lady, as spoke; it wasn't the gentleman.

LADY WILHELMINA. How singular! (*turning away*) 305

MRS WATTS. She seems mighty petickler, my dear, she's put me quite out.

MISS WATTS. La, Ma', that's because you've such a monstrous mean look. See how different she'll be to me. Pray, mem, if it i'n't impertinent, mem, do you go to the new series opperer 310 tomorrow?

LADY WILHELMINA. How incomprehensible! people of such a stamp to enquire into my engagements! what can Miss Percival mean by exposing me to such extraordinary familiarity?

SIR MARMADUKE. Some freak; a little Witch! Poor Cleveland! 315

V.296 **Rinelur** Ranelagh was "An elegant place of public entertainment near Chelsea, and frequented by the Nobility, Gentry, and citizens of the higher rank. . . . The price of admission is 2s.6d. for which tea, coffee, and other refreshments are furnished. The entertainments consist of vocal and instrumental music, by the first Professors in each way": *The London Guide, Describing the Public and Private Buildings of London, Westminster, & Southwark* (London: Fielding, 1782), 5. Matthew Bramble found little pleasure there: "What are the amusements at Ranelagh? One half of the company are following one another's tails . . . while the other half are drinking hot water, under the denomination of tea": Tobias Smollett, *The Expedition of Humphry Clinker*, ed. Lewis M. Knapp (London: Oxford University Press, 1966), 88–89.

He'll soon have his head turned. However that's no business of mine.

MISS WATTS (*to* MRS WATTS). They look as if they thought we were just a set of nobodys. Let's talk of our Coach.

MRS WATTS. So do, my dear. 320

MISS WATTS (*aloud*). I wonder if our Coach stops at the Door.

MRS WATTS. I hope never a Cart, nor nothing, will drive against it, for the paint's but just new put on, and it cost sich a deal!

MISS WATTS (*whispering*). La, Ma', you're always talking so saving! Can't you speak about our servants? I dare say, (*aloud*) 325 Robert's forgot to tell Thomas to order Richard to stop.

MRS WATTS. Yes, I dares to say Robert's forgot to tell Thomas to order Richard to stop.

MISS WATTS (*whispering*). I'm sure if that gentleman was to see me, he'd speak. I'll go nigher. 330

Approaches FRANK.

FRANK (*leaning on his elbow and not looking at her*). How do do, ma'am? Pray will you give me leave to enquire why Miss Percival has not the honour of seeing Miss Elizabeth tonight?

MISS WATTS. Sir, she's got the headache.

MRS WATTS. She's a little bit fertigued, sir, I take it, for she's 335 come from Indy this morning.

MR TIBBS. Good lauk, Tom, look at them fine gentlemen, as you call 'em! One's lying all along, as if he was sick a bed; and t'other's gaping at Cousin Peg, as if he was going to take a nap full in her face! 340

MR WATTS. Well, if they an't both the two gentlemen of my Darter Betsey's acquaintance at the Hitel! I'm sure, sir, (*to* LORD JOHN) I did not know you. Pray, sir, may I make free—

LORD JOHN. Umph?

MR WATTS. I say, sir, may I make free— 345

LORD JOHN (*affecting not to hear him*). Frank, will you step with me this way. I want to speak with you plaguely. La, la, la, la, lall—By your permission, sir!

Pushes by MR WATTS, *and exit singing.*

MR WATTS. There, now, Cousin Tibbs, you see how it is with these fine folks! They won't speak to one but just when they've 350 a mind! However this t'other'll be civil enough, I suppose; for he's one of the Muster Clevelands as had a mind to my Darter. Pray, sir,—(*to* FRANK)

FRANK. Sir, your very most obedient! Fal de ral.

Rises abruptly, and humming an air, without looking at him.

MR WATTS. They all treat me alike, you see! Ah Cousin Tibbs! Never begin to set up for a gentleman in the middle of life! I never speak to none of them great folks, of my own act, but what they sham they don't hear me! 355

MR TIBBS. Well, if it don't make my blood boil! What right have they to be deaf more than another man? Fegs, if they serve me so, I'll get me a speaking trumpet, that I war'n't me shall bring 'em back to their hearing! 360

MRS WATTS (*to* MISS WATTS, *after vainly walking up and down to attract the notice of* LADY WILHELMINA). This lady's so purdigious shy, I can't make no acquaintance with her. I'll speak to the young gentleman, I think. Pray sir, (*to* FRANK) if it isn't troublesome— 365

FRANK. My dear ma'am—can I have the honour to be of the least service to you?

Exit.

MR TIBBS. Good lauk! I never see the like! Speaking to a body, and then walking off without waiting for never an answer! 370

MISS WATTS. La, Ma', nobody'll be pelite to you, if you're so over and above civil. They find you out for a low person directly. See how I do!— I think, mem, (*to* LADY WILHELMINA) it's rather a hot evening, mem? Can you be so obliging, mem, without undressing yourself— 375

LADY WILHELMINA. Undressing myself!

MISS WATTS. As just to lend me a long pin, mem, if you've one to spare; for my Feathers feel so loose—

Enter MISS PERCIVAL.

MISS PERCIVAL. Frank—O, he's gone!— Lady Wilhelmina! I am proud to see you. I did not know your La'ship was come. How are you Sir Marmaduke? 380

MRS WATTS (*creeping forward to examine her dress*). Dear! her things are of no great value!

MISS PERCIVAL. I make no apology, Lady Wilhelmina, for having left you alone with so agreeable a party. How happy you must have been! 385

LADY WILHELMINA. Madam?

SIR MARMADUKE. She's certainly crazy! (*aside*)

MRS WATTS. I'm sure, ma'am, that's very genteel of you, what you're so kind to say of our being so agreeable.— Where's your courtsie my dear? (*courtsying low*) 390

MISS WATTS. La, Ma', don't you see?

MR WATTS (*to* MR TIBBS). This is the first of all the gentry as has ever said such a word as my being agreeable. I'm sure, ma'am, (*bowing*)— 395

MISS PERCIVAL. What pretty people! But don't I interrupt you, Lady Wilhelmina? Do be sincere now; don't I break in upon your little family chat?

LADY WILHELMINA. Miss Percival! 400

MISS PERCIVAL. I see I derange you; and it really shocks me. I must positively run away, that you may enjoy one other completely—Nay, nay, I won't be denied giving you this happiness. *Exit running.*

Manent LADY WILHELMINA, SIR MARMADUKE, MR, MRS *and* MISS WATTS, *and* MR TIBBS.

LADY WILHELMINA. This exceeds whatever I have yet met with for incredibility! An Earl's daughter—Lady Wilhelmina Tylney, classed with persons of such a description! 405

SIR MARMADUKE. I have no doubt but she will be in Bedlam within a month.— I wish the deeds had been signed for my mortgage. (*aside*)

MRS WATTS. That young lady's very much the lady of qualitie, indeed; only I don't think her gown come to half as much as mine. (*aside*) 410

LADY WILHELMINA. People of such a sort to be suffered to stay in the same room with one! (*staring at them*)

MR TIBBS. She looks fit to pysin us! How I do hate fine folks! (*aside*) 415

LADY WILHELMINA. How I detest low people! (*aside*)

MR TIBBS. They never know what they'd be at for pride and airs. (*aside*)

LADY WILHELMINA. The very sight of a mean person distresses me! (*aside*)

MR TIBBS. Harkee, Tom! If this is the best manners your fine 420

V.407 **Bedlam** St. Mary of Bethlehem Hospital for the mentally ill.

folks has got to shew us, they may keep them for one another. They won't do for me.

Exit.

Enter CLEVELAND.

LADY WILHELMINA. O my good Cleveland, how I revive in seeing you! Step this way, and let me speak with you. (*draws him aside*) Look, I beseech you, at those persons! 425

CLEVELAND. What persons, madam?— Heavens!— Mr Watts! —how could he get in here? (*aside*)

SIR MARMADUKE. Let me speak to you first, Nephew.

LADY WILHELMINA. Sir Marmaduke, I am quite uneasy for a consultation with him. 430

SIR MARMADUKE. I don't meddle with your uneasiness, Lady Wil; but I have something I want to say to him myself; and I never defer my own business. Come this way, Nephew.

Exit.

Manent LADY WILHELMINA, CLEVELAND, MR, MRS *and* MISS WATTS.

MISS WATTS. La, what a smart beau!

CLEVELAND. The females too! how amazing! What can they possibly do in this house? (*aside*) 435

Enter MISS PERCIVAL.

MISS PERCIVAL. Mr Cleveland! how kind is this call!

CLEVELAND. Kind, madam?

MISS PERCIVAL. Unless, indeed, you knew the party you were to meet. O you wicked Creature! I half suspect here were your incitements. (*pointing to the* WATTSES) 440

CLEVELAND. Upon my honour, madam,—I—I—

MRS WATTS. I wonder what her hid-dress cost! Mine's as good agen. (*aside*)

MISS PERCIVAL. Tell me the truth, now; had not some report reached you that this company would be here? 445

CLEVELAND. Company, madam?

MISS PERCIVAL. O bless me! perhaps you don't know them then? What a mistake I have been guilty of! however, I must positively make you acquainted with one another. Give me leave, Mr—Mr—how shockingly stupid I am! I can't for my life recollect this gentleman's name! 450

MR WATTS. Thomas Watts, ma'am. That's my name.

MISS PERCIVAL. Mr Thomas Watts!— Mr Cleveland, let me have the honour of presenting you to each other. 455

CLEVELAND (*bowing, and turning aside*). Confusion! What demon has been at work to bring them hither! (*aside*)

MISS PERCIVAL. Permit me, now, to have the honour of introducing you to the ladies—Mrs—Mrs—I've lost that name again!

CLEVELAND. What impertinent affectation! (*aside*) 460

MISS PERCIVAL. O! Watts—ay, Watts. Mrs Watts, will you allow me the pleasure of presenting Mr Cleveland to you?

MRS WATTS. I ha'n't no peticler objection, as I know of, mem, if the gentleman's none. (*making sundry formal courtsies*)

CLEVELAND (*after bowing respectfully*). I never was so confounded in my life! (*aside*) 465

LADY WILHELMINA. My good Cleveland, approach this way. Do you understand anything of all this? Can you unravel it? Inviting Me to such unheard of persons?

CLEVELAND. Indeed I—I—I— 470

LADY WILHELMINA. Persons one would rather be buried alive than ever speak to?

CLEVELAND. Ma'am I—I—really—

LADY WILHELMINA. I don't wonder at your distress; but let me recommend it to you, to use your influence with Miss Percival to put a period to such fancies. 475

CLEVELAND. My influence, Madam? Has not Miss Percival informed you—

LADY WILHELMINA. Who can they possibly be? Where can she have picked them up? 480

MISS WATTS. La, I thought we was going to be introduced all round! I don't know what I'm to be left out for! (*aside*)

MRS WATTS. I dare say my mignornet lace would buy all she's got on! (*aside, after closely examining all* MISS PERCIVAL'S *dress*)

MISS PERCIVAL. Come, Mrs—Mrs—Mrs Watts, come and sit upon this sofa with Lady Wilhelmina. I'm sure you must have a thousand things to say to one another. 485

MRS WATTS. Lady?— O laws! Who'd have thought of that! I've

V.483 **mignornet lace** A mispronunciation of Mignonette, a fine netted lace.

been speaking to a Lady!— I'm sure ma'am, I never guessed at the lady's being a Lady! (*courtsying again lower and lower*) 490

MISS PERCIVAL. Come Lady Wilhelmina,—

LADY WILHELMINA. Is it possible, Miss Percival, you can suppose I shall trouble this—gentlewoman to sit by Me? A—gentlewoman I have so little probability of troubling again? And whom, certainly, I never had the—accident of meeting before? 495

MISS PERCIVAL. Never meeting before? My stars, Lady Wilhelmina! you seem to know nothing of your nearest connexions.

LADY WILHELMINA. Connexions, Miss Percival?

MISS PERCIVAL. Nay, if the alliance is a secret . . .

LADY WILHELMINA. The alliance? What pleasantry is this? Can 500 you help me, Mr Cleveland, to comprehend what Miss Percival would say?

CLEVELAND. Me, madam? I—I—I—O that I were again in Calcutta! (*aside*)

MISS PERCIVAL. I must speak to Mr Cleveland myself. Pray— 505

CLEVELAND. I entreat to—to—to take my leave. A particular engagement.

MISS PERCIVAL. No; come hither, man, and don't mar your own good fortune. I have sent for you—Listen, I say!—merely to give you a meeting with the fair lady of your choice. (*in a low* 510 *voice*)

CLEVELAND. Madam?

MISS PERCIVAL. And not a meeting alone, but to contrive you a tête-à-tête. Now say whether I am good?

CLEVELAND. I—I—certainly do not doubt that—but— 515

MISS PERCIVAL. What is it you doubt, then? Am I not explicit? I have invited you solely to have the pleasure myself of procuring you a tête-à-tête with Miss Watts.

CLEVELAND. I am so astonished—so—

MISS PERCIVAL. She is coming at last! (*aside*) You won't see her, 520 then, perhaps?

CLEVELAND. Not see her?

Enter ELIZA.

MISS PERCIVAL. And won't own yourself obliged to me? (*holding out her hand*)

CLEVELAND (*kissing it*). Ah, madam! exquisitely! 525

ELIZA. Heavens! for this am I forced hither? (*aside*)

CLEVELAND (*not seeing her*). Such unexpected goodness—I want words—

ELIZA. Can I bear this? Perfidious, faithless Cleveland! (*aside*)

MISS PERCIVAL. Well, go quietly into that next room, and eat custards, till I have hussled away all others, but her whom you would keep. No thanks, man. (*pushes him out*) Miss Elizabeth! This is extremely good indeed. 530

ELIZA. I knew not how, madam, to resist the urgency of your note—though why I am summoned— 535

MISS PERCIVAL. You don't seem well?

ELIZA. My head—a little—aches—

LADY WILHELMINA. Is not this the young lady I had the pleasure to see this morning in Albermarle Street? (ELIZA *courtsies*) Allow me to enquire after your health; and pray, ma'am, (*in a low voice*)—suffer me to ask if you can conjecture who these singular persons are? 540

ELIZA. Madam!

LADY WILHELMINA. How can Miss Percival have gotten them together? I am sure you never can have seen such before. An elegant young woman like you must be offended— 545

ELIZA. Pardon me, madam—I am not quite well—I must beg a glass of water—O Cleveland! are you a party in this insult to all my feelings? (*aside*)

MISS WATTS. La, what can have brought Eliziana? 550

MRS WATTS. Why Betsey, my dear, why how come you to come?

MISS PERCIVAL (*to* ELIZA). In that Boudoir you can ring and order what you please.

Exit ELIZA, *eagerly followed by* MRS *and* MISS WATTS.

MR WATTS. I should like to know what has brought Bet, too. Ladies, your servant. 555

Exit.

Manent LADY WILHELMINA *and* MISS PERCIVAL.

MISS PERCIVAL. Delightful creatures! Do now, let me wish you joy, Lady Wilhelmina. You must like them so amazingly. How I hope I shall see you all together some evening at Ranelagh!

LADY WILHELMINA. I trust I shall never so far forget what is

V.531 **hussled** A form of "hustled," i.e., pushed.

due to my rank in life, Miss Percival, as to lose my temper; but you will have the goodness to dispense with my remaining any longer to be affronted in this extraordinary manner with persons of such a Stamp. 560

Exit.

MISS PERCIVAL *alone.*

[MISS PERCIVAL.] How deliciously she is worked! It is balm to me to behold her. And now, my dear Sir Marmaduke, a few tender words for you. Here he is. Sir Marmaduke! 565

Enter SIR MARMADUKE TYLNEY.

SIR MARMADUKE. You make me happy, my dear Miss Percival, by your call. You have been so surrounded by—new friends, I hardly dared approach you.

MISS PERCIVAL. My dear Sir Marmaduke, our love of each other's society is, I am sure, reciprocal; and so perfectly am I convinced of your kindness for me— 570

SIR MARMADUKE. You do me but justice.

MISS PERCIVAL. So satisfied of the disinterested view with which you promote my union with your Nephew— 575

SIR MARMADUKE. My dear young lady, your confidence makes me happy.

MISS PERCIVAL. Such, I say is my reliance, that not a thought entered your head but of our mutual felicity—

SIR MARMADUKE. I thank you! 580

MISS PERCIVAL. That I make not the smallest scruple to tell you —I am now wholly resolved against that mortgage engagement.

SIR MARMADUKE. What?— How?—

MISS PERCIVAL. I withdraw my consent to it. That's all.

SIR MARMADUKE. Withdraw your consent to it? And pray —Why? 585

MISS PERCIVAL. I've changed my mind.

SIR MARMADUKE. Changed your mind? But why? Pray why?

MISS PERCIVAL. I really can't tell. However, it will make no change, I know, in you. I feel equally sure of your desire to make us happy—and—of your Lincolnshire Estate. 590

Exit.

SIR MARMADUKE *alone.*

[SIR MARMADUKE.] A little vixen! Not pay off my mortgage? A little D--l! Give them my Lincolnshire Estate, indeed? Not a sixpence of it!

Re-enter MISS PERCIVAL, *with* CLEVELAND.

MISS PERCIVAL. I have dispersed all troublesome spectators now, but Sir Marmaduke; and you may dispatch him, while I prepare the young lady for the tête-à-tête I have promised you. 595

Exit by another door.

CLEVELAND. What thanks can I offer you?

SIR MARMADUKE *and* CLEVELAND.

CLEVELAND. Sir Marmaduke, may I seize this little moment to open to you my situation? 600

SIR MARMADUKE. I enter into nothing that don't concern me, Nephew: but if 'tis about the Lincolnshire Estate—I must frankly tell you—I can't part with it.

CLEVELAND. Sir!

SIR MARMADUKE. I am very sorry, my dear Cleveland; but a man's own affairs must first be consulted; and the times are so bad—one can but barely live, however careful. You are a young man, though, and if the loss of the Lincolnshire Estate throws any obstacles in your way—What hinders a little voyage back to India to mend your fortune? 605 610

CLEVELAND. A little voyage, sir, to the East Indies?

SIR MARMADUKE. Why what's half a dozen years, or so, in the life of a young man? I hate difficulties. To demur about paying off my mortgage, indeed, is a real abomination, for it puts me to a great inconvenience; but a voyage more or less to the East Indies—What is it, at your time of life? I hate a fuss about common casualties. I wonder if my rascal is come yet. If he makes me wait a single minute, I'll give him warning. I can't bear waiting. No fuss, I tell you, Nephew! no difficulties about trifles. 615

Exit.

CLEVELAND.

[CLEVELAND.] Alas! how unhappy a turn for affairs to take, at the moment Eliza seems so hurt or so offended! Can I sue back her favour, implore her returning tenderness and confidence, when a bankrupt thus abruptly in all but love? No! her decision must be noble, unsolicited, and prompt, or the cruel alternative of Sir Marmaduke must indeed be put in practice. 620 625

Enter MISS PERCIVAL, *leading in* MISS WATTS, *and whispering.*

MISS WATTS. La, with me?— A gentleman so in love?

MISS PERCIVAL. Yes, and I have promised him an opportunity of declaring his passion.

MISS WATTS. La! and I never see him but once at a distance this morning. It must be love at first sight, I think. 630

MISS PERCIVAL (*advancing*). Now then, sir, I hope to deserve the gratitude you profess, and to repay, in part, what so amply I owe! behold—

CLEVELAND. Who, madam?

MISS PERCIVAL. Miss Watts, sir! 635

CLEVELAND. Where, madam?

MISS PERCIVAL. Here!— And I leave you to the enjoyment I have promised of an uninterrupted tête-à-tête.

Exit.

CLEVELAND, MISS WATTS.

MISS WATTS. La, how droll! He's fell in love with me without knowing my name! (*aside*) 640

CLEVELAND. What execrable vengeance is this! (*aside*)

MISS WATTS. He looks quite the gentleman; but it's odd he don't begin. (*aside*)

CLEVELAND. What am I to do now? How cruel is an angry woman! (*aside*) 645

MISS WATTS. I dare say he'll say something pretty, when he's got it ready. (*aside*)

CLEVELAND. Madam, I—my confusion—

MISS WATTS. La! he's quite the lover. (*aside*)

CLEVELAND. This mistake— 650

MISS WATTS. Mistake, sir?

CLEVELAND. It is I believe—a near relation, a Sister, I imagine—of yours, that Miss Percival—

MISS WATTS. A sister? La! What, Eliziana?

CLEVELAND. Yes, madam, Miss Elizabeth. If I might be allowed —a short conference with her—how inexpressibly, should I be obliged! 655

MISS WATTS. O la, sir, pray let it be as long as you please! Don't make it short for me, I beg! I'm sure I don't care. I'll call her myself to you. Here, Sister Eliziana! I'm glad it wa'n't me, I'm sure, for I hate Lovers. Sister, I say! 660

Exit.

CLEVELAND.

[CLEVELAND.] How does my heart, how does every pulse acknowledge her power, and tremble at the use she may make of it! She comes!

Enter ELIZA.

This, at least, is condescending. 665

ELIZA. I would not refuse this once, sir, to converse a few moments with one whom—

CLEVELAND. This once, madam?

ELIZA. What more than once can I accord, or can you desire, in this altered state of things? Altered irreversibly! 670

CLEVELAND. Enough! Altered, indeed! Pardon the temerity of this last intrusion. I should not have presumed to urge it, had I not imagined it possible some elucidation—but I was mistaken. You have gathered, I conclude, if not distinctly heard, the history of my recall, and its consequences? 675

ELIZA. Yes, sir; I have gathered all I now ever wish to know.

CLEVELAND. I have only, then, madam, to supplicate you would believe that I have not entreated for this short interview—

ELIZA. It cannot be too brief!

CLEVELAND. With any formed design to harass you by solicitations— 680

ELIZA. Spare the assurance, sir! they have not been numbered in my expectations.

CLEVELAND. Ah, rather spare, Eliza, this cold cruelty! let me not, however, stray into reproach, for to that I would owe no obligation. Take therefore back all engagement! I must not offend you by acknowledgements for what is past—O that as readily I could command forgetfulness as silence! Adieu, Eliza!—My farewell, since you ordain so, must be brief—but who can tell my wounded soul when its effects may know a term? (*going*) 685 690

Enter JEMIMA.

JEMIMA. My Brother!

CLEVELAND. Stay me not!

Exit.

ELIZA, JEMIMA.

JEMIMA. What can this mean?

ELIZA. I know not! I am all astonishment. Is it for him to shew resentment? Is it his to speak of a wounded soul? 695

JEMIMA. Has he not explained to you his situation?

ELIZA. Has it not explained itself? Or has any misapprehension involved my judgement in errour? Ah, Miss Cleveland! Dear and blessed, should I call the conviction of misapprehension which should clear your brother to my view noble, firm, and honourable as I thought him this morning! 700

JEMIMA. Let us seek a quiet room—for here we shall be broken in upon every moment and permit me, dear madam, to state to you a few simple facts. 705

ELIZA. Will they bring home mistake to me—and to Cleveland honour?

JEMIMA. Will you pardon me if I say yes?

ELIZA. Pardon? I shall contest with him to which you are most a sister. 710

Exeunt.

Enter MISS WATTS.

[MISS WATTS.] I wonder what Sister Eliziana and her lover's saying together so long. La! they're gone!

Enter MR TIBBS, *with cakes in each hand.*

MR TIBBS. Well I can't but say I'm rather in better humour since I've made free with all them tidbits. I've put myself at the tip of the mode for that; and I can't but say I like it well enough. I suppose I've eat me clear a pastry cook's shop. What? Cousin Peg! why I suppose, now nobody's by, a body may ask you how you do? 715

MISS WATTS (*after looking round*). How do do, Cozen Joel?

MR TIBBS. What think you of this purdigious fine quality breeding? Walking off one by one, without never a word, except turning up their noses? If this here behaviour's what they call the thing, it's none so difficult. I warrant I could do it as well as they; it's little more than turning upon one's heel when a body speaks to one; or squealing a tune at 'em; or saying over again their own last word. 720 725

MISS WATTS. You? O, to be sure! You're very like to a person of qualitee!

MR TIBBS. Nay, I'll bet you sixpence I can do after the manner of that lord thing-um, and that t'other fine mister, as was here just now, so as you should not know one of us from t'other. 730

MISS WATTS. Don't vaunt you so, Cousin Joel. Here comes that grand lady.

MR TIBBS. Vaunt me? Have you a mind I should try?

MISS WATTS. You durst not! 735

MR TIBBS. Durst not! Fegs, you shall soon see that! What need I care?

Enter LADY WILHELMINA.

LADY WILHELMINA. How enormously unfortunate that the servants are not to be found! I know not which way to turn my eyes to avoid some disagreeable object. 740

MISS WATTS (*whispering*). Now do if you dare, I say!

MR TIBBS. Dare? Why, look, then! (*struts round to face* LADY WILHELMINA) How do do?

LADY WILHELMINA (*staring*). What?

MR TIBBS. I hope you are confounded well? 745

LADY WILHELMINA. Heavens!

MR TIBBS. O the Doose, and the Devel, and the plague and consumed! (*ludicrously imitating* LORD JOHN)

LADY WILHELMINA. What inscrutable effrontery! I'll look him into a statue. (*fixes her eyes upon him and frowns*) 750

MR TIBBS. How do, I say? (*nodding familiarly*)

LADY WILHELMINA. Dignity is lost upon such ignorance. 'Twill be better to awe him by authority—draw me that sofa this way, sir! (*imperiously*)

MR TIBBS. Sofa? Tol de rol. (*singing*) 755

LADY WILHELMINA. Astonishing! Did you not hear me, sir!

MR TIBBS. O the Doose!

LADY WILHELMINA. This is a class of person beyond any I have met with yet!

MR TIBBS. O the Divil! (*throws himself full length upon the sofa*) 760

MISS WATTS. He! He!

LADY WILHELMINA. What can that vulgar thing find to laugh at? But low people never know. However, they are beneath notice. I'll sit down myself, and force their retreat by silent contempt. (*turning round to seat herself*) What do I see? A person 765 of that description presuming to lie down upon a sofa? A sofa which I had thoughts of occupying myself!

Enter SIR MARMADUKE.

SIR MARMADUKE. The servants wet? Hang the servants! What signifies it to me if they never were dry again?

LADY WILHELMINA. O Sir Marmaduke! I have received an af- 770 front past all comparison! I am on the very point of fainting.

SIR MARMADUKE. I don't meddle with that, Lady Wilhelmina. I have always told you not to let every little inconvenience get the better of your reason—Would you believe Miss Percival has thought proper to order my servants to the public house, be- 775 cause forsooth, of the storm!

LADY WILHELMINA. The storm!— Is there a storm? O how shall I have the courage to get home?

SIR MARMADUKE. I am amazed, Lady Wil, you suffer such paltry accidents to discompose you. What matter a little bad 780 weather? It offends me to see importance given to such trifling events.

LADY WILHELMINA. Unfortunately, too, I had ordered on the new Hammercloth.

V.784 **Hammercloth** "Hammercloths are among the principal ornaments to a car-

SIR MARMADUKE. How? My new Hammercloth? Why what a diabolic thing is this! 785

LADY WILHELMINA. And John, I dare say, will get fresh cold, and must be sent back to the Country to be nursed again; for he is but half recovered from his ague.

SIR MARMADUKE. Hang his ague! Think of my new Hammercloth! I must sit down to breathe. Heigh!— Who's that fellow lying upon the sofa? Pray, sir,—may I ask—are you taken ill? 790

MR TIBBS. Ill, sir?

SIR MARMADUKE. Do you usually, sir, lie down upon Ladies' Sofas, with walking shoes on? 795

MR TIBBS. Shoes, sir?

MISS WATTS. He! He!

SIR MARMADUKE. Cleveland will have a blessed lot! But let him see to that! (*aside*)

Enter MRS WATTS.

MRS WATTS (*to* MISS WATTS). Dear, my dear, so you're here at last? Why I've been looking for you high and low. And my feet hurt me so—if I don't sit down, I'm afraid I shall tumble. Dears! What a sight is here! Joel Tibbs a-lying upon this fine couch! Out upon you, Joel! 800

MR TIBBS. Tol de rol. (*sings*) 805

MRS WATTS. Is that your manners? Singing without being asked?

MISS WATTS (*whispering*). La, Ma', what do you let people know you know him for?

MRS WATTS. Why, what right has he to take that fine couch to hisself? 810

SIR MARMADUKE. What a crew! (*aside*)

MRS WATTS. Why Joel, I say, an't you ashamed?

MR TIBBS. Hay?

MRS WATTS. Lolloping so before company!

MR TIBBS. What? 815

MRS WATTS. Why don't you offer the seat to the lady?

---

riage; they are a cloth covering to the coachman's seat, made to various patterns agreeable to the occupier's fancy": William Felton, *A Treatise on Carriages* (London: Author, 1796), 153. The costs, according to Felton, ranged from £4 10/- for plain cloths, to £18 12/0 for one of silk and lace (p. 158). In Richard Cumberland's *The West Indian* (London: Griffin, 1771, 33), Lady Rusport uses the leopard skin hammercloth when she visits the west end of town.

MR TIBBS. Umph?

MRS WATTS. Lack-a-day, why are you turned deaf all o' the sudden?

MR TIBBS. Deaf? O the Doose! 820

MRS WATTS. Yes, deaf; can't you answer? Why don't you get up, I say and make your bow?

MR TIBBS. My bow? O the Divil!

MRS WATTS. Dear, if I don't believe you're out of your head! What do you say it all over agen for? 825

MR TIBBS. Over agen? O confounded!

MRS WATTS. Yes; don't you know English, man?

MR TIBBS. English? O consumed!

MRS WATTS. Dears, if you a'n't enough to turn one's brain! One might as well talk to the post. 830

SIR MARMADUKE. Pray, madam, will you give me leave to ask—do you happen to know who that gentleman is?

MISS WATTS (*whispering*). Say no, Ma'!

MRS WATTS. Not in the least, sir. Some poor low cretur, I suppose.

MR TIBBS (*starting up*). Some poor low cretur? Fegs, that's pretty high! Why I'm afeard, Cousin Aylce, it's you as has lost your wits! 835

MISS WATTS. Come this way, Ma'!

Exit hastily.

MRS WATTS. Well, my dear, only don't go so purdigious fast.

Exit.

MR TIBBS. O fegs, but you shall hear me! 840

Exit.

SIR MARMADUKE, LADY WILHELMINA.

LADY WILHELMINA. Why do you not speak to Miss Percival yourself, Sir Marmaduke, upon this singular proceeding?

SIR MARMADUKE. Why what harm does it do to me?

Enter JEMIMA.

JEMIMA. My dear Uncle, my dear Lady Wilhelmina, I come to you with a narrative—and a proposition—upon which all my Brother's happiness depends. 845

SIR MARMADUKE. What, about my Lincolnshire Estate, I suppose? But I can't part with it now. I want it myself. And as to his happiness, he'll never be happy while he lives, if he lets himself be ruffled by every petty disappointment. He should command more fortitude. 850

JEMIMA. But, sir, if the mortgage—

SIR MARMADUKE. Don't mention it! 'Tis the cursedest provocation I ever met with. I lose all temper at it.

JEMIMA. But if a young lady should suddenly appear, still richer than Miss Percival, and still more attached to my Brother, who would instantly acquiesce in that condition— 855

SIR MARMADUKE. How—? What?— Is there anybody will pay off my mortgage?

JEMIMA. There is. A young lady the most amiable; by whose desire I have written the generous proposition to my Brother, whom I expect every instant; though to obviate his disputing it, she is occupied, at this moment, in previously arranging it with her Friends. 860

LADY WILHELMINA. But who is she? What is her Birth? 865

SIR MARMADUKE. O, hang her Birth! What is her fortune?

Enter CLEVELAND.

CLEVELAND. Jemima!— Is this possible?—my Uncle—Lady Wilhelmina—

SIR MARMADUKE. I don't understand a word of the matter. I have not seen one deed relative to what she is worth. 870

LADY WILHELMINA. I don't comprehend a syllable. I have heard nothing of her genealogy.

JEMIMA. She is here! come this way dear madam—and Sir Marmaduke—and let me unravel the history before you meet.

Exeunt, at one door, LADY WILHELMINA, SIR MARMADUKE, *and* JEMIMA: *at another,*

Enter ELIZA.

CLEVELAND. Generous Eliza! And can it be after a parting so abrupt, so desperate, that you deign thus sweetly to call me back to life—to love—to yourself? 875

ELIZA. Can you blame me for that parting?— No, Cleveland, no! when you think how cruel a combination of circumstances conspired to alarm and make me wretched— 880

CLEVELAND. Wretched? Dear, loved Eliza! You permit me then,

to hope the separation with which this eventful day has been teeming was not dreaded by me alone?

ELIZA. Ah no! why should I try to disguise, that from the moment I consented to give you my hand, you became the master of my happiness? 885

CLEVELAND. I have nothing left to wish! every hope is surpassed and my felicity is complete!

Enter JEMIMA, *followed by* SIR MARMADUKE.

JEMIMA. My dear Brother, Sir Marmaduke complies; and but that Lady Wilhelmina—you know her prejudices against the City—is just now cruelly disturbed— 890

SIR MARMADUKE. And what have I to do with that? Come hither, my dear Nephew; I'll tell thee what. Since the young lady's so generous—what a happy young rascal thou art!—since she's so generous, I say, why—sooner than lose sight of thee again,—I'll— 895

CLEVELAND. What, dear sir?

SIR MARMADUKE. Accept her proposition for paying off my mortgage—and make over to thee my Lincolnshire Estate.

CLEVELAND. This goodness, my dear Uncle, would exceed even my desire, but that I hope from it the entire consent of my Eliza's friends. 900

ELIZA. 'Tis that alone which, to me, can give value to your acquisitions. They are now in the next room, hasten, I beseech you, and acquaint them with Sir Marmaduke's munificence. 905

SIR MARMADUKE. I'll go myself, young lady.

ELIZA. How good! How kind!

SIR MARMADUKE. They'll be sure, else to make some blunder about my mortgage. (*aside*)

CLEVELAND. How exquisite is my happiness! 910

Exit ELIZA, *between* SIR MARMADUKE *and* CLEVELAND.

Enter MISS PERCIVAL, LORD JOHN, *and* FRANK CLEVELAND.

MISS PERCIVAL. What can be the meaning of this? They seem all reconciled and delighted!

LORD JOHN. O the D--l!

FRANK. Yes, yes; all is over, and they are completely happy.

MISS PERCIVAL. How abominable! 915
FRANK. We're in a shocking way here, Miss Percival!
LORD JOHN. Confoundedly shocking!
MISS PERCIVAL. How? What do you mean?
FRANK. All in the background!
LORD JOHN. Deucedly back! 920
MISS PERCIVAL. Who, I say, who?
FRANK. My dear madam—you and I!
MISS PERCIVAL. Impertinent fop!
FRANK. Adorable Creature!— Ah madam, raillery apart, what spirit would you preserve—and O what bliss might you bestow, 925 by nipping in the bud the triumph for which malice is preparing!
MISS PERCIVAL. What triumph?
FRANK. Lady Wilhelmina, finding no one here but Lord John whose rank permitted a vent to her indignation;—Lord John,—step this way. Miss Percival will be curious to hear Lady Wil's 930 rhapsody from yourself.
LORD JOHN. O the Deuce! She's consumedly tift. She dooms poor Cleveland to the bastinado. What, says she, shall a young lady of the rank of Miss Percival honour him with her passion— 935
MISS PERCIVAL. How? Passion?
LORD JOHN. And shall he reject her?—
MISS PERCIVAL. Reject her? Intolerable!— I shall die of this insolence! (*sitting down*)
FRANK (*kneeling*). Ah! by one generous stroke disperse its arrows. 940
MISS PERCIVAL. Go—Go!
LORD JOHN. And for a young Cit! says she.
MISS PERCIVAL. Monstrous!
LORD JOHN. Make the honourable Miss Percival wear the Willow!— 945
MISS PERCIVAL. The Willow?

Enter SIR MARMADUKE, CLEVELAND, ELIZA *and* JEMIMA.

FRANK (*rising*). How exulting they look!
MISS PERCIVAL. The Willow!— Nay, what do you rise just now for?

V.944–45 **wear the Willow!** "allusion to the willow as a symbol of mourning or of being lovelorn" (*OED*).

FRANK (*kneeling, and seizing her hand*). Enchanting Fair One! do you permit, then, my adoration? 950

MISS PERCIVAL. No, no!

FRANK *rises, but retains her hand.*

SIR MARMADUKE. What's this? Is Frank begging pardon for his Brother?

CLEVELAND. I trust, Miss Percival,— 955

MISS PERCIVAL. Dear sir, have you the goodness to be uneasy for me?

FRANK. Or the grace to conclude no Cleveland could be favoured by a fair lady, but yourself?

ALL. How? 960

FRANK. See your mistake, good Brother, learn to be modest—and resemble me! (*kissing* MISS PERCIVAL'S *hand*)

MISS PERCIVAL. Be quiet, you shocking Creature!

JEMIMA. Ah, dear Miss Percival, still, then, may I retain a Sister?

SIR MARMADUKE. Bravo, Frank!— They'll both be ruined in half a year: however, that's no business of mine. (*aside*) 965

Enter LADY WILHELMINA, MR, MRS *and* MISS WATTS, *and* MR TIBBS.
LADY WILHELMINA *brushes past* MR TIBBS *to enter first.*

LADY WILHELMINA. You will have the goodness, sir, to make way.

MR TIBBS. O yes, ma'am. I never force my company. I like nobody that don't like me. 970

LADY WILHELMINA. Were such vulgar wretches ever born before? Anything ever seen so disagreeable? (*half aside*)

MR TIBBS (*listening*). O yes, ma'am! as to that the World's full of disagreeable people. (*staring her full in her face*)

MR WATTS (*to* ELIZA). Well, Bet, my dear, as the Baronight will come down so handsome— 975

MRS WATTS. Dears, Tommy how rude you speak! You should say—

MISS WATTS. La, Ma', you let nobody speak but yourself! Sister Eliziana— 980

LADY WILHELMINA. Surely, Sir Marmaduke, you have not accommodated yourself with a person descended from such a tribe?

CLEVELAND. Ah Madam—look not at the root, but the flower!

LADY WILHELMINA. I can make no compromise, sir! She would ally us with the City!— O Sir Marmaduke! I shall die if you consent, I shall die! 985

SIR MARMADUKE. That's your affair Lady Wil.

LORD JOHN. Die? O the D--l!

ELIZA (*coming forward with* CLEVELAND). Ah! Cleveland! Were you less dear to me, how could I have courage to meet a prejudice so chillingly unkind, so indiscriminately unjust? 990

CLEVELAND. My Eliza, while your delicacy has had a charm which has distanced all the allurements of flattery, all the attractions of partiality, let me claim, from your true greatness of mind, a cool superiority to resentment against those who, forgetting that Merit is limited to no spot, and confined to no Class, affect to despise and degrade the natives of that noble Metropolis, which is the source of our Splendour, the seat of integrity, the foster Mother of Benevolence and Charity, and the Pride of the British Empire. 995 1000

FINIS

FANNY BURNEY AND THE THEATRE

An examination of Fanny Burney's comments on plays and acting does not indicate that she was either a scholarly or critical analyst of the stage. What it does show is that she had a lively and life-long interest in drama and an extensive knowledge of plays that was gleaned not only from reading and play going but also from an acquaintance with professional actors, managers, and playwrights. Her relationship with drama is that of an enthusiastic amateur who does not hesitate to speak with authority on whether a piece is pleasing or tedious but who does not have the professional reviewer's tendency to analyse what makes a play successful or defective.

Fanny Burney's contact with the theatre began early. Her father, Dr. Charles Burney, had been, as a young man, apprenticed to the musician and composer Dr. Arne, at whose house in London he began an acquaintance with Mrs. Cibber and David Garrick. Garrick remained a constant and beloved inmate of the Burney household, and his off-stage performances delighted the Burney children. Fanny describes a morning visit made by Garrick while Dr. Burney was having his hair dressed. Garrick, "himself in a most odious scratch wig," supervised the operation with "a look in the Abel Drugger style of *envy* and sadness," and then, "putting his stick to his mouth, and in a Raree-showman's voice," offered to hawk Dr. Burney's *History of Music*.[1] The Burneys' appreciation of Garrick extended to his professional performances. As Bayes in *The Rehearsal*, he kept them "in convulsions [with] excess of laughter . . . and we have laughed almost as much at the recollection as at the representation."[2] Fanny found him so "sublimely horrible" as Richard III that she felt herself "glow with indignation everytime I saw him."[3] He was "exquisitely great" as Lear,[4] and as Abel Drugger in Ben Jonson's *The Alchemist* he won her admiration for "the extreme meanness, the vulgarity, the low wit, the vacancy of countenance, the appearance of unlicked nature in all his motion."[5]

Garrick was not the Burneys' only contact with the stage; they knew the Colmans intimately enough for Fanny to mourn the death of Mrs. Colman;[6] and later, at Streatham, she made the acquaintance of Richard Brinsley Sheridan. Fanny's brother Charles collected a library of plays which the British Museum bought in 1818 for £13,500,[7] and Fanny herself mentions some 120 plays she has seen or read.[8]

One indication of Fanny Burney's confidence in her knowledge of plays is that she overcomes her habitual modesty and seldom hesitates to pass judgement on them. When writing about plays she has seen, Fanny Burney talks of the merits, not only of the play, but also of the production. Thus, she finds herself pleasantly surprised at a production of *Tamerlane*: "The play was much better performed than I expected"[9] and concludes that Miss Barsanti acts Charlotte Rusport in *The West Indian* "with great ease, sprightliness, and propriety."[10] Just as she found Cibber's alterations of *King Lear* objectionable,[11] she takes exception to a production of the Dryden-Davenant version of *The Tempest*:

> Shakespeare's *Tempest*, which for fancy, invention, and originality, is at the head of beautiful improbabilities, is rendered by the additions of Dryden a childish chaos of absurdity and obscenity; and the grossness and awkwardness of these poor unskillful actors rendered all that ought to have been obscure so shockingly glaring, that there was no attending to them without disgust.[12]

Fanny Burney could be tough-minded about excessive sentimentality in plays, as when she calls Dr. Delap's *Edwy and Edilda* "unreadably soft, and tender, and senseless,"[13] and when she dismisses the Reverend George Butt's *Timoleon* as "mighty common trash, and written in clumsy language, and many of the expressions afforded us much diversion by their mock grandeur, though not one affected, interested, or surprised us."[14] Sheridan's *Critic* she praises as being "full of wit, satire, and spirit," although she has not "sufficiently attended to the plays of these degenerate days to half enjoy or understand the censure or ridicule meant to be lavished on them."[15] Unfortunately, Fanny's enjoyment of wit often gives way to her disapproval of impropriety. She praises Mrs. Jordan's acting in *The Country Girl*, "but the play is so disagreeable in its whole plot and tendency, that all the merit of her performance was insufficient to ward off disgust."[16] She condemns Sir George Farquhar's *Sir Harry Wildair* as a work "wholly abounding in all that can do violence to innocence and morality,"[17] preferring George Colman the Elder's thoroughly sentimental *English Merchant*, which she calls "elegant and serious."[18] One significant aspect of Fanny Burney's evaluation of plays is that, even when she finds that a play is ill-written, she can enjoy it—often because of its weaknesses. She says of James Cobb's *Humourist* that it is "a thing without plot, character, sentiment, or invention; yet by means of ludicrous mistakes and absurd dialogues, so irresistibly comic, for one representation, that we all laughed till we were almost ashamed of ourselves."[19] She also finds Frederick Reynolds's *Cheap Living* "full of absurdities,—but at times irresistibly comic."[20] There is in this kind of judgement an indication that Fanny Burney is sometimes less concerned with the quality of a play than with the effects it produces on the playgoer.

If Fanny Burney's diaries do not often show an evaluative and critical response to plays, they do demonstrate an easy familiarity with contemporary drama. She knows Samuel Foote's *Devil on Two Sticks* well enough to write a punning ditty on it;[21] she smiles when someone asks her if she likes a 1773 production of Colman the Elder's *Occasional Prelude*, "little thinking that I have seen it near a dozen times";[22] and she frequently quotes from Colman and Garrick's popular comedy *Clandestine Marriage*.[23]

Not all Fanny Burney's experience with the theatre was at arm's length, as spectator and reader; as a young girl she took part in family entertainments and revelled in the staging of plays, though she was much given to stage fright. As early as 1770, when she was eighteen, she writes of participating in a play to be presented "by a company of comedians in Queen Square" (where the Burneys lived),[24] and in 1771 she gives a long account of a performance of Colley Cibber's *Careless Husband*. Miss Barsanti was to play Edging; Miss Allen (Fanny Burney's stepsister), Sir Charles; and Fanny herself, Lady Easy and Lady Graveairs. Although highly entertained with the spectacle of Miss Allen in men's clothes, in which "she appeared the most dapper, ill-shaped, ridiculous figure I ever saw," Fanny's nervousness caused her "to run off quite overset, and unable to speak."[25] She was persuaded to return but was in an agony of nervousness throughout her scene:

> I was almost breathless the whole scene; and O! how glad when it was over! Sir Charles' appearance raised outrageous mirth.

> Horse laughs were echoed from side to side, and nothing else could be heard. She required all her resolution to stand it. Hetty was almost in convulsions. Mr. Crisp hollowed. Mr. Featherstone absolutely *wept* with excessive laughing; and even Mademoiselle Rosat leaned her elbows on her lap, and could not support herself upright. What rendered her appearance more ridiculous was that, being wholly unused to acting, she forgot her audience, and acted as often with her back to them as her face; and her back was really quite too absurd, the [full] breadth of her height.[26]

In 1777 the Burneys were involved in yet another theatrical venture, and Fanny gives a detailed account of the costumes, setting, acting, and reception of the plays, which were Arthur Murphy's *The Way to Keep Him* and Henry Fielding's *Tom Thumb*. Once again, Fanny suffered from stage fright, which affected her acting so that "I am sure *without flattery*, I looked like a most egregious fool."[27] By the time she came to play Huncamunca in *Tom Thumb*, Fanny had regained her self-possession and "exerted myself, to the utmost of my power in tragic pomp and greatness,"[28] and "the whole concluded with great spirit, all the performers dying, and all the audience laughing."[29]

Like the diaries and letters, Fanny Burney's novels also provide ample evidence of her familiarity with drama. All four novels have numerous quotations from and allusions to the plays of Shakespeare; and *Evelina* makes references to such contemporary pieces as Hoadley's *Suspicious Husband*, Congreve's *Love for Love*, Colman the Elder's *The Deuce Is in Him*, Foote's *The Minor* and *The Commissary*, and Bickerstaffe's *Drummer*.[30] Although the later novels do not concern themselves with the London stage, Fanny Burney's continuing interest in plays manifests itself in a quotation from Mason's *Elfrida*[31] and in such scenes as the description, in *Camilla*, of a production of *Othello* by "actors . . . of the lowest strolling kind."[32]

Fanny Burney's familiarity with plays led her to use dramatic techniques in her diaries and novels. Most critics from Macaulay to Adelstein have praised her ability to provide a "transcript of life" and her method of advancing action and delineating character through dialogue,[33] and two Ph.D. dissertations have been written which take for their subject Fanny Burney's literary relationship to the theatre.[34] These critics make the point that Fanny Burney's strength as a novelist and diarist lies in her ability to write sprightly dialogue, an ability much enhanced by her keen ear and retentive memory.[35] A glance at the diaries and novels bears out the critics' judgement. The diaries provide vivid little scenes that are almost entirely dramatic. For instance, in describing a social evening at the Burneys' in November 1775, Fanny Burney reproduces the conversation with short commentaries that resemble stage directions:

> DR. BURNEY. Your Ladyship was doubtless at the Opera last night?
>
> LADY EDGECUMBE. Oh, yes! but I have not heard the Gabrielli! no; I will not allow that I *heard* her yet.
>
> DR. BURNEY. Your ladyship expected a more powerful voice?
>
> LADY EDGECUMBE. Why no; not that; the *shadow* tells me what the *substance* must be. She cannot have acquired this great name throughout Europe for *nothing*; but I repeat, I have not yet *heard* her; so I will not judge. She had certainly a bad cold.
>
> . . . .
>
> DR. KING (*pushing himself forward*). But, with submission, I humbly beg leave to ask your ladyship, if Gabrielli has yet done herself justice?
>
> LADY EDGECUMBE. Certainly not. But, Dr. Burney, *I* have heard Monticelli; *I* have heard Manzoli; and *I* have heard Mingotti; and I shall never hear them again! —*And*,—I have heard the Agujari; and I shall never hear *her* again![36]

After such a revealing dialogue, a reader already knows that Lady Edgecumbe is "clever, lively, quick" and that Dr. King "was, as usual, *fade*, imposing, and insipid."[37]

Dramatic techniques are also discernible in Fanny Burney's novels. Evelina, in her letters to her guardian, follows the pattern of Fanny Burney's own letters as she faithfully transcribes conversations and provides a minimal amount of commentary on them. The later novels depend less on dialogue than does *Evelina*, but they, too, contain lively episodes which could easily be scenes from a play. Even *Camilla*, "fashioned," as Joyce Hemlow says, "according to the analyses of human nature to be read in the semi-philosophical or educational works, the courtesy-books of the day,"[38] has sections in it which remind the reader of the author's earlier dramatic flair. The conversations of the lower-class Miss Mittins and Mr. Dubster or the aristocratic Sir Sedley provide the sort of spirited dialogue which had been so admired in *Evelina*. If, as the common critical judgement posits,

Fanny Burney's novels became successively more prosy, she never quite lost her talent for depicting foibles through revelatory dialogue.

Given her interest in plays and her mastery of dramatic technique, it is not surprising that Fanny Burney should turn to play writing; indeed, one only wonders why she waited as long as she did and why she needed so much prodding. Perhaps it was that, in spite of her success as a novelist, she still feared the exposure to criticism that a dramatist must face. Or she may have been sensitive to the fact that, although novel writing had become a respectable occupation for a lady, writing for the stage was still largely a masculine profession.[39] Whatever the reason for her reluctance, it was not until the summer of 1778 that Fanny Burney embarked on *The Witlings*, her first dramatic effort. In that summer, just as the authorship of *Evelina* became widely known, Fanny, then aged twenty-six, was to experience "the most consequential day I have spent since my birth: namely, my Streatham visit."[40] At Streatham she was introduced to Mrs. Thrale and her circle, a circle which included such luminaries as Dr. Johnson, Edmund Burke, Sir Joshua Reynolds, and Mrs. Montagu, leader of the *bas bleus*.[41] It was Mrs. Thrale who first introduced to Fanny the notion of writing a comedy, urging that it "would be something worth your time—it is the road both to honour and profit, and why should you have it in your power to gain both, and not do it?"[42] But even the encouragement of Mrs. Thrale and Dr. Johnson might not have been enough to spur Fanny's pen if an even greater incentive had not been added in the shape of a virtual guarantee of production from those two great men of the theatre, Richard Brinsley Sheridan and Arthur Murphy.[43] Fanny's account of the meeting with Sheridan in January 1779 shows the extent of his faith in her:

> Sir Joshua—["]Anything in the dialogue way, I think she must succeed in; and I am sure invention will not be wanting.["]
>
> Mr. Sheridan—["]No, indeed. I think, and say, she should write a comedy. . . .["]
>
> "Consider," continued Sir Joshua, "you have already had all the applause and fame you can have given you in the closet; but the acclamation of a theatre will be new to you.["]
>
> And then he put down his trumpet, and began a violent clapping of his hands.
>
> I actually shook from head to foot! I felt myself already in Drury Lane, amidst the hubbub of a first night.

"Oh me!" cried I, "there may be a noise, but it will be just the reverse." And I returned his salute with a hissing.

Mr. Sheridan joined Sir Joshua very warmly. . . .

Mr. Sheridan. . . .—["]She will write a comedy,—she has promised me she will!["]

FB—["]Oh!—if you run on in this manner, I shall—["]

I was going to say get under the chair, but Mr. Sheridan, interrupting me with a laugh, said,

"Set about one? very well, that's right!["]

"Ay," cried Sir Joshua, "that's very right. And you (to Mr. Sheridan) would take anything of hers, would you not?—unsight [*sic*], unseen?"

What a point-blank question! Who but Sir Joshua would have ventured it!

"Yes," answered Mr. Sheridan, with quickness, "and make her my best bow and my best thanks into the bargain."[44]

After such encouragement, it is not surprising that Fanny Burney should overcome her scruples. The conversation, the evening, were decisive; what had perhaps been random thoughts and wishes, jottings-down of character sketches or dialogue, became now a full-fledged enterprise. The meeting with Murphy a month later served to confirm a resolution already made. Not only did he enthusiastically support Mrs. Thrale's injunctions to Fanny to write a comedy; he also undertook to look it over with an eye to qualities that would most appeal to what "the sovereigns of the upper gallery will bear."[45]

For the subject of her first comedy Fanny Burney turned naturally to the new milieu in which she found herself. There were so many wits and eccentrics around her that "my opportunities for writing [grew] less and less, and my materials more and more."[46] Everything encouraged her to write a satire of wits and intellectuals. Mrs. Thrale accused her of planning to "trim us all by and by!";[47] Sir Joshua Reynolds felt "that if he were conscious to himself of any trick, or any affectation, there is nobody he should so much fear as this little Burney!";[48] and Dr. Johnson called her a little "character monger."[49] Fanny quickly learned from Dr. Johnson and Mrs. Thrale that female wits such as Mrs. Montagu were not to be unquestioningly idolized, and she could not but become imbued with some of their suspicion of, and contempt for, self-proclaimed wits, male or female. Nor could she, perhaps, resist Dr. Johnson's exhortations to pit her wit against that of the prominent bluestocking:

> "Down with her Burney!—down with her!—spare her not!—attack her, fight her, and down with her at once! You are a rising wit, and she is at the top; and when I was beginning the world, and was nothing and nobody, the joy of my life was to fire at all the established wits! . . . So at her, Burney—at her, and down with her!"[50]

So Fanny Burney, urged to write a comedy by such eminent men of the theatre as Sheridan and Murphy, encouraged to satirize intellectual pretensions by such intellectuals as Dr. Johnson and Mrs. Thrale, and herself having little respect for the parading of literary inclinations, wrote *The Witlings*, which Joyce Hemlow calls "a surprisingly sharp satire on the affectations of the Witlings . . . and especially of the *bas bleus*."[51]

The Witlings, completed in 1778,[52] is in part a delightful satire of intellectual pretensions and in part a sentimental romance. Lady Smatter, whose nephew Beaufort is in love with the heiress Cecilia, heads a literary club of would-be wits. The two plots are connected by Lady Smatter's rejection of Cecilia once she loses her fortune and by the machinations through which Beaufort and his friend Censor force her to sanction the marriage of the lovers. The strength of the play lies in the scenes which expose the ignorant pretensions of Lady Smatter and the folly of the poet Dabler. Lady Smatter, a self-proclaimed wit, explains her intellectual activities to Cecilia:

> LADY SMATTER. O, I am among the Critics. I love criticism passionately, though it is really laborious Work, for it obliges one to read with a vast deal of attention. I declare I am sometimes so immensely fatigued with the toil of studying for faults and objections, that I am ready to fling all my Books behind the Fire.
>
> CECILIA. And what authors have you chiefly criticized?
>
> LADY SMATTER. Pope and Shakespeare. I have found more errors in those than in any other.
>
> CECILIA. I hope, however, for the sake of readers less fastidious, your Ladyship has also left them some beauties.
>
> LADY SMATTER. O yes, I have not cut them up regularly through; indeed I have not, yet, read above half their Works, so how they will fare as I go on, I can't determine.[53]

Dabler, the poet of fashion, is full of conceit and devoid of talent, and he has clearly joined the literary club only to have an opportunity to thrust his execrable verse on the other members. Priding himself on his ability to write occasional verse, he pens an ode on Cecilia's sudden loss of fortune:

> *The pensive Maid, with saddest sorrow sad,*—No, hang it, that won't do!—Saddest sad will never do. With,—with—with *mildest* —ay, that's it!—*The pensive Maid with mildest sorrow sad,*—I should like, now, to hear a man mend that line!—I shall never get another to equal it.—Let's see,—sad, bad, had, Dad,—curse it, there's never a Rhyme will do! *Crystal Tears, & Sigh to Sigh did add.* Admirable![54]

The Witlings shows Fanny Burney's gift for acute observation and clever dialogue, but whether or not it would have pleased "the sovereigns of the upper gallery" Fanny never learned. For when she submitted it for approval to Dr. Burney and Mr. Crisp, "my two daddies put their heads together to concert for me that hissing, groaning, catcalling epistle" which was to be the death knell of the play.[55] Although both Sheridan and Murphy urged her to allow them to read and help revise it, Fanny was not to be moved once her two mentors had decided against the play. The fate of *The Witlings* was decided: "The fatal knell, then, is knolled, and 'down among the dead men' sink the poor *Witlings*—forever, and forever, and forever."[56]

When Fanny Burney next turned her hand to drama, it was to write verse tragedies. Her diaries indicate that the gloom of a royal family suffering from the king's illness transferred itself to her, so that her mind "would bend to nothing less sad [than tragedy], even in fiction."[57] Between October 1788 and August 1790,[58] Fanny completed *Edwy and Elgiva* (based on Hume's version of the story of the Saxon king Edwy[59]). By the end of 1791 she had written two other tragedies—*Hubert de Vere, a Pastoral Tragedy* and *The Siege of Pevensey* —and had begun work on another, *Elberta.* These tragedies, with their contrived action and stilted language, do not add to Fanny Burney's reputation as a dramatist; Hemlow remarks that "when we have said that Fanny Burney wrote three she-tragedies, but that as a poet, she was not so fortunate as to evade the dangers inherent in this species of composition, we shall, perhaps, have achieved an adequate summary of the matter."[60] Of these tragedies, only one was performed; *Edwy and Elgiva* opened at Drury Lane on 21 March 1795 and was, as Mrs. Thrale uncharitably put it, "hooted off the stage."[61] Fanny Burney herself conceded its imperfections: "It was not written with any idea of the stage, & my illness & weakness & constant *ab-*

sorbment in the time of its preparation, occasioned it to appear with so many *undramatic* [ef]fects, from my inexperience of Theatrical requisites & demands, that when I saw it, I perceived myself a thousand things I wished to *change*."[62] The piece was withdrawn after one performance.

In her next dramatic venture, Fanny Burney returned to comedy. *Love and Fashion*, written between 1798 and 1799,[63] while the author was happily settled at Camilla Cottage with husband and child, is the most sentimental of Fanny Burney's comedies. It deals with the choice between true love and wealth. The heroine, Hilaria, must choose between her young lover Valentine and her old but wealthy suitor Lord Ardville. The outcome is never really in doubt, and the whole action of the play is concerned with Hilaria's fluctuations as she is tempted by Lord Ardville's splendid gifts but reclaimed by Valentine's strictures on the right way to choose a husband. There are comic scenes, of course, largely concerning servants, but the main concern of the play is a serious exploration of a moral choice. Fanny Burney uses the opportunity to make some biting remarks about fashionable life. Sometimes, the criticism is presented indirectly through the superficial values of fashionable people, but more often Fanny allows the hero Valentine to make sober speeches castigating fashionable mores:

> The votaries, the general votaries of Fashion, weak rather than wicked are less the slave of their own follies than of those of others. They do not, therefore, in their matrimonial choice, enquire whom they prefer, or whom they dislike; their sole solicitude is to gather whom their associates will approve, or will scorn. For themselves, if self-consulted, they might perhaps, acknowledge, that an amiable companion would make them happier than the trappings of a coach horse; but when they ask what is said around them, they find the equipage alone considered—the Companion not thought of.[64]

This kind of moralizing and the sentimentality that irks a modern reader would not have irritated the admirers of *Jane Shore* and *The English Merchant*. Such, at least, was the opinion of Thomas Harris, manager of Covent Garden, who accepted the play for production in November 1799. But once again Fanny's hopes for seeing her work staged were to be unfulfilled. She postponed all her plans when her beloved sister Susan died in January 1800, and Harris seems after that to have forgotten the project altogether, for Fanny wrote to her sister Esther on 17 March 1801: "Even yet I know not what is purposed as to *time*, or even whether at *any* it will be heard of!"[65]

In spite of the collapse of plans for producing *Love and Fashion*, Fanny Burney was not disheartened as she had been after the "death knell" of *The Witlings*, and she was spurred on because the d'Arblays were in financial straits. When, in October 1801, General d'Arblay went to France to seek employment, Fanny began to write again. The products of her industry were two more comedies, *The Woman-Hater* and *A Busy Day*, which disprove the usual evaluation that Fanny Burney's writing deteriorated with each new work.[66]

In *The Woman-Hater*, Fanny constructed a much more complex plot than she had hitherto attempted in her comedies. Sir Roderick, who is the woman-hater of the title, has been a misogynist ever since he was rejected by Lady Smatter, a character based on the learned lady in *The Witlings*. His anger at Lady Smatter is such that he has disowned his own sister Eleonora for having married Lady Smatter's brother Wilmot. He now vents his resentment on all women and on young Jack Waverley, who is to be his heir if he eschews all women. Meanwhile, the Wilmots, who had gone to the East Indies to seek their fortune, have separated because Wilmot has (unjustly) accused his wife of infidelity. She has fled with their daughter Sophia, and Wilmot has been unknowingly raising the nurse's daughter Joyce as his own child. When the play opens, Eleonora and Sophia have returned to England in hopes of finding support from either Lady Smatter or Sir Roderick. Wilmot, too, has come back, having discovered that his suspicions of Eleonora's perfidy were unfounded.

There is much room for intrigue here, and Fanny Burney exploits the complications of the plot to create a far richer play than she had written earlier. It is an indication of her progress as a dramatist that she is able to untangle this tortuous plot without straining our credulity or attention span. She does this by making sure that each scene somehow contributes to the unwinding of the plot—from a comic confrontation between Waverley and Sir Roderick to a dramatic encounter between Eleonora and her husband. Unlike *The Witlings*, which is episodic, and unlike *Love and Fashion*, which has no suspense, *The Woman-Hater* consistently involves the audience by provoking interest in the characters and curiosity as to how all the problems of the plot can be solved. In the end, the Wilmots are reconciled and even Sir Roderick and Lady Smatter are betrothed, but the conventional happy ending is so often in jeopardy that one cannot help but be concerned.

The seriousness of the Wilmot intrigue does not mean that there is no comedy in the play. On the contrary, the comic scenes in *The Woman-Hater* are more carefully integrated with the sentimental plot than in the earlier plays. Sir Roderick is in some ways the obverse, comic side of Wilmot; he, too, has suffered from his involvement with a woman, and though the excess of his reaction makes him a figure of fun, his plight serves to balance that of Wilmot. In Lady Smatter one sees a softened version of the earlier portrait. Significantly, although the first Lady Smatter was left in a humiliating position at the end of the play, this one is reintegrated into society, opting for reconciliation with Sir Roderick rather than isolation with her books.

Unlike *The Witlings* and *Love and Fashion*, *The Woman-Hater* would have needed very little revision before being staged. It has all the elements of a successful comedy of the period: it combines comedy of humours with that of manners, and it includes a good dose of sentiment as well as farce. These various elements are handled deftly, and, as Hemlow says, "Of Fanny Burney's plays, *The Woman-Hater* would have best pleased contemporary theatre-goers."[67]

These two last plays, *The Woman-Hater* and *A Busy Day*, with every chance of success on stage, were fated to suffer the same oblivion as Fanny Burney's earlier comedies. No sooner had she completed them than General d'Arblay's affairs took the family to France, where she remained for ten years. When she returned to England in August 1812, she was busy with the completion of *The Wanderer*, and a look at the current stage would have convinced her that her domestic comedies were not likely to find a place among the popular costume dramas and extravaganzas then prevailing.[68] So her two "very good plays, which might have realized the 'golden dreams' almost realized in 'Love and Fashion,'" remained unperformed and unpublished.[69] Fanny Burney's career as playwright spanned more than twenty years; that it should have been so obscure and unsuccessful is due to a combination of ill advice and ill luck rather than inability, and one can now only conjecture as to the effect on her literary reputation if circumstances had permitted a public display of her dramatic talents.

STAGING

A BUSY DAY

Fanny Burney was concerned with the social and moral issues conveyed by her play, but she never lost sight of the fact that the play was meant to be performed. Her concern for the produceability of the play led her not only to choose a popular subject and to create sprightly dialogue but also to keep in mind how the play would look and sound. A reading of *A Busy Day* shows that Fanny Burney's knowledge of practical stagecraft was significant.

The London theatrical world for which Fanny Burney was writing at the turn of the century was one on the verge of change but yet comfortably following the patterns and customs of the eighteenth-century stage. The upheavals caused by the Licensing Act of 1737 had largely subsided, leaving the patent theatres, Drury Lane and Covent Garden, securely exercising their exclusive rights to produce legitimate theatre in London. Only the Haymarket had a license to compete with the patent theatres, and its season began when the two others closed for the summer. There was, as yet, no intimation of the competitive agitation that would lead to the revocation of the Licensing Act in 1843.[1] Thomas Harris at Covent Garden and Richard Brinsley Sheridan and John Philip Kemble at Drury Lane could run the two companies with the assumption that, in London, they had only each other as rivals for the favours of a large audience, the many fine actors, and the new plays being written. Nor was this an intense competition. Frederick Reynolds characterized the relationship between Harris and Sheridan as one of mutual cooperation: "So decorous were they in their rivalry, and so convinced was each, that he himself should only be injured by a hostile conduct towards the other, that the *stars* of the one house more than once performed with the *stars* of the opposing company."[2]

Still, there were distinctions between the two companies; and, for reasons both practical and sentimental, *A Busy Day* was written for Covent Garden, as is evident from the list of actors Fanny Burney provides.[3] In part, Fanny Burney would have been attracted to Covent Garden because its manager sought out new plays. Thomas Dutton refers to Harris's interest in new plays when he compares the two theatres' offerings for the 1799/1800 season: "In the article of *novelties*, Covent Garden decidedly distanced her rival; Drury Lane producing only *two* new pieces, and both of those *after-pieces* . . . whilst Covent Garden brought forward *five*, and two of them regular five-act Dramas."[4] To a company looking for new plays, a new comedy by someone of Fanny Burney's reputation would be most welcome. Harris had previously accepted *Love and Fashion*, and although it was never produced, his enthusiasm for it would indicate an inclination on his part to commit himself to Fanny Burney's work.[5] Harris was neither an actor-manager like Kemble nor a playwright-manager like Sheridan, but Fanny Burney could rely on his skill at revising plays. Reynolds pays tribute to Harris's ability to improve a playwright's manuscript:

> To the late Mr. Harris, I am indeed materially indebted for the success of this comedy [*Notoriety*]. He proposed many important alterations, curtailments, and additions; all of which, both by the author, and actors, were immediately adopted. We knew he had experience, and we knew that he had profited by it; his taste was unexceptionable, and his judgment was never sullied by prejudice. . . . he worked for the *general* interest.[6]

Harris's tact and the loyalty he evoked from his company are demonstrated by the fact that, even when the actors lost a case of complaint against him,[7] only one of the eight aggrieved players left the management because of the dispute. Such stability in a company would be important to Fanny Burney, who was writing for financial gain.

Perhaps Fanny Burney was also influenced in her choice of company by the memory of the failure of *Edwy and Elgiva*, which, despite the best efforts of the management at Drury Lane, closed after one dismal performance on 21 March 1795.[8] Nor should one discount one other factor: Covent Garden was the theatre most frequented by George III and his family.[9] Fanny Burney's attachment to the royal family is well documented in her journals and letters, and it rose, not only from her genuine respect and affection for them, but also from her desire to retain their favour and her annual pension of one hundred pounds. It is therefore not unlikely that she would want to write for a company which stood in such good grace with George III and Queen Charlotte.

Of course, the audience for which Fanny Burney wrote *A Busy Day* included many others besides the royal family. It was an audience both large and varied. In spite of the "refined and sentimental" nature of much of the drama of the late eighteenth century, "the size of the theatre-going public was steadily increasing throughout the century."[10] Hogan works out that, in 1790, with a total London population of nine hundred thousand, there were approximately five thousand playgoers in each of the patent theatres on an average night.[11] This large audience was drawn from various strata of society, each stratum concentrating in one location in the auditorium. Booth says:

> Socially the eighteenth-century patent theatre audience was remarkably stable: the fashionable aristocracy and upper middle class in the boxes, the middle class, professional and literary people in the pit, and the lower middle class, servants, journeymen, apprentices, sailors, etc. in the galleries.[12]

The pit was not the exclusive province of critics and professionals. A nobleman who wished to scan the boxes at leisure might choose to sit in it, and, as in *Cecilia*, aristocratic ladies too would occasionally make use of it.[13] Usually however, "the boxes were the proper gathering place for those persons [i.e., the fashionable upper classes] who because of late dinner parties or a late sitting of Parliament could not, on many a night, find themselves able to be at the play until well after it had begun."[14] The habitual tardiness of the fashionable set was a practical reason for having them sit in boxes, for the latecomers could use the separate entrances and thus cause less disturbance; but of course these people also cared about their comfort and about being seen.[15] The upper gallery was the province of the "gods" referred to in many an eighteenth-century prologue, and in spite of their occasional misbehaviour and cheap seats, both playwrights and actors were eager to please them. Noise and inattention could be detected in all parts of the auditorium, and Thomas Holcroft characterized a typical audience as being "composed of a large mixture of the illiterate, the inconsiderate, and persons educated among the vulgar; or only half informed at best."[16] It is clear from contemporary accounts that in the eighteenth century the audience could be both riotous and cooperative; Dutton describes an incident which demonstrates the less-than-docile attitude of the audience:

> A serious disturbance took place at the Theatre [Covent Garden] this evening, in consequence of the *tardiness* of the performers to comply with the demands of the audience . . . the performers, by an *inverted* mode of argument, apprehending they were the *mistresses* and *masters*, not the *servants* of the public, and that they had a right to *control* those, by whose munificence they are *fed*, thought proper to *lord* it over the spectators. This *revolutionary* principle by no means accorded with the sentiments of the audience; opposition only tended to render them more clamorous in the assertion of their undoubted *right*. . . . Mr. Pope came forward with a kind of apology, but was pelted, hissed, and hooted off the stage.[17]

In contrast to this episode, which shows the recalcitrance of the audience, an account from Goede shows the audience's good humour and easy fellowship with the actors:

> I was once at the little theatre in the Haymarket, when two gentlemen in a box quarrelled; to the great annoyance of the co., there being no police. . . . While they were boxing the uproar was so great, that neither the spectators could understand the actors nor the actors each other. Upon which Fawcett came forward, and raising his voice, called out, "Hey day! be quiet!" The audience laughed at and applauded Fawcett, and an end was put to the tumult by one of the parties being boxed out into the lobbies.[18]

Given Fanny Burney's frequent attendance at plays, one may assume that she had the various elements of the audience clearly in mind when she wrote *A Busy Day*. For the critics and professional literary people, she wrote a play which had lively dialogue and realistic action; for the aristocrats and wealthy merchants in the boxes, she wrote the kind of social satire which would enable them to laugh at each other or perhaps even at themselves. For the gods in the galleries, who must be kept entertained, she put in scenes which are almost pure farce—as when Mr. Tibbs baits Lady Wilhelmina. And, since all parts of the audience liked and were accustomed to a high moral tone and a degree of sentiment, she put in enough elevated dialogue to ensure that her play would be considered morally and emotionally satisfying.

Nor did Fanny Burney forget that the success of a play depended greatly on the abilities of the actors. The number of performers in London was not large, and the normally lifelong attachment of actors to one of the two patent theatres naturally led to a degree of rapport on stage. Still, the late eighteenth century was clearly a time of displays of individual histrionic talent, as is evident from the chapter headings chosen by the writers of *The Revels History of Drama in English*: "The Garrick Era" and "The Kemble Religion." Garrick, whose style of acting influenced players for the rest of the century, brought a new vivacity and variety to a stage which "had come to seem 'unnatural' because the monotony of [earlier actors'] gesticulation and declamation tended to make their emotions appear static."[19] By the time Kemble and his sister Mrs. Siddons came on the stage (1785 and 1775), audiences had come to expect a certain amount of realism from actors, and this they were given. But the hugeness of the rebuilt theatres at the end of the century caused difficulties for the actors. Drury Lane seated 2,300 in 1791 and expanded to 3,600 in 1794; and Covent Garden expanded from 2,500 seats in 1782 to 3,013 in 1792.[20] These changes indicate that financially the theatres were doing well, but the enormous halls demanded an exaggeration of manner that necessarily strained the actors' abilities to be both subtle and intelligible. George Colman the Younger pointed to this problem when he said:

> To produce in very large theatres the desired and instantaneous effects of the voice, more [effort] is requisite . . . but to send post-haste intelligence in a smile, to forward dispatches by a glance, to print, as it were, a Gazette in the face, that it may reach eager politicians, so far distant from the spot whence information must be transmitted, is a much more arduous undertaking.[21]

This "arduous undertaking" resulted in styles of acting which today might seem most "unnatural." Kemble's style was characterized by a "mixture of statuesque repose and sudden emotional shock,"[22] and "staggering dramatic pathos and intensity were . . . the very hallmarks of the art of Sarah Siddons."[23] Of course, not all the actors of the late eighteenth-century stage followed the Kembles' lead; the comic actors, in particular, were able to retain a more natural style, in part because comedies were usually written in less elevated language. The lively antics of William Thomas Lewis and Joseph Shepherd Munden were their own invention, as was the "rich, genial, vinous spirit" of Mrs. Jordan.[24]

The variety of talent and style available to eighteenth-century playwrights made it customary for them to write plays for particular actors. This habit of playwrights may have led to financial success, but two contemporary critics take dramatists to task for it. Dutton speaks of "the absurdity, except with a view to immediate gain, of writing plays by an *inverted process*; i.e. of *writing* parts for particular actors, instead of leaving it to the actor to *suit* himself to the part."[25] W. C. Oulton, criticizing Thomas Morton's *Secrets Worth Knowing* (1798), calls the play "inferior, having been evidently written *for the actors* (Messrs. Lewis, Quick, Fawcett, Munden, Knight, Pope, Holman, &c.) and not *for the public*; the delineation of characters thus invented, must be imperfect, and the business arising from them confused."[26] It is difficult, at this late date, to determine whether Fanny Burney chose the actors before or after she wrote *A Busy Day*, but the names from the Covent Garden company she pencilled in were shrewdly chosen: Thomas Knight as Lord John Dervis; Alexander Pope as Cleveland; William Thomas Lewis as Frank; Joseph Shepherd Munden as Mr. Watts; John Fawcett as Mr. Tibbs; Isabella Mattocks as Lady Wilhelmina; Mary Ann Davenport as Mrs. Watts; Maria Ann Pope as Eliza. The choice of Pope (1763–1835) and his wife (1775–1803) as the ingénues of the piece may have been dictated as much by the sentimental value of presenting husband and wife as lovers as by their abilities. Pope generally played tragic roles but had also appeared as Joseph Surface in Sheridan's *School for Scandal* (1798), as Bevil in Steele's *Conscious Lovers* (1787), and as Delaval in Holcroft's *He's Much to Blame* (1798).[27] The two latter roles are much like that of Cleveland—young lovers notable for good hearts and fine intentions rather than for wit and wisdom. Mrs. Pope in her brief acting career (1797–1803) had created the role of Delaval's sister Maria (1798), a woman much wronged by a faithless lover; her experience in a part calculated to elicit sympathy may have influenced Fanny Burney's desire to have her play the role of the heroine.

In her choice of comic actors, Fanny Burney was astute. Lewis (1748–1811), who became the deputy manager at Covent Garden in 1782, was also its principal comedian. He had played Sir George Versatile in *He's Much to Blame* (1798), Beverley in Colman the Elder's *Man of Business* (1774), and Sir Harry Flutter in Mrs. Sheridan's *Discovery* (1763), all parts that require spirit and energy.[28] Contemporary reviews indicate that Lewis had the liveliness needed to make a success of these roles,[29] and Dutton, in the *Dramatic Censor*, talks of Lewis's "inimitable style of acting, in parts distinguished by whim and volatile eccentricity."[30] The part of Frank Cleveland clearly calls for an actor who can convey volatility without seeming too fantastic; the self-centred eccentricities of Frank need the services of a spirited actor to make one enjoy his machinations and applaud his eventual success in finding a rich wife. The scenes in which Frank absurdly woos Eliza are written comically enough, and they would certainly be well served by an actor who could carry off impertinence with style. Lewis, it appears, was just such an actor, and even if the part was not written specifically for him, this would have been a happy conjunction of role and player. The play's other town fop, Lord John Dervis, was assigned to Thomas Knight (d. 1820), whose past performances included Sir Benjamin Backbite in *School for Scandal* (1798), Tony Lumpkin in Goldsmith's *She Stoops to Conquer* (1798), and Dick Dowlas in Colman the Younger's *Heir at Law* (1797). One reviewer wrote that Knight was "too graceful for clowns and too clownish for beaus," which quality would be appropriate for the clownish beau Lord John.[31]

The two "low" male characters, Mr. Watts and Mr. Tibbs, are also well suited to the talents of the actors Munden and Fawcett. Joseph Munden (1758–1832), who joined Covent Garden in 1790, made his name in such roles as Quidnunc in Murphy's *Upholsterer* (1790), Sir Anthony Absolute, Hardcastle, and Zekiel Homespun in *Heir at Law* (1797).[32] The first three characters are like Mr. Watts in that each is what may be characterized as a "heavy father." As Homespun, Munden would have had to show a command of low dialect as well as an honest forthrightness, qualities present in the part of Mr. Watts. Hunt praises Munden as "a genuine comedian . . . with a considerable degree of insight into character as well as surface,"[33] and Lamb talks of his variety of comic grimaces:

> When you think he has exhausted his battery of looks, in unaccountable warfare with your gravity, suddenly he sprouts out an entirely new set of features, like Hydra. . . . in the grand grotesque of farce, Munden stands out as single and unaccompanied as Hogarth.[34]

The oddness of Munden's expressions would have contributed to the fun of those scenes in which Miss Percival is horrified by Mr. Watts's appearance. Equally useful would be the physical idiosyncrasies of Fawcett (1768–1837), who specialized in low comedy at Covent Garden and whose "talent lies chiefly in vehement middle-aged gentlemen, in boisterous eccentricities of all kinds, and in merry-hearted footmen."[35] Fawcett was the actor for whom Colman the Younger wrote the part of Dr. Pangloss in *Heir at Law*,[36] a part which calls for the same sort of buffoonery that is required by the characterization of Mr. Tibbs. The part of Mr. Tibbs is not a large one—he has some sixty lines compared to Mr. Watts's ninety—but he is the one who must carry the climactic comic scene in the play (when he imitates fashionable manners), and Fanny Burney clearly wanted someone whom the audience saw as a constant source of laughter.

The two contrasting comic female roles—Lady Wilhelmina and Mrs. Watts—were assigned to two popular comic actresses of the time. Mrs. Mattocks (1746–1826) had played Lady Vibrate in *He's Much to Blame* (1798) and Mrs. Knightley in *The Discovery* (1763),[37] parts which require, if not the stately snobbishness of Lady Wilhelmina, at least the same kind of dignified impertinence and the strength of a personality used to having her own way. Mrs. Davenport (1765–1843) made a speciality of portraying talkative and vulgar women such as Mrs. Hardcastle (1794), Mrs. Malaprop (1795–96), and Deborah Dowlas in *The Heir at Law* (1797).[38] Of her, Leigh Hunt says, in what must be an understatement, that she could be supposed to be "leaning . . . by the way she digs at her words as if she were rooting up horse-radish, to comedy."[39]

If Fanny Burney cared about who was to play each role, she also cared, as the manuscript shows, *how* they should play their parts. In a period when much license was granted to actors, who usually interpreted parts as they pleased,[40] Fanny Burney seems to have given unusually complete and specific stage directions. These do not merely indicate entrances and exits; they indicate movements around the stage, physical contact with other players, and even the tone of voice and manner of expression an actor should use. Some of the directions regarding movement are merely logical extensions of the text (walking to the person addressed, or walking away when someone requires privacy) but many of them are also interpretative, as when the manuscript directs that Cleveland or Eliza should walk about in agitation (II.384; III.376, 726). At other times, the instructions are more detailed and specific. In the scene at Kensington Gardens, when Cleveland vainly attempts to speak with Eliza, the stage directions clearly block out the movements, so that, even without dialogue, the progress of the scene is clear: "[Cleveland] is drawing [Jemima] towards the further seat [where Eliza is]; when Miss Percival rushes in, and, catching the hand of Jemima throws herself against the shoulder of Cleveland, without looking at him" (III.following 427). When Miss Percival has run off, Cleveland tries again: "They move towards the further seat. Eliza looks down; Miss Watts bends forward to stare: and Mrs Watts rises and courtsies low" (III.following 460). This second attempt is thwarted when Miss Percival again runs in, and finally "runs off, one hand covering her face, the other holding by Cleveland" (III.following 573). There are also a number of phrases directing the players to bow or sit or sing or throw themselves on chairs, as well as instructions directing physical contact between players, instructions which bear witness that Fanny Burney was acutely aware that plays are more than words.

Perhaps the most surprising stage directions, coming from a new playwright, are those indicating how the actors should move or speak or look. There are, of course, the usual directions regarding asides and whispers, but Fanny Burney goes further and tells the actors how to interpret the piece. Thus, a waiter is to "Exit loiteringly" (I.following 124), Mrs. Watts is to "Exit, hobbling" (III.following 583), and Mr. Watts is to "Exit, bowing awkwardly around" (IV.following 542). Lord John must yawn while speaking to Lady Wilhelmina (II.187); Eliza must sigh when speaking to Jemima of Cleveland (IV.15), and Lady Wilhelmina is to speak "imperiously" to Mr. Tibbs (V.754). Even facial expressions are specified, as when Cleveland is "looking uneasily toward Eliza" (III.following 491) and Lady Wilhelmina questions Eliza while "still stiffly looking at her" (IV.28–29).

What is clear from the stage directions provided is that Fanny Burney felt she knew enough about acting to instruct actors. A comparison with other plays of the time shows how much Fanny Burney did in this respect. Cecil Price's edition of *The School for Scandal*, which is based on manuscripts in Sheridan's hand,[41] shows that Sheridan contented himself with indicating only exits and entrances, with a very few directions regarding manner of action. In George Colman the Younger's *The Heir at Law*, one finds the same paucity of specific stage directions, since the author limits himself to indicating an occasional gesture.[42] Holcroft, in *He's Much to Blame*, includes the kind of directions that Fanny Burney uses, but compared to *A Busy Day*, his play has very few. John Burgoyne's *Heiress*, on the other hand, has almost as many directions as *A Busy Day*, and they are of the same type: interpretations of actions and states of mind. Thus Miss Alton "*comes forward modestly*" and Mrs. Blandish "*writes, as pleased with her Thought.*"[43] It is possible that the less experienced dramatists, such as General Burgoyne and Fanny Burney, were more optimistic about their influence on the actors; the significant point, however, is that playwrights did not routinely provide the kind of detailed directions found in *A Busy Day*, and Fanny Burney deliberately chose to direct the actions of the players more extensively than was common among dramatists of the time.

Fanny Burney's concern for the proper production of her play did not lead her to issue instructions regarding sets and costumes; Fanny Burney is no George Bernard Shaw, and her directions are both general and simple. The sets needed for *A Busy Day* are four standard interiors and one outdoor scene representing Kensington Gardens. The first act, which takes place in a hotel, needs a minimum of furniture—there must be a table and a chair, since Eliza sits down to write a note to her father (I.following 149). The second act, in the Tylneys' drawing room, needs finer furnishings than the hotel apartment and calls for a desk with writing materials at which Lord John sits (II.636), plus the usual chairs and tables. The third act specifies two benches in the gardens, on which are seated the Watts party and the Cleveland party (III.39, 381). The fourth act is in Jemima's dressing room, which, if it resembles that of Lydia Languish, would be furnished with a toilet table, closet, sofa, bolster, books, and various feminine props.[44] The last act takes place in "an elegantly fitted-up apartment" (V.preceding 1) in Miss Percival's house and could easily use some of the furniture used in Act II. The stage directions specify some furniture on which Frank, Lord John, and Miss Percival relax: two great chairs and a sofa (V.189–94), which becomes the bone of contention between Mr. Tibbs and Lady Wilhelmina in their comic confrontation.

The matter of costumes and props, too, is left largely to the discretion of the company, since Fanny Burney says little of them. There are only general indications of clothing—clearly the Wattses are vulgarly overdressed and Mr. Tibbs is dressed to show his relative poverty. In any event, Fanny Burney probably knew that "each actor had more-or-less his own choice of what he wore,"[45] and therefore she did not attempt to influence the player's choice. In this, Fanny Burney follows the usage of other dramatists of the period, who usually do not specify furnishings and costumes. Sometimes, particulars regarding sets and costume are required, as when Joseph Surface hides Lady Teazle behind a screen,[46] or when, in *The Heiress*, Miss Alscrip's vulgarity is underlined by her dress of "Otahaite feathers," "Italian flowers," and "knots of pearl that gathered up the festoons";[47] but generally playwrights of the period are as reticent about sets and costumes as is Fanny Burney.

Since each act of *A Busy Day* has a new set, the play would have required the sophisticated stage machinery available in the late eighteenth century.[48] Eighteenth-century scenery consisted of painted flats and wings, each resting on sets of grooves on the stage floor and in the flies. When it was time to change the scene, the flats could be pulled off from the sides or a new flat could cover the previous one. The wings, too, could be slid in and out on grooves. *A Busy Day* requires such changes only after each act, so the process of changing the flats and wings would occur behind "a curtain painted in a conventionally ornamental design and located immediately behind the proscenium curtain."[49] All these scene changes, as well as the plays themselves, took place not in the darkness familiar to the modern playgoer but in a candle-lit auditorium. The lighting of the stage itself could be varied by placing metal shields over the lights on either side of the stage or by lowering the metal trough which contained the footlights.[50] *A Busy Day* would make no extraordinary demands on the lighting system, since the only direction about lighting is in the fifth act, which is set in a "brilliantly lit" room, an effect easily achieved by adding more candles, presumably on the stage itself.

One other point needs to be made regarding the staging of *A Busy Day*: Fanny Burney seems to have controlled carefully the pacing of the action so that there are very few long, tedious stretches which might bore the audience. There are a minimum of short soliloquies and very few long conversations. Altogether, there are some 170 entrances and exits in the play, which indicates a considerable flow.[51] The stage business as sketched in the manuscript is enough to prevent the actors' merely standing about making speeches to each other, and there are few moments when a character has the opportunity to be idle and inattentive on stage. That actors were often inattentive is clear from contemporary accounts; Thomas Holcroft complains:

> Among performers, who are favorites with the public in particular, it is far from uncommon to see them so totally forget decency, the respect due to an audience, and the contempt which they bring upon themselves, as to look about them, into the boxes and the pit, in order to discover who they know, or even, at some times, impudently to make slight nods, signs, or grins.[52]

One may conjecture that, with many years of attentive playgoing behind her, Fanny Burney was aware of the vagaries of actors and determined to do all she could to prevent lax or wrong-headed performance.

Fanny Burney had had one theatrical failure (*Edwy and Elgiva*) and had given up opportunities for two possible successes (*The Witlings* and *Love and Fashion*). With *A Busy Day*, it seems, she was determined to make up for the earlier disappointments. The designation of appropriate actors, the explicit stage directions, and the lack of demanding or unrealistic scenery and props indicates an awareness as well as determination: Fanny Burney knew what were the exigencies of the late eighteenth-century stage, and she fashioned a production that would meet the requirements for success.

DESCRIPTION OF THE MANUSCRIPT

The manuscript of *A Busy Day*, in General d'Arblay's hand, is "written with great care, neatness, and legibility."[1] The corrections are in Fanny Burney's hand, and there are no other marks on the manuscript other than bold horizontal lines marking the end of each act. The absence of stray marks, together with the neat uniformity of the five notebooks (one for each act), suggests that this is a final draft.

The paper used in the notebooks seems to come from the same lot, as the quality is uniform, the chain lines being 2.5 cm. apart and the only watermark being a fleur-de-lys (Heawood 1479). The paper may belong to the printing demy group which was being produced in England in 1781.[2] Since the chain lines are parallel to the spine and since the watermark appears only partially at the bottom or top of pages, one can assume that the paper was cut in half perpendicular to the chain lines and then folded.

The sheets are folded in half to make two leaves, each measuring 20.5 cm. by 12.6 cm. Each folded sheet is placed beside the next, folds together. Then one folded sheet encloses the inner leaves to form the outer cover. The whole is then stabbed and sewn at the spine. Thus, Notebook 1 contains ff. 1/28 and ff. 2/3 to 26/27; Notebook 2, ff. 1/30 and ff. 2/3 to 28/29; Notebook 3, ff. 1/34 and ff. 2/3 to 32/33; Notebook 4, ff. 1/30 and ff. 2/3 to 28/29; and Notebook 5, ff. 1/40 and ff. 2/3 to 38/39. There are no blank leaves, so it is likely that the play was written on loose gatherings which were afterwards bound.

In Notebook 1, f. 1^{r} has the title in General d'Arblay's hand: "A BUSY DAY / or / AN ARRIVAL from INDIA. / A / COMEDY / IN FIVE ACTS." "Persons of the Drama" in Fanny Burney's hand are listed on f. 1^{v}. Act I appears on ff. 2^{r}–28^{r}. Notebook 2 has a half title on f. 1^{r}: "A Busy Day / or / An arrival from India / Act. 2. / ⏟ ." Act II appears on ff. 2^{r}–30^{v}. Notebook 3 has the half title on f. 1^{r}: "A

Busy Day / or / An arrival from India / Act.3^{d}.” Act III is on ff. 2^{r}–33^{r}. Notebook 4 has a half title on f. 1^{r}: “A Busy Day / or / An arrival from India. / Act.4 ⏟ / .” Act IV is on ff. 2^{r}–30^{r}. Notebook 5 has a half title on f. 1^{r}: “A Busy Day / or / An arrival from India. / Act. V.” Act V is on ff. 2^{r}–40^{r}. The careful marking of each notebook with half title may be due to General d’Arblay’s tidy habits (the manuscripts of the other comedies are marked with Roman numerals indicating acts, but no other identification) or it may indicate that the manuscript was to be submitted to an acting company.

The numbering of the manuscript supports the theory that the play was written on loose gatherings. Each gathering is numbered on the recto of the first leaf, and the numbering runs consecutively through the notebooks. Notebook 1 has numbers 1–13 on the recto of each gathering’s first leaf and 14 on f. 28^{r}; Notebook 2 is numbered 16–29 from f. 4^{r} to f. 30^{r}; Notebook 3 is numbered 30–45 from f. 2^{r} to f. 32^{r}; Notebook 4 is numbered 46–60 from f. 2^{r} to f. 30^{r}; and Notebook 5 is numbered to 79 from f. 2^{r} to f. 40^{r}. The numbers are written in the same hand and ink as the manuscript play, and appear in the middle of the top margin of the page.

EDITORIAL CHANGES

Approaching the task of editing an unpublished manuscript is both exhilarating and worrisome. It is, of course, enormously gratifying to know that one is breaking new ground, but the very newness of the work fills a scholar with trepidation, and every choice becomes a dilemma. *A Busy Day* is aimed, by author and editor, at a wide and general audience which includes scholars as well as those who want to read for pleasure only. Therefore, in editing *A Busy Day*, I have aimed for two things: (1) a "clean" text which is easily accessible to a modern reader but which retains the flavour of its time; (2) a record of the changes made so as to indicate the details of the manuscript in a straightforward way.

The manuscript of *A Busy Day* is written in the hand of General Alexandre d'Arblay, whose clear and attractive script is a boon to any editor. Once one becomes accustomed to his handwriting, it is so legible as to obviate the need for conjectural readings. The changes and corrections made by Fanny Burney are also, if not so quickly, accessible to those familiar with her hand. Not so easily deciphered, however, are the portions of the text that Fanny Burney deleted. When she wanted to cancel a line, or a paragraph, or even a whole page, she did not merely draw a line through the rejected material; rather, as Joyce Hemlow points out, "it was her custom to cover line by line with a series of interlocking and obliterating *o*'s, *e*'s, or *m*'s."[1] Therefore, a good deal of the cancelled sections is unrecoverable, even with the aid of strong light and magnifying glass.

Given the general clarity of the manuscript, it has been possible to present the text with a minimum of fuss. The textual notes refer to insertions by Fanny Burney (+FB) or General d'Arblay (+AA) and to deletions (*del.*). When the cancellations are not recoverable, I have indicated the length of the deletion, and a conjectural reading of a deleted word is indicated by a question mark before the word. There are few editorial changes in spelling; like the fictional editor of the correspondence in *Anna St. Ives* (1792), this editor too "has used his own judgment, in suffering various words to retain their primitive dress; the better to preserve what would otherwise have been too much unlike its author."[2] Therefore, I have retained such common eighteenth-century forms as "dropt" or "connexion" as well as consistent idiosyncrasies such as "ackward." I have changed General d'Arblay's Gallicisms—for example, "desagreeable"—and recorded the change. The only other spelling change is the regularization of the various spellings of the proper nouns Aylice/Aylce, Tilney/Tylney, and Piccadilly. Except for these occasional changes, then, the spelling of this edition is the spelling of the manuscript.

The punctuation and capitalization of the manuscript present a more difficult problem. Like many eighteenth-century writers (or, indeed, twentieth-century ones), Fanny Burney is not consistent in her use of abbreviations, exclamation marks, and capitals, and the question arises as to how many of these irregularities are those of General d'Arblay. The editor's problem here is twofold: how to regularize enough for accessibility without losing the eighteenth-century texture, and how to avoid replacing the inconsistencies of the manuscript with an inconsistency of one's own. As an eighteenth-century printer might have done, I have silently changed the abbreviations such as "&" and "L^{y}" and "p^{r}" by writing out the word, and "M^{r}" and "M^{rs}" have been changed to the more familiar "Mr" and "Mrs." I have changed full-stops to question marks when a line of dialogue is clearly a query (for example, I.323 and I.492), added full-stops and commas when they are clearly required to make sense of the text (II.605, V.673, IV.67), and deleted the occasional apostrophe after "La" (III.3 and 101). Dashes of various lengths are silently reduced to a one-em dash.

There are a number of silent changes in capitalization, but they all fall into one of four categories: (1) The manuscript is inconsistent in the capitalization of terms of address such as "sir" and "madam" and "gentlemen"; these have all been put in lower case. On the other hand, "Lord," "Lordship," "Lady," and "Ladyship," also inconsistently capitalized as terms of address, are all in upper case. (2) Family titles such as "Mother" and "Sister" appear throughout the manuscript in both upper and lower case. In this edition, the capitals are retained when the words refer to a specific family relationship (e.g., I.89, I.98) and lower case when the reference is generic, as in "younger brother" (e.g., II.382). (3) Many common nouns appear in both upper and lower case, often on the same page of the manuscript. They have been left in upper case only when the capital adds emphasis or provides the necessary sense of labelling, as in "Heiress" (I.325).

(4) Lower-case letters following exclamation points are retained, but lower case after full-stops and question marks are capitalized.

Two other changes are silent: all numerals are written out, so that "5" becomes "five" and "80,000 pounds" becomes "eighty thousand pounds"; and words such as "any thing," "every body," and "up-stairs" are compounded to one word.

It seemed to me that it was possible to take greater liberties with the stage directions than with the speeches, since these are aimed at actors and managers rather than at the audience. The aim in this edition has been to make them consistent and visually clear. Thus the names of speakers, which are usually underlined in the manuscript, are given in capital letters, and stage directions have been italicized. When the directions follow the name of the speaker, they are in parentheses and italicized, without any punctuation of their own, for example, "1ST WAITER (*within*)." When the directions stand alone, they are italicized, begin with a capital letter, and end with a fullstop, for example, "*A side door opens, and* ELIZA *enters, with* DEBORAH, *who endeavours to support her*." Since the manuscript usually specifies who is left on stage after an exit, I have retained this feature, but without the framing lines of the manuscript, so that

Cleveland, Eliza

becomes

CLEVELAND, ELIZA

The necessity for keeping an eye to detail without losing sight of larger concerns is what makes an editor's life taxing as well as interesting. As Michael Millgate said at the 1977 Conference on Editorial Problems, "Clearly, there is no such thing as pure editing. The editor, who must necessarily start by being a bibliographer, must become in some measure a critic and even a biographer too, even while thinking of himself all the while as a galley slave."[3] In editing *A Busy Day*, I have tried to take into consideration the convenience of the general reader and the curiosity of the scholar while keeping in mind that it is a document which was written for production in 1801–02, not for publication in 1984. If, in editing, I have not been so faithful as Sterne would have liked,[4] I hope at least Fanny Burney's practical mind would forgive the changes I have made.

Textual Notes

I.16–19 London . . . Street?] +FB, **replacing del.** London
I.40 with] +FB
I.51 to] +FB
I.58 dare say—] **del.** when I come to go to bed
I.60 ask] +FB, **replacing del.** help
Mungo] **del.** ascertain
I.65 young] +FB
I.90 channel] **del. punctuation**;
I.97 so] +AA
I.120 Did you, meme?] **del.** I believe you did. I had quite forgot it.
I.155 afraid] **del. second** f
I.156 never] **del. one illegible word**
I.159–60 I . . . messenger.] +FB. **After this there are 16 deleted and illegible lines, given to Cleveland. From the cancelled stage direction** *reads*, **one may conjecture that Cleveland reads aloud the letter Eliza has written.**
I.161 Ay . . . go.] +FB, **replacing del.** No, no, give me the letter.
I.172 quit him;] **del. 7 illegible lines**
but] +FB
I.172–74 so . . . passed] +FB, **replacing del. one illegible line**
I.176 Tell . . . means—] +FB; **del. 4 illegible lines**
I.177 CLEVELAND . . . rigidly] +FB
I.178 Portsmouth,] **del.** that
I.179 loitered, that,] **del.** I might **and one illegible word**
I.179–80 I might] +FB
I.180 But . . . at] +FB, **replacing del.** When I learnt at
I.181–82 Browns . . . me] +FB, **replacing del.** Browns, my alarm **and 2 illegible lines**
I.185 the accident which] +FB, **replacing del.** what
I.186 House.] +FB, **replacing del.** Hotel.
I.187 must not] **del. one illegible word**
I.199 much self-occupied] +FB, **replacing del. one illegible word**
I.200 any great] +FB, **replacing del.** much
I.209 develop] **ms. reads** devellop
I.211–12 Your high . . . him] +FB, **replacing del.** He must be
I.214 Daughter] +FB, **replacing del.** family
I.229 industry.] **del. 4 illegible lines**
I.249 you take him.] +FB, **replacing del. punctuation**;
I.258 Yes . . . here!] +FB
I.preceding 260 FRANK] **del.** Cleveland
I.285 I warrant] I +FB

I.287 if] **del.** yo
I.294 few] +FB
I.319–20 Alderson] **ms. reads** Anderson. **This must be a slip of the pen, since everywhere else in the play Eliza's guardian is called Alderson.**
I.345 as] **ms. reads** has
I.401 *has entered*)] **del.** Mada
I.411 half] **del.** an
I.415 Eliziana] **del. punctuation;**
I.453 (*weeps*)] **del.** MISS WATTS. La, Pa' what did you ask her for? you are always in sich a hurry. I'd have asked myself presently. Don't mind Pa' Sister Elizeana. **These lines may have been cancelled because they indicate a degree of sensitivity on Miss Watts's part which is not evident elsewhere in the play.**
I.454 Pray, my dear,] +FB, **replacing del. 2 illegible lines**
got] +FB, **replacing del.** brought
I.461 with you?] **del.** MISS WATTS. La, Ma', they're some acquaintance to be sure. / ELIZA. No; they're—
I.462 (*advancing*).] **del. one illegible word**
I.475 the] +FB
I.479 you're] **ms. reads** your
I.484 MISS WATTS.] **del.** Yes, yes
I.514 MR WATTS.] **del. 3 illegible words**
I.532 my dear] +FB, **replacing del.** Peggy
gown.] **del.** MISS WATTS (*in a whisper*). What do you call me Peggy for?
I.536 the little . . . prattle?] +FB, **replacing del.** Bet?
I.548–49 But . . . Aylce?] +FB; **del. 9 illegible lines**
I.551 I see.] +FB
I.560 at home!] **del. 2 illegible lines**
I.561 your neighbours.] +FB, **replacing del.** other folks, what ever you may think of it.
I.562 stop] +FB, **replacing del.** stand there
I.602 man's] 's +FB, **replacing del.** is
I.607 face!] **del.** Water!
I.629–30 of it . . . Come,] +FB, **replacing del.** of it. Come,

II.24 so I] I +AA
am:] **del.** I;
II.38 morning] **del.** in the deepest distress
II.41 man!] **del.** he is much to be lamented.
II.42 for it!] +FB, **replacing del.** of hand
II.43 his] **del.** poor
II.51 yesterday] **del.** ?morning

II.58 put] **del.** that
II.62 sufferers!] **del. 2 illegible lines**
II.63 there are.] +FB, **replacing del.** it is.
II.64 accident.] **del.** I can't bear a pother.
II.65 Poor] +FB, **replacing del.** And
II.74 carriages.] **del.** Why should she expect to be spared more than her neighbours?
II.76 head] +FB, **replacing del.** Hair
II.77 off] **del.** his head
II.101 and stage direction My . . . AARON] +FB. **She may have decided to have Sir Marmaduke exit here because it is unlikely that he would silently attend to a dialogue between Miss Cleveland and Lady Wilhelmina which does not concern himself.**
II.105 Garman] **ms. reads** German
II.109 of that nature] +FB
II.113 disagreeable] **ms. reads** desagreeable
events.] **del.** SIR MARMADUKE. My little Hay-rick!
II.119 a] +FB, **replacing del. one illegible word**
II.139 romance] **del. 2 illegible lines**
II.144 it] +FB
II.152 list.] **del.** LORD JOHN. The mode of your entry is so entirely
II.155–56 one of] +AA
II.following 160 *Enter* SIR MARMADUKE.] +FB
II.161 SIR MARMADUKE] +FB, **replacing del.** MISS CLEVELAND
II.175 meddle] **del.** upon
II.194 family] **del. 2 illegible lines**
II.222 faith] **del. 6 illegible lines**
II.364 born a] **del.** ?Peeress
II.365 I see,—] **del. one illegible line**
II.366 madam,—] **del. 2 illegible lines**
II.369 sentiments] **del.** which I share
II.370 Wilhelmina,—] **del.** I assure you **and 2 illegible words**
II.383 who . . . house—] +FB
II.387–88 to preserve . . . City.] +FB, **replacing del. 2 illegible lines**
II.398 have] +FB
II.399 and] +FB
II.428 on] +AA, **replacing del.** of
II.435 Miss Percival] +FB, **replacing del.** she
II.437 agreeable] **second** e +AA
II.453 mutual] +FB
II.470 a] +AA
II.472–74 CLEVELAND . . . reserve.] +FB, **replacing del.** CLEVELAND. Fear me not **and one illegible word**
II.475 hard] +AA

II.497–98 You . . . what] +FB, **replacing del.** What
II.545 City?] **del.** Who is there that holds the City in more respect.—
II.555 yourself.] **del. 6 illegible lines**
It] +FB
II.563–64 Why . . . about?] +FB
II.567 FRANK . . . to?] +FB
II.580 unintelligible] +FB, **replacing del.** fatheaded
II.584 Marmaduke] **ms. reads** Marmaduc
II.587 for?] **del.** And what am I to do if she should receive me now?
II.601 very] +FB, **replacing del.** same
II.606 a] +AA
II.609 the] +FB, **replacing del.** they
II.623 should] +FB
II.644 *deserving*] **del. second** *s*
II.647 What] +FB, **replacing del.** Why
II.651 Cleveland.] **del.** LORD JOHN. Hol! y.u.n.g. is that right? / FRANK. Not quite **and 3 illegible words**
II.653 ; young what, did you say?] +FB
II.654 FRANK.] **del.** Well now put down
to be sure.] +FB
II.663 writ] **del.** nev
II.742 Kensington] **ms. reads** Kinsington

III.26 me] +FB, **replacing del.** I
III.28 down?] **del.** MISS WATTS. La, Pa, can't you read it and see!
III.29 are Mr] +FB, **replacing del. 2 illegible words**
III.36 read] **del.** th
III.52 be] +AA
III.178 MRS WATTS . . . enough.] +FB
III.188 gentleman.] **del. 3 illegible words**
III.199 , I believe!] +FB, **replacing del. punctuation.**
III.211 Muster] **del.** M:
III.223 often] **del.** which
III.244 you] **del. one illegible word and** them
III.264 your] **del.** ?wife
III.277 last] +AA, **replacing del.** ?lost
III.278 Tommy] **ms. reads** Tom̄y
III.286 but she] **del. one illegible word**
III.313 shabby.] **del. one illegible word**
III.324 little.] **del. one illegible word**
III.328 I've] +FB, **replacing del. one illegible word**
III.329 hear me.] **del. one illegible word**
III.337 blushes] +AA, **replacing del.** ?Blushes
III.339 they're] +AA, **replacing del.** they've

III.340 for] +AA
III.364 by . . . Baronet!] +FB, **replacing del.** was a baronet
III.380 or not.] **del.** (a
III.395 can] +AA
III.410 soon be] **del.** en
III.431 conjuncture] +FB, **replacing del.** ?conjucture
III.443 Ah!] **del.** I
III.469 CLEVELAND.] **del.** Me? no madam
III.470 Did] **del.** you
III.471 I] +FB, **replacing del.** Me
III.following 473 *running*] **del** ?*running and* ?*throwing herself upon Cleveland*
III.476 O] **ms. reads** Ô
III.506 JEMIMA.] **del.** Yes, for
III.509 would . . . encounter] +FB, **replacing del. one illegible line**
III.518 seems] +FB
III.536 honour] **del. second** n
III.581 Why how you] +FB, **replacing del. one illegible line**
III.586 been] **del.** something
III.596 they'll] **del. one illegible word**
III.612 La, Pa',] **del. punctuation** —
III.660 FRANK.] **del.** Miss Percival to be sure
III.660–61 Miss . . . sure.] +FB
III.703 such] +AA
III.715 rid] **del.** off
III.724 all description] +FB, **replacing del. 2 illegible words**
III.728 I am] **del.** affra
III.740 that] **del.** has
thus] +FB
III.743–44 , the Loves . . . Goddesses—] +FB
III.744 Calcutta] +FB, **replacing del.** Bengal

IV.25 keenly] +FB, **above uncancelled** hardly
IV.34 *staring*] +FB, **replacing del. one illegible word**
IV.49 Ma'am, I—] **del. one illegible word**
IV.91 I] +FB, **replacing del.** Me
IV.112 this morning] **del. underline**
IV.118 Cleveland!] **del.** he has my pity; he deserves it for the horrour he confessed at the thought of a connexion so unfitting for our family, and he has an added [**one illegible word**] from the rational fear he must entertain lest it
IV.120 how . . . lest it] +FB; **del.** should **in FB's hand**
IV.122 ELIZA.] **del.** Good Heavens!
IV.135 ma'am, your] **del.** ?Lordship

IV.184 La'ship] d **del. after** La
IV.186–87 that . . . should] +FB, **replacing del.** at the discourse which must
IV.188 repay] **del.** s
IV.193 who] +AA
IV.201 tormenting!] +FB, **replacing del.** provoking!
IV.202 Heaven!] **del.** this
is the] **del.** very
who was] +FB
IV.254 not] +AA
IV.257 afraid] **del. second** f
IV.259 gentleman] **del. 2 illegible letters**
IV.289 the] +AA; **del.** e **before** very
IV.291 such a] **del. one illegible letter**
IV.302 Very well] **del. punctuation,**
IV.311 to my] **del.** to my
IV.326 pinnacle] **ms. reads** piñacle
IV.355 *entering*] **ms. reads** *intering*
IV.357–58 *and . . . scene*] +FB
IV.378 agreeable] **ms. reads** agreable
IV.398 What I] **del.** ?cannot
IV.414 *raising*] **ms. reads** *rising*
IV.432 *forward*] +AA
IV.460 under] **del.** unde
IV.461 beseech] **del.** you
IV.515 two] **ms. reads** too
IV.535 I] **del. one illegible word**
IV.536 sure] **del. punctuation,**
Frank] **del. punctuation,**
IV.555 Quiz is!] **del. punctuation?**
IV.574 on] +AA
IV.579 bad] +FB, **replacing del.** bid
IV.592 Yet I] I +FB
IV.626 Sel] **written over** salt
IV.707 begin to] **del.** to
IV.719 an] +AA
IV.730 virtue—] **del.** (*Exit*)
IV.730–31 don't . . . her!] +FB
IV.following 731 End of] **del.** the

V.12 LORD JOHN.] **del.** De
V.preceding 15 *Enter* MISS PERCIVAL.] **del.** Who's that?
V.36 wait upon you] +FB, **replacing del.** come
V.68 Albermarle] **del. one illegible word**

V.69 dilemma] **del. punctuation** —
V.82 Wil] **del. second** l.
V.83 utter] +AA
V.90 them] **del.** ?ke
V.116 fretful] **del. second** l
V.139 FRANK.] **del.** I go.— And yet,—might not his presence
V.preceding 149 *Re-enter*] = +AA
V.176 gaping] **del. second** p
V.185 nonsense] +FB, **replacing del.** ?non sense
V.196 the] +AA
V.231 their] **ms. reads** thier
  cheres] +AA, **replacing del.** chezes
V.237–38 So . . . her.] +FB
V.241 man] +FB, **replacing del.** ?man
V.254 wish] **del. 2 illegible letters**
V.262 at] +AA
V.264 my dear,] **del. one illegible word**
V.292 'em] +FB
V.297 about in] **del. punctuation** —
V.305 singular!] **del.** ?turning
V.323 paint's] +AA, **replacing del.** ?paints
V.335 fertigued] +FB, **replacing del.** fatigued
V.364 *attract . . . of*] +FB, **replacing del. one illegible word**
V.389 (*aside*)] +FB
V.471 buried] **del. second** r
V.503–504 Calcutta!] +AA, **replacing del.** Bengal!
V.523 own] +AA
V.527 unexpected] **ms. reads** inexpected
V.540 ma'am,] **del.** in
V.590 of your] **del.** desire
V.600 open to] to +AA
V.621 seems so] so +AA
V.658 let] **del.** me
V.660–61 I'm sure . . . say!] +FB
V.679 too] **ms. reads** to
V.684 rather] **del.** ?,
V.698 misapprehension] **ms. reads** mysapprehension
V.725 squealing] **ms. reads** squeling
V.742 look] +AA, **replacing del. one illegible word**
V.764–65 contempt] +FB, **replacing del.** confusion
V.771 I am] **del.** the
V.820 O the Doose!] +FB
V.823 O the Divil!] +FB
V.826 O confounded!] +FB

V.828 O consumed!] +FB
V.853–54 provocation I] **del.** met
V.following 874 *Exeunt*] +AA, **replacing del.** *Exit*
V.875 Generous Eliza!] **del. underline**
V.958 Cleveland] **del.** would
V.972 (*half aside*)] +FB
V.973 (*listening*)] +FB
V.977–78 should say—] **del.** MR TIBBS. Fegs, Tom, if a wife of mine was to [**one illegible word**] me to be sure [**one illegible word**]—(*apart to Mr Watts*) / MR WATTS. [**one illegible line**] / MRS WATTS. Why Tommy, I say—
V.986 City!— O] O +FB, **replacing del. 3 illegible words. The following 9 lines are deleted and illegible.**
V.1001 the] +FB

NOTES

Fanny Burney and the Theatre

1. *The Early Diary of Frances Burney, 1768–78*, ed. Anne Raine Ellis (London: Bell, 1907), 2: 28–31. Subsequently referred to as *ED*.

2. *ED*, 1: 163–64.

3. *ED*, 1: 186.

4. *ED*, 1: 199.

5. *ED*, 1: 265.

6. *ED*, 1: 111–12. George Colman the Elder (1732–94) was a popular dramatist whose works include *A Clandestine Marriage* (with Garrick) and *The English Merchant*.

7. See William Younger Fletcher, *English Book Collectors* (New York: Franklin, 1969), 308: "Dr. Burney also amassed from three hundred to four hundred volumes containing materials for a history of the British Stage, and several thousand portraits of literary and theatrical personages. On the death of the Doctor his library was purchased for the British Museum for the sum of thirteen thousand five hundred pounds."

8. See App. V for a list of plays mentioned in Fanny Burney's writings.

9. *ED*, 1: 32.

10. *ED*, 1: 265.

11. *ED*, 1: 200. Her remark shows Fanny Burney's familiarity with Shakespeare's works, for she says "I am sorry that this play is acted with Cibber's alterations, as every line of his, is immediately to be distinguished from Shakespeare." For a discussion of the declining popularity in "improved" Shakespeare in the last half of the eighteenth century, see Christopher Spencer, "Introduction," *Five Restoration Adaptations of Shakespeare* (Urbana: University of Illinois Press, 1965), 1–7.

12. *The Diary and Letters of Madame d'Arblay, 1778–1840*, ed. Charlotte Barrett, with preface and notes by Austin Dobson (London: Macmillan, 1904–05), 1: 288. Subsequently referred to as *DL*.

13. *DL*, 1: 339.

14. *DL*, 1: 369. Neither Dr. Delap's play nor the Reverend Butt's was performed or published; Fanny Burney had read them both in manuscript. Her judgement of *Timoleon* seems to have been justified, for although Butt was eager to stage it, "by the opinion of Mr. Garrick, it was not put into perfor-

mance": David Erskine Baker, *Biographia Dramatica* (London: Longmans, Hurst, Rees, Orme, and Brown, 1812), 1: 80.

15. *DL*, 1: 450.
16. *DL*, 4: 47.
17. *DL*, 4: 54.
18. *DL*, 4: 361.
19. *DL*, 3: 401–02.
20. *The Journals and Letters of Fanny Burney (Madame d'Arblay)*, ed. Joyce Hemlow et al. (Oxford: Clarendon, 1972–82), 4: 29. Subsequently referred to as *JL*.
21. *ED*, 1: 57.
22. *ED*, 1: 191.
23. Ellis notes that "no single play is so often quoted throughout the early, and later Diaries, and letters, of Fanny Burney, as that highly successful comedy": *ED*, 1: 68 n 1.
24. *ED*, 1: 104.
25. *ED*, 1: 129.
26. *ED*, 1: 130.
27. *ED*, 2: 167.
28. *ED*, 2: 177.
29. *ED*, 2: 179.
30. Frances Burney, *Evelina; or, The History of a Young Lady's Entrance into the World*, ed. Edward A. Bloom (London: Oxford University Press, 1968), 25, 78, 82, 188, 352.
31. Frances Burney, *Cecilia; or, Memoirs of an Heiress* (London: Bell, 1904), 1: 261.
32. Frances Burney, *Camilla; or, A Picture of Youth*, ed. Edward A. Bloom and Lillian D. Bloom (New York: Oxford University Press, 1972), 318.
33. See Thomas Babington Macaulay, "Madame d'Arblay," *Critical, Historical and Miscellaneous Essays and Poems*, 3 vols. (New York: Burt, 1880); Will Taliaferro Hale, "Madame d'Arblay's Place in the Development of the English Novel," *Indiana University Studies* 3 (January 1916), Study no. 28; Eugene White, *Fanny Burney, Novelist: A Study in Technique. Evelina, Cecilia, Camilla, the Wanderer* (Hamden, Conn.: Shoe String, 1960); Michael E. Adelstein, *Fanny Burney* (New York: Twayne, 1968).
34. Marjorie Lee Morrison, "Fanny Burney and the Theatre," Ph.D. diss., University of Texas, 1957; Elizabeth Yost Mulliken, "The Influence of the Drama on Fanny Burney's Novels," Ph.D. diss., University of Wisconsin, 1969. Both dissertations emphasize the light the plays shed on Fanny Burney's novelistic techniques.
35. See, e.g., Adelstein, *Fanny Burney*, 152.
36. *ED*, 2: 104.
37. *ED*, 2: 103–4. A comparison with two contemporary diarists points up Fanny Burney's special skills as a diarist. Mrs. Piozzi's *Thraliana* reflects

more than it records, and conversations are rephrased and interpreted rather than reported. Boswell, whose *London Journal* provides vivid details of eighteenth-century London, emphasizes the self-analytical aspect of diaries: "A man cannot know himself better than by attending to the feelings of his heart and to his external actions, from which he may with tolerable certainty judge 'what manner of person he is.' I have therefore determined to keep a daily journal": James Boswell, *Boswell's London Journal, 1762–1763*, ed. Frederick A. Pottle (New York: McGraw-Hill, 1950), 39. Fanny, who is less reflective than Mrs. Thrale and less self-conscious than Boswell, provides us with amusing and revealing dialogue with relatively little intrusion of self.

38. Joyce Hemlow, *The History of Fanny Burney* (Oxford: Clarendon, 1958), 259.

39. The successes of such female playwrights as Aphra Behn (?1640–89) and Susannah Centlivre (1667–1723) would not have encouraged Fanny Burney, since both these ladies had led lives that were hardly respectable and wrote plays which would undoubtedly have shocked her. Mrs. Frances Sheridan (1724–66) could have been a more encouraging example in terms of propriety of behaviour, but her intimacy with the stage was far longer and more professional than was Fanny Burney's.

40. *DL*, 1: 53.

41. See Hemlow, *History*, 105–38.

42. *DL*, 1: 148.

43. By 1778, Richard Brinsley Sheridan (1751–1816) was not only part owner and manager of Drury Lane Theatre but also the author of three very successful plays: *The Rivals* (1775), *The Duenna* (1775), and *The School for Scandal*, which began its long run on 8 May 1778. Arthur Murphy (1727–1805) began as an actor at Covent Garden in 1754 but gave up performing after two years and began to write a series of popular comedies, including *The Way to Keep Him* (1760), *The Citizen* (1763), and *Three Weeks after Marriage* (1776).

44. *DL*, 1: 149–50.

45. *DL*, 1: 205.

46. *DL*, 1: 85.

47. *DL*, 1: 118.

48. *DL*, 1: 185.

49. *DL*, 1: 90.

50. *DL*, 1: 115.

51. Hemlow, *History*, 133. Although the idea for *The Witlings* may have come from observation, it is likely that there were literary influences at work as well. There are some parallels between *The Witlings* and Molière's *Les femmes savantes*, especially in the characters of Lady Smatter and Dabler, who resemble Philamente and M. Trissolin. Dabler, of course, has other parallels as well—Bayes of *The Rehearsal* and Sir Fretful Plagiary of *The Critic*.

52. *DL*, 1: 207–09, 259–61.

53. "The Witlings," act II, 28–29, Berg Collection, New York Public Library.

54. Ibid., 67.

55. *DL*, 1: 260.

56. *DL*, 1: 256.

57. *DL*, 4: 118.

58. *DL*, 4: 118, 362.

59. Hemlow, *History*, 219.

60. Joyce Hemlow, "Fanny Burney: Playwright," *University of Toronto Quarterly* 19 (1949–50): 176.

61. Hester Lynch Piozzi, *Thraliana: The Diary of Mrs. Hester Lynch Thrale (later Mrs. Piozzi)*, ed. Katharine C. Balderston (Oxford: Clarendon, 1942), 2: 916. Mrs. Thrale's judgement was shared by Mrs. Siddons, who had played Elgiva and who wrote: "Oh there never was so wretched a thing as Mrs. D'Arblay's Tragedy. . . . The Audience was quite Angelic and only laughed where it was *impossible* to avoid it": Miriam Benkovitz, "Introduction," *Edwy and Elgiva* (Hamden, Conn.: Shoe String, 1957), xi.

62. *JL*, 3: 99.

63. *JL*, 4: 65.

64. "Love and Fashion," act V, sc. iii, p. 203, Berg Collection, New York Public Library.

65. *JL*, 4: 477.

66. Adelstein (*Fanny Burney*) attributes the deterioration of the quality of the novels to Fanny Burney's lack of critical judgement and to her "turning from satirical to serious fiction, and from writing about the world that she knew to a world beyond her" (p. 148). White (*Fanny Burney, Novelist*) adds: "Her years at court, her acclaim as an author, her developing consciousness of the instructional function of the novel, her experiences in Revolutionary France all had their effect in changing her outlook. She affected a style or unconsciously adopted one that retained and exaggerated all that was bad in her early writing and lost much of what had given it originality and freshness" (p. 3). A recent article on the subject explores the connection between Fanny Burney's psychological difficulties and her loss of the "creative spark": Lillian D. Bloom and Edward A. Bloom, "Fanny Burney's Novels: The Retreat from Wonder," *Novel: A Forum on Fiction* 12 (Spring 1979): 215–33.

67. Hemlow, "Playwright," 189.

68. See Robertson Davies, "Playwrights and Plays," in *The Revels History of Drama in English*, ed. Clifford Leach and T. W. Craik (London: Methuen, 1975–78), 6: 209–12. Davies points out that the popular taste at this time ran to adaptations from poetry and to extravaganza and pantomime.

69. Hemlow, *History*, 312.

Staging *A Busy Day*

1. See Michael R. Booth, "Public Taste, the Playwright and the Law," in *The Revels History of Drama in English*, ed. Clifford Leach and T. W. Craik (London: Methuen, 1975–1978), 6: 41.

2. Frederick Reynolds, *The Life and Times of Frederick Reynolds. Written by Himself*, 2d ed. (London: Henry Colburn, 1827), 2: 230.

3. See "Persons of the Drama."

4. Thomas Dutton, *The Dramatic Censor; or, Weekly Theatrical Report* (London: Roach and Chapple, 1800), 2: 304.

5. See "Fanny Burney and the Theatre," pp. 158–59.

6. Reynolds, *Life and Times*, 2: 126.

7. *A Statement of Differences Subsisting between the Proprietors and Performers of the Theatre-Royal, Covent Garden* (London: Willes, 1800). The dispute involved the right of the actors to free passes to plays, the raising of the amount paid by actors to the management for benefit nights, and the fine levied on actors for refusing to take a part. The lord chamberlain supported Thomas Harris on all counts.

8. See pp. 157–58.

9. See C. A. G. Goede, *The Stranger in England; or, Travels in Great Britain* (London: Matthews and Leigh, 1807), 2: 260.

10. Leo Hughes, *The Drama's Patrons: A Study of the Eighteenth-century London Audience* (Austin: University of Texas Press, 1971), 155.

11. Charles Beecher Hogan, "Introduction," to Part 5, "1776–1800," in Arthur Scouten et al., eds., *The London Stage, 1660–1800* (Carbondale: Southern Illinois University Press, 1968), 1: ccix.

12. Michael R. Booth, "Introduction," *English Plays of the Nineteenth Century* (Oxford: Clarendon, 1973), 1: 1.

13. Frances Burney, *Cecilia; or, Memoirs of an Heiress* (London: Bell, 1904), 1: 129.

14. Hogan, "Introduction," xxxi.

15. James J. Lynch, *Box, Pit and Gallery: Stage and Society in Johnson's London* (New York: Russell and Russell, 1953), 201–3.

16. Thomas Holcroft, *The Theatrical Recorder* (New York: Burt Franklin, 1968), 1: 415.

17. Dutton, *Dramatic Censor*, 1: 268.

18. Goede, *Stranger in England*, 2: 253–54.

19. Frederick Marker and Lisa-Lone Marker, in *Revels*, 6: 98; also 97 nn 29, 30.

20. Hogan, "Introduction," xliii.

21. Richard Brinsley Peake, *Memoirs of the Colman Family* (London: Richard Bentley, 1841), 225.

22. Marker and Marker, in *Revels*, 6: 118.

23. Ibid., 116.

24. William Hazlitt, *The Complete Works*, ed. P. P. Howe (London: Dent, 1930–34), 18: 229.

25. Dutton, *Dramatic Censor*, 2: 237–38.

26. W. C. Oulton, *A History of the Theatres of London* (London: Chapple and Simpkin and Marshall, 1818), 2: 26.

27. *The Dictionary of National Biography*, ed. Leslie Stephen and Sir Sidney Lee (London: Oxford University Press, 1917–50), 16: 129. (Hereafter *DNB*.) See also *London Stage*, Part 5, 1: 1039, 3: 2044.

28. See cast lists of these plays in Mrs. Elizabeth Inchbald, ed., *The Modern Theatre: A Collection of Successful Modern Plays, as Acted at the Theatres Royal, London* (London: Longmans, Hurst, Rees, Orme, and Brown, 1811); *The Dramatic Works of George Colman* (London: Becket, 1777); *Bell's British Theatre* (London: Cawthorn, British Library, 1797). See also *London Stage*, Part 5, 3: 2056, 2044, 1039, 2044, 2056, 2111, 2029.

29. Leigh Hunt, who saw Lewis act when the player was fifty-seven years old, said, "It must however be universally surprising that of the only two actors on the stage who can represent the careless vivacity of youth [Ellison and Lewis] an old man is the most lively": *Critical Essays on the Performers of the London Theatres* (London: John Hunt, 1807), 74.

30. Dutton, *Dramatic Censor*, 2: 237.

31. I am grateful to Professor Philip Highfill for allowing me access to the unpublished notes towards *A Biographical Dictionary of Actors, Actresses, Musicians, Dancers, Managers and Other Stage Personnel in London, 1660–1800*, being published by Southern Illinois University Press.

32. *DNB*, 13: 1195–98.

33. *Leigh Hunt's Dramatic Criticism, 1808–1831*, ed. Lawrence Huston Houtchens and Carolyn Washburn Houtchens (New York: Columbia University Press, 1949), 101.

34. *The Works of Charles and Mary Lamb*, ed. E. V. Lucas, (London: Methuen, 1903), 2: 148.

35. *Hunt's Dramatic Criticism*, 102.

36. *DNB*, 6: 1122–23.

37. *DNB*, 13: 72–74. A contemporary critic, quoted in the notes for *A Biographical Dictionary*, condemns her "drawling accents," "glares in her eyes," and "false ambition to appear well bred"; these are all idiosyncracies which fit the role of Lady Wilhelmina.

38. *A Biographical Dictionary of Actors, Actresses, Musicians, Dancers, Managers and Other Stage Personnel in London, 1660–1800*, ed. Philip Highfill, Kalman A. Burnim, and Edward A. Langhans (Carbondale: Southern Illinois University Press, 1973–80), 4: 191–93.

39. *Hunt's Dramatic Criticism*, 90. Highfill adds that Mrs. Davenport never had to descend to second-rate parts because "her mastery of the mannerisms of loquacious underlings, affected social climbers, tedious grandams, and a whole group of the elderly odd fish beloved of English audiences kept her securely a favorite": *A Biographical Dictionary*, 4: 192.

40. Hogan, "Introduction," cliii–cliv.
41. *The Dramatic Works of Richard Brinsley Sheridan*, ed. Cecil Price (Oxford: Clarendon, 1973), 1: 349–50.
42. George Colman the Younger, *The Heir at Law*, in *The British Theatre*, ed. Mrs. [Elizabeth] Inchbald (London: Longmans, Hurst, Rees, and Orme, 1808), 21: 11, 13.
43. General John Burgoyne, *The Heiress*, in *British Theatre*, ed. Inchbald, 22: 39, 7.
44. Sheridan, *Dramatic Works*, 1: 84.
45. Hogan, "Introduction," lxix.
46. Sheridan, *Dramatic Works*, 1: 421.
47. Burgoyne, *Heiress*, 30.
48. See Richard Southern, "Theatres and Stages," *Revels*, 6: 70.
49. Hogan, "Introduction," lix.
50. Ibid., lxv–lxvi.
51. A random sampling of other plays shows that Fanny Burney does indeed include more exits and entrances than other dramatists of the time: Murphy's *Citizen* (1763) has 28; Colman and Garrick's *Clandestine Marriage* (1766) has 81; Kelly's *False Delicacy* (1768) has 47; and Cumberland's *West Indian* (1771) has 88.
52. Holcroft, *Theatrical Recorder*, 1: 339–40.

Description of the Manuscript

1. Joyce Hemlow, *The History of Fanny Burney* (Oxford: Clarendon, 1958), 300 n 3.
2. Philip Gaskell, *A New Introduction to Bibliography* (Oxford: Clarendon, 1972).

Editorial Changes

1. *JL*, 1: xl.
2. Thomas Holcroft, *Anna St. Ives*, ed. Peter Faulkner (London: Oxford University Press, 1970), 19 n.
3. Michael Millgate, "The Making and Unmaking of Hardy's Wessex Edition," in *Editing Nineteenth-century Fiction*, Papers given at the thirteenth annual Conference on Editorial Problems, University of Toronto, 4–5 November 1977, ed. Jane Millgate (New York: Garland, 1978), 79–80.
4. Laurence Sterne, *A Sentimental Journey through France and Italy, by Mr. Yorick*, ed. Gardner D. Stout, Jr. (Berkeley and Los Angeles: University of California Press, 1967), 54. Sterne commands the printer of *Political Romance*: "do not presume to alter or transpose one Word, or rectify one false Spelling, nor so much as add or diminish one Comma or Tittle."

PLAYS SEEN OR READ BY FANNY BURNEY

The following list of plays has been culled from the *Early Diaries*, the *Diaries and Letters*, and the *Journals and Letters* of Fanny Burney as well as from the files in the Burney Room at McGill University, Montreal. The list undoubtedly does not include all plays that Fanny Burney saw or read, since there must have been ones she did not mention. Presumably, she read more of Shakespeare's works than is indicated here, and her knowledge of contemporary drama may have been wider than is suggested by this list. Dates given are dates of first performance or first edition.

Addison, Joseph. *Cato*. 1713.
———. *The Drummer; or, The Haunted House*. 1716.
———. *Rosamond*. 1707.
Artois, François-Victor-Armand d', and Jean-Henri Dupin. *La belle Allemande*. 1812.
Baillie, Joanna. *The Country Inn: A Comedy*. 1804.
———. *De Montfort: A Tragedy*. 1798.
———. *The Tryal: A Comedy*. 1798.
Bickerstaffe, Isaac. *Lionel and Clarissa*. 1768.
———. *The Padlock: A Comic Opera*. 1768.
Bickerstaffe, Isaac, and Samuel Foote. *Dr. Last in His Chariot*. 1769.
Brueys, David-Augustin de. *L'avocat Patelin, comédie*. 1706.
———. *Le grondeur, comédie*. 1691.
Burges, Sir James Bland. *Riches; or, The Wife and Brother*. 1810.
———. *Tricks upon Travellers*. 1810.
Butt, George. *Timoleon* (not printed or acted).
Capelle, Pierre, and Louis Mézières. *Journée aux aventures*. 1816.
Carey, Henry. *Chrononhotonthologos*. 1734.
———. *The Contrivances; or, More Ways than One*. 1715.
———. *The Dragon of Wantley: A Burlesque Opera*. 1740.
Charagnac, Michel-Joseph-Gentil de, and Mare-Antoine-Madeleine Desangiers. *Je fais mes farces*. 1815.
Chateaubriand, François-René de. *Atala, ou les amours de deux sauvages dans le désert*. 1801.

———. *Les martyrs*. 1809.
Cibber, Colley. *The Careless Husband*. 1704.
———. *The Tragical History of King Richard III*. 1700.
Cobb, James. *Doctor and Apothecary*. 1788.
———. *The Humourist*. 1785; (not printed).
Coffey, Charles. *The Devil to Pay; or, The Wives Metamorphosed. A Ballad Farce*. 1731.
Collier, Sir George, and Thomas Linley. *Selima and Azor*. 1776.
Colman, George, the Elder. *The Clandestine Marriage*. 1766.
———. *The Deuce Is in Him*. 1763.
———. *The English Merchant*. 1767.
———. *The Man of Business*. 1774.
———. *The Occasional Prelude*. 1776.
———. *Polly Honeycomb*. 1760.
Colman, George, the Elder, and David Garrick. *The Jealous Wife*. 1761.
———. *The Musical Lady*. 1762.
Colman, George, the Younger. *The Heir at Law*. 1797.
———. *The Iron Chest*. 1796.
Corneille, Pierre. *Rodogune*. 1645.
Cowley, Hannah. *The Belle's Stratagem*. 1780.
———. *Who's the Dupe?* 1778.
Crisp, Henry. *Virginia*. 1754.
Cumberland, Richard. *The West Indian*. 1771.
Dalayrac, Nicolas. *Maison à vendre*. 1800.
Delap, John. *The Captives*. 1786.
———. *The Royal Suppliants*. 1781.
Desmoustier, Charles-Albert. *Les femmes*. 1793.
Destouches, Philippe. *La fausse Agnès*. 1716.
———. *L'irrésolu*. 1713.
Duval, Georges-Louis-Jacques. *Une journée à Versailles, ou le discret malgré lui*. 1814.
———. *La maison à vendre*. 1819.
Farquhar, Sir George. *Sir Harry Wildair*. 1701.
Fielding, Henry. *The Mock Doctor; or, The Dumb Lady Cured*. 1732.
———. *Pasquin*, 1736.
———. *Tom Thumb; or, The Tragedy of Tragedies*. 1730.
Fontenelle, Bernard Le Bovier de. *Abdolonime*. 1751.
Foote, Samuel. *The Commissary*. 1765.
———. *The Devil upon Two Sticks*. 1768.
———. *Handsome Housemaid; or, Piety in Pattens*. 1773.
———. *The Minor*. 1760.
Garrick, David. *Bucks, Have at Ye All; or, The Picture of a Playhouse*. 1784.
———. *The Country Girl*. 1766.

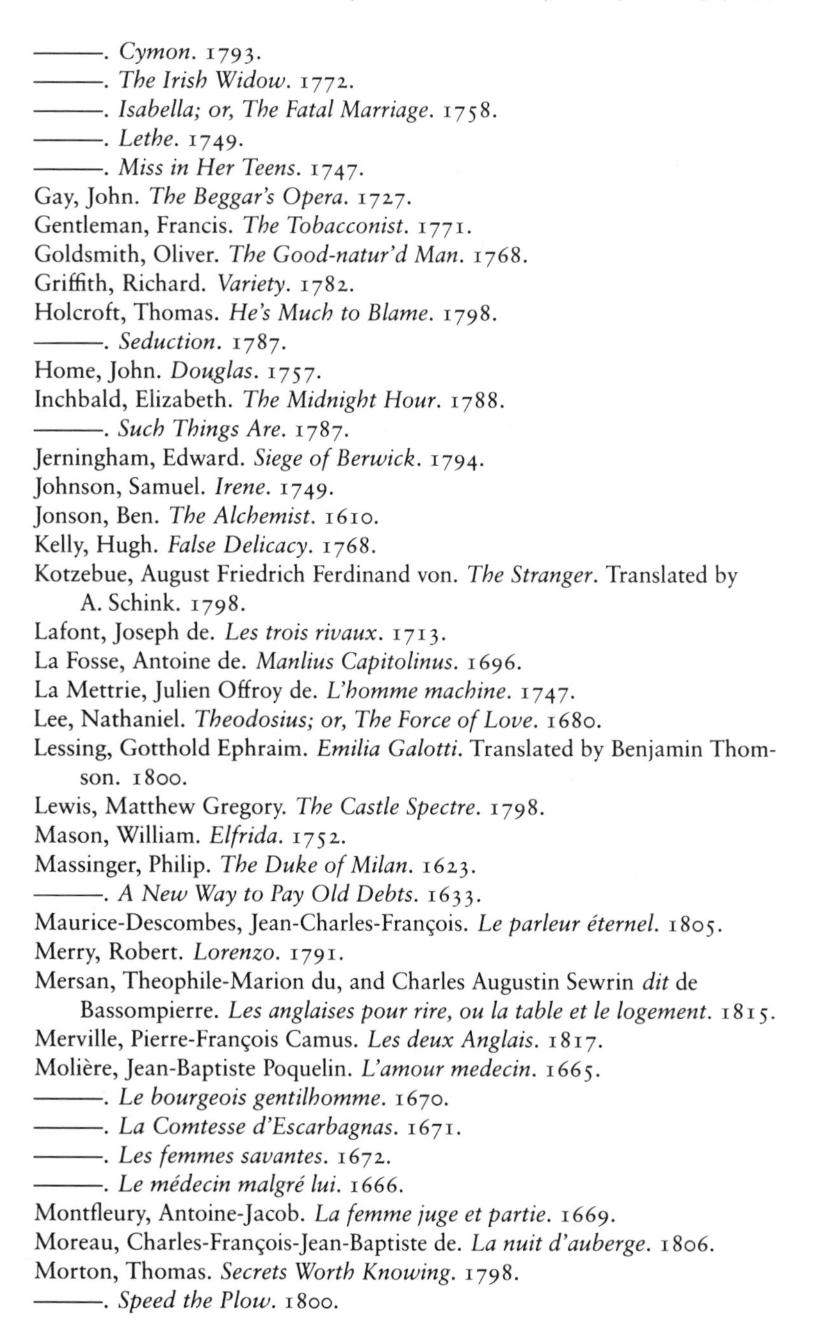

———. *Cymon.* 1793.
———. *The Irish Widow.* 1772.
———. *Isabella; or, The Fatal Marriage.* 1758.
———. *Lethe.* 1749.
———. *Miss in Her Teens.* 1747.
Gay, John. *The Beggar's Opera.* 1727.
Gentleman, Francis. *The Tobacconist.* 1771.
Goldsmith, Oliver. *The Good-natur'd Man.* 1768.
Griffith, Richard. *Variety.* 1782.
Holcroft, Thomas. *He's Much to Blame.* 1798.
———. *Seduction.* 1787.
Home, John. *Douglas.* 1757.
Inchbald, Elizabeth. *The Midnight Hour.* 1788.
———. *Such Things Are.* 1787.
Jerningham, Edward. *Siege of Berwick.* 1794.
Johnson, Samuel. *Irene.* 1749.
Jonson, Ben. *The Alchemist.* 1610.
Kelly, Hugh. *False Delicacy.* 1768.
Kotzebue, August Friedrich Ferdinand von. *The Stranger.* Translated by A. Schink. 1798.
Lafont, Joseph de. *Les trois rivaux.* 1713.
La Fosse, Antoine de. *Manlius Capitolinus.* 1696.
La Mettrie, Julien Offroy de. *L'homme machine.* 1747.
Lee, Nathaniel. *Theodosius; or, The Force of Love.* 1680.
Lessing, Gotthold Ephraim. *Emilia Galotti.* Translated by Benjamin Thomson. 1800.
Lewis, Matthew Gregory. *The Castle Spectre.* 1798.
Mason, William. *Elfrida.* 1752.
Massinger, Philip. *The Duke of Milan.* 1623.
———. *A New Way to Pay Old Debts.* 1633.
Maurice-Descombes, Jean-Charles-François. *Le parleur éternel.* 1805.
Merry, Robert. *Lorenzo.* 1791.
Mersan, Theophile-Marion du, and Charles Augustin Sewrin *dit* de Bassompierre. *Les anglaises pour rire, ou la table et le logement.* 1815.
Merville, Pierre-François Camus. *Les deux Anglais.* 1817.
Molière, Jean-Baptiste Poquelin. *L'amour medecin.* 1665.
———. *Le bourgeois gentilhomme.* 1670.
———. *La Comtesse d'Escarbagnas.* 1671.
———. *Les femmes savantes.* 1672.
———. *Le médecin malgré lui.* 1666.
Montfleury, Antoine-Jacob. *La femme juge et partie.* 1669.
Moreau, Charles-François-Jean-Baptiste de. *La nuit d'auberge.* 1806.
Morton, Thomas. *Secrets Worth Knowing.* 1798.
———. *Speed the Plow.* 1800.

Mulso, Thomas. *Callistus; or, The Man of Fashion and Sephronius; or, The Country Gentleman*. 1768.
Murphy, Arthur. *All in the Wrong*. 1761.
———. *The Citizen*. 1761.
———. *The Grecian Daughter*. 1772.
———. *Know Your Own Mind*. 1777.
———. *The Orphan of China*. 1759.
———. *The Upholsterer; or, What News?* 1758.
———. *The Way to Keep Him*. 1760.
Noue, J. B. de la. *La coquette corrigée*. 1756.
O'Brien, William. *Cross Purposes*. 1772.
O'Hara, Kane. *Two Misers*. 1775.
O'Keeffe, John. *Agreeable Surprise*. 1781.
Otway, Thomas. *Venice Preserved*. 1680.
Perrault, Charles. *La belle au bois dormant*. 1697.
Picard, Louis Benoît. *Médiocre et rampant*. 1796.
Racine, Jean. *Andromaque*. 1667.
———. *Athalie*. 1691.
———. *Bérénice*. 1670.
———. *Britannicus*. 1669.
———. *Esther*. 1689.
———. *Mithridate*. 1673.
Reynolds, Frederick. *Cheap Living*. 1797.
———. *The Dramatist; or, Stop Him Who Can*. 1789.
Richardson, Elizabeth. *The Double Deception*. 1778.
Rousseau, Jean-Jacques. *Le devin du village*. 1753.
Rowe, Nicholas. *Tamerlane*. 1701.
Royou, Jacques-Corentin. *Phocion*. 1817.
Sarti, Giuseppe. *Le nozze de Dorina*. 1789.
Saurin, Bernard-Joseph. *Le mariage de Julie*. 1772.
Scribe, Augustin-Eugène, and Charles-François-Jean-Baptiste de Moreau de Commagny. *Deux précepteurs*. 1828.
Scribe, Augustin-Eugène, and Charles-Gaspard Delestre-Poirson. *Le Comte d'Ory*. 1816.
Scribe, Augustin-Eugène, and Désaugiers, Marc Antoine Madeleine. *Tous les vaudevilles, ou chacun chez soi*. 1817.
Scribe, Augustin-Eugène, and Jean-Henri Dupin. *Combat de Montagnes, ou la folie beaujou*. 1817.
Sewrin, Charles Augustin *dit* de Bassompierre. *Les petits marionettes, ou la loterie*. 1815.
Shakespeare, William. *As You Like It*. 1598.
———. *Comedy of Errors*. 1590.
———. *Coriolanus*. 1608.
———. *First Part of Henry IV*. 1597.

———. *Hamlet.* 1601.
———. *Julius Caesar.* 1599.
———. *King John.* 1594.
———. *King Lear.* 1605.
———. *Macbeth.* 1605.
———. *Merchant of Venice.* 1597.
———. *Midsummer Night's Dream.* 1595.
———. *Much Ado about Nothing.* 1599.
———. *Othello.* 1604.
———. *The Tempest.* 1611.
———. *Twelfth Night.* 1600.
Sheridan, Mrs. Frances. *The Discovery.* 1763.
Sheridan, Richard Brinsley. *The Critic.* 1779.
———. *Pizzaro.* 1799.
———. *The Rivals.* 1775.
———. *The School for Scandal.* 1777.
———. *A Trip to Scarborough.* 1777.
Southerne, Thomas. *Isabella; or, The Fatal Marriage.* 1694.
Steele, Sir Richard. *The Lying Lover; or, The Ladies' Friendship.* 1703.
Thompson, Benjamin. *The Stranger.* 1798.
Townley, James. *High Life below Stairs.* 1759.
Vanbrugh, Sir John. *The Relapse.* 1696.
Vanbrugh, Sir John, and Colley Cibber. *The Provoked Husband; or, A Journey to London.* 1728.
Villiers, George, 2d duke of Buckingham. *The Rehearsal.* 1671.
Voltaire (François Marie Arouet). *L'ecossaise.* 1760.
———. *Mort de César.* 1794.
———. *Tancrède.* 1760.
———. *Zaïre.* 1732.
Walpole, Horace. *The Mysterious Mother.* 1768.
Webster, John. *Appius and Virginia.* 1625–30.

SELECTED BIBLIOGRAPHY

Addison, Joseph, and Richard Steele. *The Spectator*. Edited by Donald F. Bond. 5 vols. Oxford: Clarendon, 1965.

Adelstein, Michael E. *Fanny Burney*. New York: Twayne, 1968.

Altick, Richard D. *The Shows of London*. Cambridge, Mass.: Harvard University Press, 1978.

Arnold, Janet. *Perukes and Periwigs*. London: Her Majesty's Stationery Office, 1970.

Austen, Jane. *The Novels of Jane Austen*. Edited by R. W. Chapman. 5 vols. 3d ed. London: Oxford University Press, 1932–34.

Baird, John D., ed. *Editing Texts of the Romantic Period*. Papers given at the seventh annual Conference on Editorial Problems, University of Toronto, November 1971. Toronto: Committee for the Conference on Editorial Problems, 1972.

Baker, David Erskine. *Biographia Dramatica*. 4 vols. London: Longmans, Hurst, Rees, Orme, and Brown, 1812.

Baker, Henry B. *History of the London Stage and Its Famous Players (1576–1903)*. London: Routledge, 1904.

Bateson, F. W. *English Comic Drama, 1700–1750*. Oxford: Clarendon, 1929.

Bayne-Powell, Rosamond. *Eighteenth-century London Life*. New York: Dutton, 1938.

Benkovitz, Miriam. "Dr. Burney's *Memoirs*." *Review of English Studies* 10 (1959): 257–68.

Bernbaum, Ernest. *The Drama of Sensibility: A Sketch of the History of English Sentimental Comedy and Domestic Tragedy, 1696–1780*. Boston: Ginn, 1915.

Besant, Sir Walter. *London in the Eighteenth Century*. London: Black, 1902.

Bevis, Richard W., ed. and introd. by. *Eighteenth-century Drama: Afterpieces*. London: Oxford University Press, 1970.

A Biographical Dictionary of Actors, Actresses, Musicians, Dancers, Managers and Other Stage Personnel in London, 1660–1800. Edited by

Philip D. Highfill, Kalman A. Burnim, and Edward A. Langhans. 6 vols. Carbondale: Southern Illinois University Press, 1973–80.

Bloom, Lillian D., and Edward A. Bloom. "Fanny Burney's Novels: The Retreat from Wonder." *Novel: A Forum on Fiction* 12 (Spring 1979): 215–33.

Boaden, James. *Memoirs of Mrs. Siddons*. London: Gibbings, 1893.

———. *Memoirs of the Life of John Philip Kemble*. 2 vols. London: Longmans, Hurst, Rees, Orme, Brown, and Green, 1825.

Booth, Michael R., ed. *English Plays of the Nineteenth Century*. 4 vols. Oxford: Clarendon, 1973.

Boswell, James. *Boswell's London Journal, 1762–1763*. Edited by Frederick A. Pottle. New York: McGraw-Hill, 1950.

———. *Life of Johnson, Including Boswell's Journal of a Tour to the Hebrides and Johnson's Diary of a Journey into North Wales*. Edited by George Birkbeck Hill. 6 vols. Oxford: Clarendon, 1887.

Brewer's Dictionary of Phrase and Fable. Rev. ed. London: Cassell, 1959.

Burgoyne, General John. *The Heiress*. In Inchbald, *British Theatre* vol. 22.

Burney, Frances. *Camilla; or, A Picture of Youth*. Edited by Edward A. Bloom and Lillian D. Bloom. New York: Oxford University Press, 1972.

———. *Cecilia; or, Memoirs of an Heiress*. 2 vols. London: Bell, 1904.

———. *The Diary and Letters of Madame d'Arblay, 1778–1840*. Edited by Charlotte Barrett, with preface and notes by Austin Dobson. 6 vols. London: Macmillan, 1904–5.

———. *The Early Diary of Frances Burney, 1768–78*. Edited by Annie Raine Ellis. 2 vols. London: Bell, 1907.

———. *Edwy and Elgiva*. Edited by Miriam J. Benkovitz. Hamden, Conn.: Shoestring, 1957.

———. *Evelina; or, The History of a Young Lady's Entrance into the World*. Edited by Edward A. Bloom. London: Oxford University Press, 1968.

———. *The Journals and Letters of Fanny Burney (Madame d'Arblay)*. Edited by Joyce Hemlow, et al. 10 vols. Oxford: Clarendon, 1972–82.

———. Manuscripts of unpublished plays in the Berg Collection of the New York Public Library:
"The Witlings"
"Edwy and Elgiva"
"Elberta"
"Hubert De Vere"
"The Siege of Pevensy"
"A Busy Day"
"Love and Fashion"
"The Woman-Hater"

———. *Memoirs of Doctor Burney*. 3 vols. London: Moxon, 1832.

———. *The Wanderer; or, Female Difficulties.* 5 vols. London: Longmans, 1814.

Byrd, Max. *London Transformed: Images of the City in the Eighteenth Century.* New Haven, Conn.: Yale University Press, 1978.

Campbell, Thomas. *Life of Mrs. Siddons.* 2 vols. London: Wilson, 1834.

Chamberlin, E. R. *Guildford: A Biography.* London: Macmillan, 1970.

Churchill, W. A. *Watermarks in Paper in Holland, England, France etc., in the XVII and XVIII Centuries and Their Interconnection.* Amsterdam: Hertzberger, 1965.

Cibber, Colley. *An Apology for the Life of Mr. Colley Cibber, Comedian, and Late Patentee of the Theatre-Royal. With an Historical View of the Stage during His Own Time. Written by Himself.* London: John Watts, 1740.

Collier, Jeremy. *A Short View of the Immorality and Profaneness of the English Stage.* Edited by Arthur Freeman. Facsimile of 1698 ed. New York: Garland, 1972.

Colman, George [the elder]. *The Dramatic Works of George Colman.* 4 vols. London: Becket, 1777.

Connolly, L. W. *The Censorship of English Drama, 1737–1824.* San Marino, Calif.: Huntington Library, 1976.

Connolly, L. W., and J. P. Wearing. *English Drama and Theatre, 1800–1900: A Guide to Information Sources.* American Literature, English Literature, and World Literatures in English Information Guide Series, vol. 12. Detroit: Gale Research, 1978.

Copeland, Edward G. "Money in the Novels of Fanny Burney." *Studies in the Novel* 8 (1976): 24–37.

Cowley, Hannah. *Who's the Dupe?* In Inchbald, *Collection of Farces* vol. 1.

Cox, James E. *The Rise of Sentimental Comedy.* Springfield, Mo.: Author, 1926.

Crane, Ronald S. "Suggestions toward a Genealogy of 'The Man of Feeling.'" *ELH* 1 (1934): 205–30.

Cumberland, Richard. *The West Indian: A Comedy. As It Is Performed at the Theatre Royal in Drury Lane.* London: Griffin, 1771.

Cunningham, George H. *London: Being a Comprehensive Survey of the History, Tradition and Historical Associations of Buildings and Monuments Arranged under Streets in Alphabetical Order.* London: Dent, 1927.

Dennis, John. *The Critical Works.* Edited by Edward Niles Hooker. 2 vols. Baltimore: Johns Hopkins University Press, 1939.

The Dictionary of National Biography. Edited by Leslie Stephen and Sir Sidney Lee. 22 vols. London: Oxford University Press, 1917–50.

Dobson, Austin. *Fanny Burney.* London: Macmillan, 1904.

Donohue, Joseph W., Jr. *Dramatic Character in the English Romantic Age.* Princeton, N.J.: Princeton University Press, 1970.

Dowling, S. W. *The Exchanges of London*. London: Butterworth, 1929.

Downer, Alan S. "Nature to Advantage Dressed: Eighteenth-century Acting." *PMLA* 58 (1943): 1002–37.

Draper, John W. "The Theory of the Comic in Eighteenth-century England." *Journal of English and German Philology* 37 (April 1938): 207–23.

Dutton, Thomas. *The Dramatic Censor; or, Weekly Theatrical Report. Comprising a Complete Chronicle of the British Stage, and a Regular Series of Theatrical Criticism, in Every Department of the Drama*. 4 vols. London: Roach and Chapple, 1800.

Ehrlich, Blake. *London on the Thames*. Boston: Little, Brown, 1966.

The English Dialect Dictionary. Edited by Joseph Wright. London: Oxford University Press, 1961.

Erickson, James P. "*Evelina* and *Betsy Thoughtless*." *Texas Studies in Literature and Language* 6 (Spring 1964): 96–103.

Felton, William. *A Treatise on Carriages; Comprehending Coaches, Chariots, Phaetons, Curricles, Gigs, Whiskies, &c. Together with their proper Harness. In Which the Fair Prices of Every Article Are Accurately Stated*. London: Author, 1796.

Firminger, Walter A. "Madame d'Arblay and Calcutta." *Bengal Past and Present* 9 (July–December 1914): 244–49.

Fitzgerald, Percy. *The Kembles: An Account of the Kemble Family*. 2 vols. London: Tinsley, 1969.

Fletcher, Richard M. *English Romantic Drama, 1795–1843: A Critical History*. New York: Exposition, 1966.

Fletcher, William Younger. *English Book Collectors*. 1902. Reprint. New York: Burt Franklin, 1969.

Foote, Samuel. *Devil upon Two Sticks: A Comedy in Three Acts. As It Is Performed at the Theatre-Royal in the Haymarket*. London: Cadell, 1778.

Furneaux, J. H., ed. *India: A Grand Photographic History of the Land of Antiquity, the Vast Empire of the East. . . .* London: International Art, 1896.

Garrick, David. *Letters*. Edited by David Mason Little and George Morrow Kahrl. 3 vols. Cambridge, Mass.: Harvard University Press, Belknap, 1928.

Gaskell, Philip. *A New Introduction to Bibliography*. Oxford: Clarendon, 1972.

Genest, John. *Some Account of the English Stage in 1660–1830*. 10 vols. Bath: Carrington, 1832.

German, Howard Lee. "Fanny Burney and the Late Eighteenth-century Novel." Ph.D. diss., Ohio State University, 1957.

Ghoshal, Tara. "An Introduction to Fanny Burney's Comedies." Master's thesis, University of Toronto, 1975.

Goede, C. A. G. *The Stranger in England; or, Travels in Great Britain.* 3 vols. London: Matthews and Leigh, 1807.

Goldoni, [Carlo]. *Four Comedies.* Translated and introduced by Frederick Davies. Harmondsworth: Penguin, 1968.

———. *Memoirs of Carlo Goldoni, Written by Himself.* Translated from original French by John Black. Edited and introduced by William A. Drake. New York: Knopf, 1926.

Goldsmith, Oliver. *Collected Works of Oliver Goldsmith.* Edited by Arthur Freedman. 5 vols. Oxford: Clarendon, 1966.

———. "Essay on the Theatre; or, A Comparison between Sentimental and Laughing Comedy." *Westminster Magazine*, 1773.

Gould, William, ed. *Lives of the Georgian Age, 1714–1837.* Compiled by Laurence Urdang Associates. New York: Harper and Row, 1978.

Gray, Charles H. *Theatrical Criticism in London to 1795.* Columbia University Studies in English and Comparative Literature, no. 101. 1931. Reprint. New York: Blom, 1971.

The Gray's-Inn Journal. 2 vols. London: Vaillant, 1756.

Hahn, Emily. *A Degree of Prudery: A Biography of Fanny Burney.* Garden City, N.Y.: Doubleday, 1950.

Hale, Will Taliaferro. "Madame d'Arblay's Place in the Development of the English Novel." *Indiana University Studies* 3 (January 1916), study no. 28.

Hazlitt, William. *The Complete Works.* Edited by P. P. Howe, after the edition of A. R. Waller and Arnold Glover. 21 vols. London: Dent, 1930–34.

Heawood, Edward. *Watermarks, Mainly of the 17th and 18th Centuries.* Monumenta Chartae Papyraceae, vol. 1. Hilversum, Holland: Paper Publications Society, 1950.

Hemlow, Joyce. *A Catalogue of the Burney Family Correspondence, 1749–1878.* New York: New York Public Library [1971].

———. "Fanny Burney and the Courtesy Books." *PMLA* 65 (1950): 732–61.

———. "Fanny Burney: Playwright." *University of Toronto Quarterly* 19 (1949–50): 170–89.

———. *The History of Fanny Burney.* Oxford: Clarendon, 1958.

Hibbert, Christopher. *London: The Biography of a City.* London: Longmans, Green, 1969.

Hill, Constance. *Fanny Burney at the Court of Queen Charlotte.* London: John Lane, 1907.

———. *The House in St. Martin's Street.* London: John Lane, 1907.

———. *Juniper Hall.* London: John Lane, 1904.

Hill, Douglas. *A Hundred Years of Georgian London from the Accession of George I to the Heyday of the Regency.* London: Macdonald, 1970.

The History and Description of Guildford, the County-town of Surrey. 2d ed., corrected and enlarged. Guildford: Russell [1800].

Holcroft, Thomas. *Anna St. Ives.* Edited by Peter Faulkner. London: Oxford University Press, 1970.

———. *The Theatrical Recorder.* 2 vols. 1805. Reprint. New York: Burt Franklin, 1968.

Holzman, James M. *The Nabobs in England: A Study of the Returned Anglo-Indian, 1760–1785.* New York: N.p., 1926.

Hughes, Leo. *A Century of English Farce.* Princeton, N.J., Princeton University Press, 1956.

———. *The Drama's Patrons: A Study of the Eighteenth-century London Audience.* Austin: University of Texas Press, 1971.

Hume, Robert D., ed. *The London Theatre World, 1660–1800.* Carbondale: Southern Illinois University Press, 1980.

Hunt, Leigh. *Critical Essays on the Performers of the London Theatres, including General Observations on the Practise and Genius of the Stage.* London: John Hunt, 1807.

———. *Leigh Hunt's Dramatic Criticism, 1808–1831.* Edited by Lawrence Huston Houtchens and Carolyn Washburn Houtchens. New York: Columbia University Press, 1949.

Inchbald, Mrs. [Elizabeth], ed. *The British Theatre; or, A Collection of Plays, Which Are Acted at the Theatres Royal, Drury-Lane, Covent Garden, and Haymarket. Printed under the Authority of the Managers from the Prompt Books.* 25 vols. London: Longmans, Hurst, Rees, and Orme, 1808.

———, ed. *A Collection of Farces and Other Afterpieces.* 7 vols. London: Longmans, Hurst, Rees, Orme, and Brown, 1815.

———, ed. *The Modern Theatre: A Collection of Successful Modern Plays, as Acted at the Theatres Royal, London. Printed from the Prompt Books under the Authority of the Managers.* 10 vols. London: Longmans, Hurst, Rees, Orme, and Brown, 1811.

Jones, Louis C. *The Clubs of the Georgian Rakes.* New York: Columbia University Press, 1942.

Jump, John D. *Burlesque.* London: Methuen, 1972.

Kelly, Hugh. *False Delicacy: A Comedy. As It Is Performed at the Theatre-Royal in Drury Lane. By His Majesty's Servants.* 4th ed. London: Baldwin, Johnston, and Kearsly, 1768.

Kronenberger, Louis. *The Thread of Laughter.* New York: Knopf, 1952.

Krutch, Joseph Wood. *Comedy and Conscience after the Restoration.* New York: Russell and Russell, 1924.

Lamb, Charles, and Mary Lamb. *Elia and the Last Essays of Elia.* Vol. 2 of *The Works of Charles and Mary Lamb.* Edited by E. V. Lucas. 7 vols. London: Methuen, 1903.

Leach, Clifford, and T. W. Craik, eds. *The Revels History of Drama in English*. 6 vols. London: Methuen, 1975–78.

Lewis, Wilmarth Sheldon. *Three Tours through London in the Years 1748, 1776, 1797*. Westport, Conn.: Greenwood, 1971.

Loftis, John. *Comedy and Society from Congreve to Fielding*. Stanford, Calif.: Stanford University Press, 1959.

———. *Sheridan and the Drama of Georgian England*. Cambridge, Mass.: Harvard University Press, 1977.

The London Guide, Describing the Public and Private Buildings of London, Westminster, & Southwark; Embellished with an Exact Plan of the Metropolis, and an Accurate Map Twenty Miles Round. To Which Are Annexed, Several Hundred Hackney Coach Fares, the Rates of Watermen &c. London: Fielding [1782].

The London Stage: A Collection of the Most Reputed Tragedies, Comedies, Operas, Melo-dramas, Farces, and Interludes. Accurately Printed from Acting Copies, as Performed at the Theatres Royal, and Carefully Collated and Revised. 4 vols. London: Sherwood, Jones [1824].

Luton Museum and Art Gallery. *The Turnpike Age*. Luton: Author, 1970.

Lynch, James J. *Box, Pit and Gallery: Stage and Society in Johnson's London*. 1953. Reprint. New York: Russell and Russell, 1971.

Macaulay, Thomas Babington. "Madame d'Arblay," *Critical, Historical and Miscellaneous Essays and Poems*. 3 vols. New York: Burt, 1880.

MacCarthy, Bridget G. *The Female Pen*. New York: Salloch, 1948.

MacMillan, Dougald, and Howard Mumford Jones. *Plays of the Restoration and Eighteenth Century*. New York: Holt, Rinehart and Winston, 1931.

Macqueen Pope, W. J. *Theatre-Royal, Drury Lane*. London: Allen, n.d.

Manvell, Roger. *Sarah Siddons: Portrait of an Actress*. London: Heinemann, 1970.

Margetson, Stella. *Regency London*. New York: Praeger, 1971.

Marshall, Dorothy. *Eighteenth Century England*. London: Longmans, 1962.

———. *English People in the Eighteenth Century*. London: Longmans, Green, 1956.

Melville, Lewis. *More Stage Favourites of the Eighteenth Century*. London: Hutchinson, 1929.

Merchant, W. Moelwyn. *Comedy*. London: Methuen, 1972.

The Microcosm of London; or, London in Miniature. 3 vols. London: Methuen, 1904.

Millgate, Jane, ed. *Editing Nineteenth-century Fiction*. Papers given at the thirteenth annual Conference on Editorial Problems, University of Toronto, 4–5 November 1977. New York: Garland, 1978.

The Modern British Drama. 5 vols. London: William Miller, 1811.

Moler, Kenneth L. "Fanny Burney's *Cecilia* and Jane Austen's *Jack and Alice*." *English Language Notes* 3 (1965–66): 41.

Molière, Jean-Baptiste Poquelin. *The Works of Molière.* 6 vols. London, 1714. Reprint. New York: Blom, 1967.

Montague, Edwine, and Louis L. Martz. "Fanny Burney's *Evelina*." In *The Age of Johnson: Essays Presented to Chauncey Brewster Tinker*, edited by F. W. Hilles. New Haven, Conn.: Yale University Press, 1949.

Moore, John Brooks. *The Comic and the Realistic in English Drama*. Chicago: University of Chicago Press, 1925.

Morley, Edith J. *Fanny Burney*. The English Association, Pamphlet No. 60. London: Oxford University Press, 1925.

Morrison, Marjorie Lee. "Fanny Burney and the Theatre." Ph.D. diss., University of Texas, 1957.

Mulliken, Elizabeth Yost. "The Influence of the Drama on Fanny Burney's Novels." Ph.D. diss., University of Wisconsin, 1969.

Murphy, Arthur. *The Citizen: A Farce. As It Is Performed at the Theatre Royal in Covent Garden*. London: Kearsly, 1763.

Nash, Mary. *The Provoked Wife: The Life and Times of Susannah Cibber*. London: Hutchinson, 1977.

Nettleton, George Henry. *English Drama of the Restoration and Eighteenth Century (1642–1780)*. New York: Macmillan, 1928.

The New English Theatre. 12 vols. London: Rivington, 1777.

Nicoll, Allardyce. *British Drama: An Historical Survey from the Beginnings to the Present Time*. London: Harrap, 1947.

———. *English Drama: A Modern Viewpoint*. London: Harrap, 1968.

———. *A History of English Drama, 1660–1900*. 6 vols. Cambridge: Cambridge University Press, 1952–59.

———. *A History of Late Eighteenth Century Drama, 1750–1800*. Cambridge: Cambridge University Press, 1927.

———. *The Theory of Drama*. London: Harrap, 1931.

O'Brien, William. *Cross Purposes*. In Scouten, Stone, and Hogan, *London Stage*, vol. 4.

O'Keeffe, John, and Samuel Arnold. *Agreeable Surprise: A Comic Opera in Two Acts*. 5th ed. London: N.p., 1796.

Oulton, W. C. *A History of the Theatres of London, containing An Annual Register of New Pieces, Revivals, Pantomimes, &c. With Occasional Notes and Anecdotes. Being a Continuation of Victor's & Oulton's Histories, from the Year 1795 to 1817 Inclusive*. 2 vols. London: Chapple and Simpkin and Marshall, 1818.

Overman, A. A. *An Investigation into the Character of Fanny Burney*. Amsterdam: Paris, 1933.

Parnell, Paul E. "The Sentimental Mask." *PMLA* 78 (1963): 529–35.

Peake, Richard Brinsley. *Memoirs of the Colman Family*. London: Richard Bentley, 1841.

Phillips, Hugh. *Mid-Georgian London: A Topographical and Social Survey of Central and Western London about 1750*. London: Collins, 1964.

———. *The Thames about 1750*. London: Collins, 1951.

The Pictorial Handbook of London: Comprising Its Antiquities, Architecture, Arts, Manufacture, Trade, Social, Literary, and Scientific Institutions, Exhibitions, and Galleries of Art; Together with Some Account of the Principal Suburbs and Most Attractive Localities. London: Bohn, 1854.

Piozzi, Hester Lynch. *Thraliana: The Diary of Mrs. Hester Lynch Thrale (later Mrs. Piozzi)*. Edited by Katharine C. Balderston. 2 vols. Oxford: Clarendon, 1942.

Reynolds, Frederick. *The Life and Times of Frederick Reynolds. Written by Himself*. 2 vols. 2d ed. London: Henry Colburn, 1827.

Richards, Kenneth, and Peter Thomson, eds. *The Eighteenth-century English Stage*. Proceedings of a symposium sponsored by the Manchester University Department of Drama. London: Methuen, 1972.

———, eds. *Essays on Nineteenth Century British Theatre*. Proceedings of a symposium sponsored by the Manchester University Department of Drama. London: Methuen, 1971.

Rosenfeld, Sybil. "Dramatic Advertisements in the Burney Newspapers, 1660–1700." *PMLA* 51 (1936): 123–52.

Sawyer, Newell W. *The Comedy of Manners from Sheridan to Maugham*. Philadelphia: University of Pennsylvania Press, 1931.

Scholes, Percy A. *The Great Dr. Burney*. 2 vols. New York: Oxford University Press, 1948.

Scouten, Arthur H., George Winchester Stone, and Charles Beecher Hogan, eds. *The London Stage, 1660–1800. A Calendar of Plays, Entertainments, and Afterpieces. Together with Casts, Box Receipts and Contemporary Comment*. 5 pts. Pt 5, *1776–1800*. Edited by Charles Beecher Hogan. 3 vols. Carbondale: Southern Illinois University Press, 1968.

Shaftesbury, Anthony, earl of. *Characteristicks of Men, Manners, Opinions, Times*. 3 vols. 3d ed. London: Darby, 1723.

Sheldon, Esther K. *Thomas Sheridan of Smock-Alley. Recording His Life as Actor and Theater Manager in Both Dublin and London; and Including a Smock-Alley Calendar for the Years of His Management*. Princeton, N.J.: Princeton University Press, 1967.

Sherbo, Arthur. *English Sentimental Drama*. East Lansing: Michigan State University Press, 1957.

Sheridan, Richard Brinsley. *The Dramatic Works of Richard Brinsley Sheridan*. Edited by Cecil Price. 2 vols. Oxford: Clarendon, 1973.

———. *The Letters of Richard Brinsley Sheridan*. Edited by Cecil Price. 3 vols. Oxford: Clarendon, 1966.

Shorter, Alfred H. *Paper Mills and Paper Makers in England, 1495–1800.* Monumenta Chartae Papyraceae, vol. 6. Hilversum, Holland: Paper Publications Society, 1954.

Smollett, Tobias. *The Expedition of Humphry Clinker.* Edited by Lewis M. Knapp. London: Oxford University Press, 1966.

Snuggs, Henry L. "The Comic Humours: A New Interpretation." *PMLA* 62 (March 1947): 114–22.

Spencer, Christopher, ed. *Five Restoration Adaptations of Shakespeare.* Urbana: University of Illinois Press, 1965.

A Statement of Differences Subsisting between the Proprietors and Performers of the Theatre-Royal, Covent Garden. London: Willes, 1800.

Steele, Richard. *The Conscious Lovers.* In *The Plays of Richard Steele,* edited by Shirley Strum Kenny. Oxford: Clarendon, 1971.

Steeves, Harrison R. *Before Jane Austen.* New York: Holt, Rinehart and Winston, 1965.

Sterne, Laurence. *A Sentimental Journey through France and Italy, by Mr. Yorick.* Edited by Gardner D. Stout, Jr. Berkeley and Los Angeles: University of California Press, 1967.

Stevenson, Allan Henry. *Observations on Paper as Evidence.* Lawrence: University of Kansas Libraries, 1961.

Stratman, Carl J. *Bibliography of English Printed Tragedy, 1565–1900.* Carbondale: Southern Illinois University Press, 1966.

Stratman, Carl J., David G. Spencer, and Mary Elizabeth Devine. *Restoration and Eighteenth Century Theatre Research: A Bibliographical Guide, 1900–1968.* Carbondale: Southern Illinois University Press, 1971.

Sutherland, Lucy Stuart. *A London Merchant, 1695–1774.* London: Oxford University Press, 1933.

Theatrical Guardian (London), nos. 1–4 (March 1791).

Thornbury, Walter. *Old and New London: A Narrative of Its History, Its People, and Its Places.* 6 vols. London: Cassell Petter and Galpin, 1872–78.

Thorndike, Ashley H. *English Comedy.* New York: Macmillan, 1929.

Tompkins, J. M. S. *The Popular Novel in England, 1770–1800.* 1932. Reprint. London: Methuen, 1969.

Vanbrugh, Sir John, and Colley Cibber. *The Provoked Husband; or, A Journey to London.* Edited by Peter Dixon. Lincoln: University of Nebraska Press, 1974.

Watson, Ernest Bradlee. *Sheridan to Robinson: A Study of the Nineteenth-century London Stage.* Cambridge, Mass.: Harvard University Press, 1926.

White, Eugene. *Fanny Burney, Novelist: A Study in Technique. Evelina, Cecilia, Camilla, the Wanderer.* Hamden, Conn.: Shoestring, 1960.

White, T. H. *The Age of Scandal.* London: Cape, 1950.

Wimsatt, W. K., ed. *The Idea of Comedy: Essays in Prose and Verse, Ben Jonson to George Meredith*. Englewood Cliffs, N.J.: Prentice-Hall, 1969.

Wood, Frederick T. "The Beginnings and Significance of Sentimental Comedy." *Anglia* 55 (July 1931): 368–92.

———. "Sentimental Comedy in the Eighteenth Century." *Neophilologus* 18 (October 1932–July 1933): 37–44, 281–89.

The World, nos. 2188–2342 (1 January 1794 to 30 June 1794).